Collective Bargaining Comes to the Campus

Collective Bargaining

Comes to the Campus

ROBERT K. CARR

DANIEL K. VAN EYCK

AMERICAN COUNCIL ON EDUCATION • *Washington, D.C.*

© 1973 by American Council on Education
One Dupont Circle, Washington, D.C. 20036

Library of Congress Cataloging in Publication Data
Carr, Robert Kenneth, 1908–
    Collective bargaining comes to the campus.
    Bibliography: p.
    1. Collective bargaining—College teachers.
I. VanEyck, Daniel K., 1932–   joint author.
II. Title.
LB2334.C63   331.89′041′37812   73–4409
ISBN 0–8268–1401–5

Printed in the United States of America

Contents

Tables

Foreword

COLLECTIVE BARGAINING BY FACULTIES CAME TO HIGHER EDUCATION IN the United States in the latter half of the 1960s as a result of new statutes in some of the states and a reinterpretation of the federal labor relations laws by the National Labor Relations Board. Although faculty bargaining has as yet reached relatively few of the nation's four-year colleges and universities, public and private, in but a dozen states, there have been many predictions that it will spread rapidly to a significant number of institutions. Its effects on the academic profession and its potentials for strengthening or weakening the institutions and for helping or hindering teaching, research, and service are still not fully known. What is known is that the ramifications extend far beyond "wages, hours, and other terms and conditions of work" as they are understood in industrial bargaining.

Although collective bargaining is new in higher education, the statutes are on the books, and the case law is accumulating from labor board hearings and rulings. In this early stage of development, it becomes essential for the members of the academic community—faculty, administrators, boards of trustees, students—and for those outside the academic community who must administer or deal with the law to inform themselves as completely as they can about this new alternative means of conducting labor relations, for the results may be far-reaching.

The authors of this book offer thoroughgoing and dispassionate analyses of the elements that bear on faculty collective bargaining in four-year colleges and universities. Until now there has been much discussion, many articles have been written, many cases heard, many rulings made, and, in those institutions where faculty bargaining has been adopted, many hours spent on bargaining unit determination and on contract negotiation and administration. In preparing this book, Robert K. Carr and Daniel K. VanEyck have brought to their task expertise gained in the subject itself and the practical experience of having been both faculty members and administrators.

I am grateful to the Ford Foundation for the grant of funds which has made this valuable study possible. Nowhere else has faculty collective bargaining been examined in its many aspects that must be considered if wise decisions are to be made about the governance of institutions and the conditions of work of its professionals. This book is needed and I commend it to the attention of the academic community.

ROGER W. HEYNS, *President*
American Council on Education

Preface

WITH THIS VOLUME, WE HOPE TO MAKE AVAILABLE A REASONABLY AC-
curate and comprehensive account of faculty collective bargaining at
public and private four-year colleges and universities in the United
States as it has developed from its beginnings in 1968 through June
1972. Faculty bargaining is an exceedingly diverse and diffuse development, thus far limited to a few states and to a relatively small segment of the total higher education establishment. Its structure and
processes are still in formative stages. The uncertainty of the outcome—both the extent to which faculty collective bargaining will be
adopted among American colleges and universities, and the impact it
will have on institutions where it is adopted—creates widespread and
profound interest and concern. In attempting to respond to this interest and concern, we fully recognize that our account must break off
arbitrarily at what may prove to be an early point in an unfolding
story. We have managed at certain points to introduce information
about developments as late as February 1973, but when we say "now"
or seemingly write of the present, it is the situation at the end of the
1971–72 academic year that is being described.

An undeniable need exists for an orderly and generally dispassionate
account of what has been happening. We have collected and read the
pertinent documentary and interpretive literature and have attempted
to examine the available information concerning the background, the
emergence, and the effect of faculty bargaining at a number of institutions. We have analyzed the changes in federal and state laws that
have made this development possible and have examined the application of the laws to higher education by federal and state labor boards.
We have considered with care the bargaining unit disputes, the resulting labor board hearings and rulings, and their impact on a variety of
institutions. We have visited a number of education associations and
several campuses and, in the process, have had the benefit of scores of
interviews with faculty members, administrators, trustees, and labor
organization representatives.

Without exception, the individuals with whom we talked displayed an impressive, indeed, a surprising willingness to share information and judgments with us. Many of them startled us by their eagerness to answer our questions and to tell their stories. Whether this testified to pride in achievements or apprehension about consequences was not always easy to discern. Probably everyone who has played a part in the coming of faculty collective bargaining feels a bit of both.

Our approach has been to analyze the broad issues affecting institutions, rather than to develop comprehensive case studies of all the colleges and universities involved in this process; as a result, for purposes of illustration, some institutions have been discussed in greater depth than others. Similarly, although we have tried to provide a useful indication of the scope and content of faculty collective bargaining contracts, we have stopped well short of systematic statistical summaries or content analyses. Further, because faculty bargaining is recent, limited in adoptions, specific to individual institutions and local conditions, it does not yet lend itself to the collection and quantification of substantial data, to be organized either as hard facts or attitudes in the language of the statistician or the behavioral scientist.

Two considerations influenced our decision to concentrate on the four-year colleges and the universities and to make but occasional reference to the experience of two-year colleges with faculty bargaining. First, the two-year college constitutes an important but nonetheless distinctive area of American higher education, with its own educational purposes and programs and its own manpower needs and arrangements. Thus, its experience with faculty bargaining is, in our judgment, a separate story that deserves to be carefully told as such. Second, our lack of professional experience in the two-year college field, as well as the limited time and resources available to us for our task, led us to decide that we should limit our attention to faculty bargaining above the two-year level.

Neither did we deal with collective bargaining between teaching assistants and their institutions. Only fragmentary information about this phenomenon is available. We are not persuaded that it is properly part of the story of *faculty* collective bargaining. In any event, we leave a careful account of this phase of labor relations in higher education for others to examine. We suspect that it is a bit early for the task.

Candor so characterized the interviews we conducted that it seems
desirable not to try to identify here everyone with whom we talked,
either at institutions or organizations. We must and do acknowledge,
however, our great appreciation to all of the people with whom we
talked or corresponded. We feel that we must name a few who supplied information or offered suggestions and encouragement on frequent occasions over much of the period of our undertaking. Thus, at
the risk of omitting names that ought to be included, we acknowledge
our obligation to Neil S. Bucklew, Bertram H. Davis, Matthew W.
Finken, Anthony J. John, Donald D. O'Dowd, Alfred D. Sumberg,
Donald F. Walters, and Belle Zeller. The manuscript was read and
criticized in its entirety by Professors David L. Shapiro and Lloyd L.
Weinreb of the Harvard Law School. Professor Shapiro's understanding of labor law enabled him to put us straight at many points where
we might otherwise have been in error. Professor Weinreb served also
as a friend and scholar with whom we were in close consultation from
start to finish.

All of the persons named above offered significant help, difficult to
state precisely in every instance and impossible in all cases to acknowledge adequately. None, however, pressed any point of view on us, or
has any responsibility for the judgments we determined to express in
these pages, or contributed to the errors of fact or interpretation we
persisted in making in spite of their help. For the errors that careful
readers will discover, we offer only the excuse that the record of
faculty collective bargaining continues to sprawl to a virtually unmanageable degree and has refused to "stay put" long enough for
anyone to subject it to scrutiny by means of a truly scholarly appara-
tus. We invite the forbearance of our readers where we have clearly
gone astray; in particular, we invite the assistance of those who feel
moved to let us know where the facts are other than they are here
recorded.

We wish to offer our appreciation to the Ford Foundation which
provided complete funding for this enterprise and to the American
Council on Education which invited us to carry on our work under its
auspices. We must emphasize, however, that we were at all times free
from influence or restraint by either organization. Responsibility for
the direction and scope of our study, as well as for our findings, our
judgments, and our mistakes, is entirely our own.

A final word of gratitude must be offered to two remarkable

women. Our secretary, Mrs. Virginia Anstead, efficiently assembled and made available to us research notes and files that forever threatened to become unmanageable. She also typed and retyped manuscript drafts with speed and accuracy and thereby enabled us to hit upon whatever orderly presentation of materials and useful emphases and judgments may be encountered in this book. We wish, too, to acknowledge to Olive Mills, senior editor of the Council's Publications Division, a contribution that can be called "nominal" or "routine" only at a level of high professional standards.

R.K.C.
D.K.V.

CHAPTER ONE

Collective Bargaining in the United States

COLLECTIVE BARGAINING HAS TAKEN HIGHER EDUCATION BY SURPRISE. IT reached the campus long after it had arrived in industry, entering through a side gate when the focus of attention was on the explosive confrontations taking place at education's front door. Although there were logical and predictable reasons for its intrusion, its foothold in academe is still uncertain. Many persons have deplored collective bargaining as a wholly inappropriate way to handle employment relationships between educational institutions and their faculties. Yet some early results suggest that collective bargaining may become a principal means for bringing one important element in a strife-torn academic community back to a welcome condition of stability—stability that is essential to an attack on the problems causing the controversies at the front door. On the other hand, at some institutions collective bargaining could aggravate already desperately strained budgets or governance situations.

Collective bargaining as a system for conducting labor-management relations gained initial recognition in American law some four decades ago. No one then had in mind the possibility that faculties might one day adopt it as the means of carrying on important aspects of policy making and administration at their institutions. From the early 1930s to mid-1960s—the formative years of collective bargaining—the process was shaped by law and practice without any thought given to its suitability or applicability to higher education. Indeed, collective bargaining took shape as a means of enabling the great mass of workers, principally blue-collar ones, to confront their employers on something approaching even terms in establishing the conditions of their employment. By the mid-1930s, some white-collar workers were joining unions and engaging in collective bargaining, but until the end of World War II the main effort of the labor movement was centered on organizing rank and file workers in factories, mills, and mines. Only with the passage of the Taft-Hartley Act in 1947 did federal labor law expressly

1

recognize both that "professional" employees could engage in collective bargaining and that if a majority so voted, they had the right to exclude themselves from a larger bargaining unit containing nonprofessional workers.

COLLECTIVE BARGAINING LAWS ILL-SUITED TO HIGHER EDUCATION?

Academic communities that have turned to formal collective bargaining as a promising way of dealing with certain of their relationships have found themselves compelled to operate within the existing legal framework. Virtually no help has come from legislatures in the form of modified statutes applicable to the needs of the college or university as a special kind of corporate enterprise. For concessions and adjustments in the law, faculties and their institutions have been almost totally dependent on the understanding and cooperation shown by the labor boards that administer the statutes. The courts might have provided some help, but thus far they have been called on to decide few cases concerning faculty collective bargaining.

One illustration will show the difficulties encountered in applying collective bargaining law to higher education. The National Labor Relations Act contains a precise definition of "supervisor." It then excludes supervisors from membership in an "employee" bargaining unit, even though they are, in the ordinary sense, part of the work force of an enterprise. In several early cases, the National Labor Relations Board seriously questioned whether this statutory provision does not require that department chairmen and even members of certain faculty committees be excluded from bargaining units. Although the NLRB has tried to base its rulings in each case on local circumstances, it has nonetheless been applying to the academic community statutory criteria that were originally devised by Congress and then applied through the years by the NLRB and the courts without regard to their appropriateness to the composition of a faculty bargaining unit. As a result, faculty collective bargaining under law carries with it the threat that the realities of academic life may be seriously distorted to the disadvantage of faculty interests. It has been widely suggested that the benefits of collective bargaining to academic people and their institutions are likely to be fully realized only if new or unique models are developed which differ significantly from the industrial models evolved over nearly four decades. But does the law permit the development of such models? That question must be borne in mind throughout this analysis of faculty collective bargaining.

Collective bargaining is, then, more than a phrase suggesting a challenging way for an academic community to conduct an experiment in group dynamics. It might be said that many faculties have long engaged in one form or another of collective bargaining with their administrations and governing boards concerning their compensation and their role in determining institutional policies and programs. But this use of the words is now questionable, for *collective bargaining* designates a definite process shaped by history and defined by law. It is a specific means by which persons identified with a particular enterprise, separated into management and labor components, are enabled, in a highly formalistic way, to discuss certain issues (or "relations") that lie between them, to reach binding agreement on how to handle these issues, and then to be governed by that agreement in the work relationship for a fixed period. It is thus essential to summarize the origin and development of collective bargaining in the industrial sector of the American economy before examining its application to labor-management relations in higher education.

COLLECTIVE BARGAINING, A PARTICULAR SYSTEM OF CONTROLLING LABOR-MANAGEMENT RELATIONS

Collective bargaining is one of several systems for controlling the work relationship between employer and employees—between what the law calls "management" and "labor"—with reference to the fixing of wages, hours, and other conditions of employment.[1] There are other ways, or "systems," by which wages, hours, and work conditions in private industry can be fixed. These include unilateral determination by the employer of the conditions of employment, which the worker must then accept if he wants a job with that employer; bilateral bargaining between the employer and the individual employee concerning the conditions under which the latter works; and prescription by the government of wages, hours, and conditions of employment, and per-haps, out of necessity, of prices and profits as well. These systems

---

1. The National Labor Relations Act states that the employer and the repre-sentative of the employees shall bargain "with respect to wages, hours, and other terms and conditions of employment." Most state collective bargaining statutes use similar language.

may be discrete; they may also be found in varying combinations as mixed systems.

The beginnings of collective bargaining can be traced to the closing years of the nineteenth century, when an occasional employer would voluntarily recognize the right of his employees to join a labor union and then to negotiate with him through that union concerning wages and other terms of employment. But such examples were not numerous, for the law did not guarantee workers the right to organize, let alone require employers to negotiate with them. In fact, in the early decades of the nineteenth century, the law—in the form of court decisions— sometimes held labor unions, particularly when they used such weapons as picketing, strikes, and boycotts, to be criminal conspiracies.[2]

The Wagner Act and After

Collective bargaining became a leading system of controlling the employment relationship in the American economy in 1935 when Congress passed the National Labor Relations Act, known as the Wagner Act. It is usually cited as marking the beginning of collective bargaining under federal law, but the first such statute was the National Industrial Recovery Act, passed in 1933, in the first days of the New Deal. The references to collective bargaining in the NIRA were part of a bold and comprehensive program of the government during the Great Depression to "manage the economy" through stimulants and controls intended to increase employment, wages, prices, and the production and distribution of goods and services. It was under this statute that the National Labor Relations Board was established in 1934 by Presidential order. The NIRA guaranteed workers the right to organize and bargain collectively through representatives of their own choosing, but it did not provide any means to enforce these rights against employers who refused to engage in "good faith" bargaining.

In 1935, the Supreme Court declared the NIRA unconstitutional even though its two-year term was about to expire. Thereafter, Con-

2. The literature on the American labor movement and collective bargaining in industry is extensive. For a recent account intended for the general reader, see Derek C. Bok and John T. Dunlop, *Labor and the American Community. The Developing Labor Law,* ed. Charles J. Morris et al. is a 1054-page systematic presentation of the federal "law"—statutes, administrative rulings, and court decisions—on collective bargaining since 1935. A good brief analysis of the federal law appears in *Primer of Labor Relations: A Guide to Employer-Employee Conduct,* 18th ed. These three volumes have been most useful in the preparation of the present volume.

gress renewed legislative efforts to stimulate the economy, but did so on a more selective, step-by-step basis. The Wagner Act of 1935 and the Fair Labor Standards Act (Wages and Hours Act) of 1938 were part of this new effort, and their constitutionality was ultimately affirmed by the Supreme Court, the Wagner Act being upheld in 1937 in *NLRB* v. *Jones & Laughlin Steel Corp.*[3]

The Wagner Act took the crucial step forward of making it an "unfair labor practice" for an employer to refuse to bargain collectively with the workers. The Taft-Hartley Act (1947) and the Landrum-Griffin Act (1959) amended and extended the Wagner Act in significant ways. They were enacted only after long and bitter debates between labor and management about the nation's experience under the law. Sections of the former were designated the "Labor-Management Relations Act, 1947," and of the latter, the "Labor-Management Reporting and Disclosure Act"; but those parts of the now much-amended federal statute that deal with collective bargaining have always been referred to as the "National Labor Relations Act."[4]

Today the federal law controlling much industrial collective bargaining consists of a complex of statutory provisions, administrative rulings, and court decisions interpreting and applying these provisions. It is not necessary to identify the specific contributions of the 1935, 1947, and 1959 statutes to the law that applies to faculty collective bargaining; it is useful to remember that the federal law is the product of a long and often controversial political, legal, and constitutional evolutionary development.

The NLRB and Collective Bargaining in the Private Sector

The administrative rulings have been the work of the National Labor Relations Board, commonly referred to as "the NLRB." As the principal enforcement agency of the federal statute, it consists of five members appointed by the President for five-year terms. The Board conducts

3. 301 U.S. 1. The Railway Labor Act of 1926 and the Norris-LaGuardia Act of 1932 were other forerunners of the Wagner Act. The former required railway managements to bargain collectively with their employees; the latter sought to promote employer recognition of unions and voluntary collective bargaining in private industry generally by sharply curtailing intervention by the federal courts in labor disputes.

4. The United States Code citation of the present-day statute is: 29 U.S.C. §§ 151–68 (1970).

much of its work through three-member panels. The original 1935 statute was criticized on the ground that it permitted the NLRB to operate as prosecutor, judge, and jury in the enforcement of the law. This criticism led to changes in 1947, in the Taft-Hartley Act, which restricted the Board primarily to the exercise of a so-called judicial function. The investigative and prosecutorial functions were transferred to a new officer, the General Counsel. This officer, too, is appointed by the President, for a four-year term, and is wholly independent of the Board itself. Both the Board and the General Counsel, however, carry on much of their work through thirty-one regional and three subregional offices, located throughout the country. For example, the board has delegated its authority in representation hearings and elections to regional directors for first exercise at the local level in individual cases, with the Board retaining a right of review.[5]

As noted, the Board's present function is principally judicial in that it holds hearings and makes rulings in cases involving disputed representation matters (determining the proper membership of worker bargaining units and designating or "certifying" bargaining agents) and complaints that employers or employees have engaged in certain "unfair labor practices" expressly forbidden by statute. The latter rulings are subject to review by the federal courts; the former, with few exceptions, are not. Over the years court review of NLRB rulings has resulted in the development of a large body of judge-made labor law, much of it determined finally by the Supreme Court. The faculty and governing board of a college or university who find themselves bargaining collectively under federal supervision must recognize, then, that the law controlling troublesome aspects of the relationship may prove far broader and more complex than the words of the statute (which themselves are far from simple).

The National Labor Relations Act is concerned exclusively with collective bargaining in the private sector of the economy. The act expressly exempts federal, state, and local governments from its application. Moreover, the federal law applies only to those private enterprises that are directly engaged in interstate commerce or that "affect" such commerce. This limitation proceeds from the fact that the federal labor laws find their constitutional justification in the power of Congress to regulate interstate commerce. Since 1935, the application of

5. An excellent chapter in Morris, *The Developing Labor Law* describes the organization, jurisdiction, and work of the NLRB and the General Counsel (see pp. 820–40).

the National Labor Relations Act to local businesses has depended on two variables: the changing attitude of the Supreme Court toward the extent of the federal government's authority to regulate commerce and the exercise by the NLRB of discretionary authority vested in it by Congress to establish the standards or limits within which it will accept jurisdiction over cases. The Board has defined its limits from time to time in terms of the dollar volume of goods the employer buys from or ships to other states, or of the dollar volume of the total business. Thus, the NLRB declines to take jurisdiction over nonretail enterprises where the gross outflow or inflow of revenue across state lines is less than $50,000 a year. When, in 1970, it brought private colleges and universities within the scope of federal labor law, it limited its jurisdiction to institutions having a gross annual operating revenue of at least $1 million.

Bargaining for Public Employees

The extension of the right to collective bargaining under law to employees in the public service and in private enterprises that fall outside the jurisdictional limits set by the NLRB has depended on other governmental measures than the National Labor Relations Act. Through Executive orders by President Kennedy in 1962 and President Nixon in 1969, federal employees have been granted a substantial right to join unions and engage in collective bargaining with the agencies for which they work. The right of state and local employees and of workers in private enterprises outside NLRB jurisdiction is controlled by state laws. These are of two types. By the end of 1972 some thirty-seven states, either by statute or administrative ruling, permitted some degree of bargaining or "conferring" by state or local employees and the agencies for which they worked. About fifteen states had laws authorizing collective bargaining in private enterprises not covered by federal law. The latter were originally known as "little Wagner Acts,"[6]

---

6. Chap. 2 indicates as accurately as possible the states that have laws that authorize collective bargaining by faculties at public institutions. It is difficult, however, to count, analyze, and classify these laws and the "little Wagner Acts" as of any given date because state laws of both types lack uniformity of purpose and language and have been varyingly interpreted and applied by state courts and labor boards.

Labor lawyers, counseling their clients, must give attention to the line that divides federal and state jurisdiction over collective bargaining in private enterprises, for sometimes the two overlap. For a good analysis of the so-called doctrine of federal preemption (and its exceptions), see Morris, *The Developing Labor Law*, chap. 29.

a usage still common though no longer accurate. Only in a rare instance is faculty collective bargaining carried on under "little Wagner Acts."

What must be borne in mind is that, with very few exceptions, faculty collective bargaining at private institutions takes place under federal law whereas at public institutions it takes place under state laws. Thus the *right* to engage in collective bargaining is available to faculties at all private institutions except those falling below the NLRB jurisdictional standard, whereas it is available to faculties at public institutions only in states whose public employment bargaining laws are deemed applicable to faculties.

Statutes authorize collective bargaining only in the sense that the employees of enterprises covered by the law exercise the right at their own discretion. The law does not compel them to use collective bargaining as the exclusive or even preferred means of reaching agreement with their employer concerning conditions of work.[7] They may choose other methods; they may even elect to engage in a kind of voluntary bargaining on a group basis outside the statutory framework. There are hazards (to be discussed later) in following the latter course, and also a real question whether such negotiations should be categorized as "collective bargaining."

Bargaining as "Private Government" Encouraged by Public Government

Individual bargaining, by which each worker negotiates the conditions of his employment with his employer, has never been a feasible option or "system" for blue-collar workers. Without collective bargaining, these workers seldom have any choice but to accept the conditions unilaterally set by employers if they wish to gain employment or to stay on the job. But in the professional and middle management ranks of industrial enterprises (as in higher education), individual bargaining has often been the means for setting salaries and other conditions

---

7. The exercise of the right by faculties is voluntary in every instance. It is sometimes said that certain state laws "mandate" collective bargaining, particularly between school teachers and school boards. The term seldom means, however, that both parties are compelled to engage in bargaining. Employees invoke the right if they please, and the employer is then compelled to bargain with them. See Robert E. Doherty and Walter E. Oberer, *Teachers, School Boards, and Collective Bargaining: A Changing of the Guard* for an excellent account of the development of collective bargaining in public schools up to 1966.

of employment, subject only to such limitations as an enterprise's job classification system, salary schedules, and quotas for appointments at various levels or ranks. Individual bargaining is frequently aggressive—particularly prior to original appointment, or when the individual has a job offer from another enterprise—and involves a sequence of offer, counterdemand, and final agreement.

Individual and collective bargaining are not necessarily incompatible, and thus no sharp line can be drawn between situations where individual bargaining can take place and those where employees find that they must use collective strength to win what they deem to be satisfactory conditions of employment. In middle management and professional employment areas, there is the possibility, for example, that after basic or minimum conditions of employment have been set through collective bargaining, individual bargaining may ensue. Probably the condition most essential to individual bargaining is that the candidate for appointment or retention on the job demonstrate some distinct competence or usefulness. If he is not readily "fungible," he enjoys a vantage point that makes it worthwhile or essential for the employer to bargain with him.

Collective bargaining statutes do not dictate the terms of an agreement between management and labor, or even require that an agreement be reached. In the words of the federal statute, the two parties have a "mutual obligation . . . to meet at reasonable times and confer in good faith" in an effort to reach agreement. What constitutes "good faith" bargaining is controlled by a vast body of administrative and judicial determinations. In general, each party must be prepared to make genuine offers and counteroffers, but neither side is required "to agree to a proposal" made by the other side or to make "a concession." If an agreement is reached, federal law provides that either party may request the "execution of a written contract."[8]

Although one purpose of the National Labor Relations Act is to provide means to avoid or substantially to reduce "industrial strife which interferes with the normal flow of commerce and with the full production of goods and services for commerce," the law recognizes that when collective bargaining does not produce an agreement, the two sides may turn to traditional modes of labor-management warfare,

8. Quotations in this paragraph are taken directly from the National Labor Relations Act.

such as the strike and the lockout. Thus, although collective bargaining offers a means for labor and management to resolve their differences through discussion, compromise, and agreement, the threat that a strike or a lockout may follow if an impasse occurs helps make collective bargaining work. On the other hand, successful negotiations at the table also depend on mutual good will and a shared belief that open warfare will do injury to both sides.

Collective bargaining statutes are only part of the public law under which labor-management relationships are controlled or regulated. Other important laws set minimum wage and maximum hour standards, establish safety controls in hazardous forms of employment, provide for unemployment insurance, and forbid discrimination in one form or another against women, the aged, and racial and other minorities. Such laws prescribe in significant ways the actual substance of the employer-employee relationship. They contrast sharply with labor relations acts, which, though prescribing the mechanism for management-labor bargaining, leave the parties free to decide the substance of agreements. Thus, in a private enterprise economy, a labor relations law attempts to encourage and protect self-government by the interested parties as the preferred means of determining many of the conditions under which work takes place.

Collective bargaining, viewed in this light, is an aspect of "private government," or "industrial democracy," a part of a process by which a free society tries to curb a seemingly inexorable trend toward government control of all social relationships that are not self-regulating. It may be said to provide a rational means by which wages, hours, and, indirectly, prices are determined privately in a free market rather than by law. The reality of collective bargaining, however, suggests that at best it is a mixed system for the making of important social and economic determinations, the private side of the process depending for its very existence and character on statutory provisions, and its operation depending on large measures of public supervision by administrative agencies and courts. But even in such a mixed system, individuals and groups may exercise more freedom of choice, particularly in the economic marketplace, than they would be able to achieve in the total absence of governmental involvement. However, the extent to which public authorities control the outcome of an essentially private process is crucial. This is particularly true in higher education, where it has long been thought desirable that individual institutions should enjoy great freedom to shape their own purposes and programs. Moreover, it is clear that faculties had as much to do with this free or voluntary shaping of the process and content of higher education as had any of the other elements within the academic community.

There are ominous signs that self-government in higher education is coming to an end. If colleges and universities, public and private alike, are indeed becoming subject to much greater measures of governmental control, it may matter little that one of the attractions of collective bargaining is said to be the emphasis it places on self-government within the academic community. The contention is already being put forward that the issues to be resolved through faculty collective bargaining are too important for the academic community to decide and should, accordingly, be settled directly by public authority at the state or national level through statutes, administrative regulations, and court orders.

The question should be raised here about the government agencies established by, or utilized for the enforcement of, collective bargaining statutes. Are they consistent with the "private government" view of the process, or at least with the "mixed system" view? Typically, one of these agencies, such as the National Labor Relations Board, supervises the process of collective bargaining. It may help determine the precise membership of a bargaining unit and it may supervise the election in which the workers choose a bargaining agent to represent them. It may enforce statutory provisions prohibiting unfair labor practices on the part of both management and labor.[9] But the labor board does not sit at the bargaining table as a "third force"; it does not by direct or indirect means help shape the substance of an agreement. Neither does it attempt to settle an impasse in negotiations, decide the conditions on which a strike shall be ended, or supervise the administration of an agreement while it is in effect.[10]

9. In the federal domain, NLRB rulings in unfair labor practice cases may be appealed to the federal courts, and much of the law that controls in unfair labor practice situations has been made by the U.S. Supreme Court. The present discussion of unfair labor practice cases ignores the extent to which investigatory and prosecutive powers under federal law are vested in the General Counsel rather than the Board.

10. There are exceptions. Under some state laws, the state labor board or other government agencies are given a direct role in the impasse-breaking process. Moreover, state officials do suggest, and in some situations in effect compel the acceptance of, compromise agreements on the disputed issues.

PRINCIPLES OF EXCLUSIVE REPRESENTATION
AND FAIR REPRESENTATION

The principle that all workers in a bargaining unit shall be represented by a single labor organization has been part of the U.S. labor
movement's credo for nearly a century. This principle of "exclusivity,"
as it is often called, has been recognized since 1935, in the National
Labor Relations Act. Section 9(a) of the statute provides that the
labor organization that wins the support of a majority of the members
of a bargaining unit (following, if necessary, a run-off election between
the two top organizations in the first election) shall be certified as the
exclusive bargaining agent for all of the workers in the unit, including
those who did not vote for the victorious organization.[11] State collective bargaining laws, with a few execptions, also incorporate the
principle. On the other hand, that some kind of joint or "council"
bargaining can be carried on where labor is represented by more than
one union is demonstrated in several nations in western Europe. In
France, for example, each union is simply given the right to represent
its own members, and collective bargaining normally takes place
through uneasy coalitions among the three major labor federations.

In this country, the case for exclusive representation is now seldom
questioned. Even in states where exclusivity is not required by law—
New York is one—employers and employees usually agree to observe
it. The advantage to labor is readily understood. If more than one
labor organization took part in the negotiation and administration of a
contract, on a proportional representation basis, the employer might
attempt "divide and conquer" tactics against the workers. Multiple
bargaining agents might also transfer to the bargaining table the task
of ironing out differences within the labor group that, under exclusive
representation, would be resolved at the time the bargaining agent is
chosen, or at least within the councils of the labor group before its
representatives go to the bargaining table.

Employers readily accept the principle for a variety of reasons. In
so doing, they avoid the "whipsaw" tactics that might be used against
them where two or more unions were competing against one another

11. The act does allow individual workers to present grievances to the employer and to have such grievances adjusted, without the intervention of the bargaining agent, provided the adjustment is not inconsistent with the collective
bargaining contract and provided a representative of the bargaining agent is given
opportunity to be present when the grievance is considered and adjusted.

during the negotiation of an agreement, each anxious to demonstrate its superior effectiveness to the workers and thus tempted to escalate labor's demands at the table. The confidentiality of delicate negotiations is easier to preserve. A single union can be presumed able to maintain stability within the work force during the period that a contract is in effect, by keeping dissident minorities in line and by preventing wildcat strikes and jurisdictional disputes.

The exclusive representation arrangement, which has become such an integral part of collective bargaining under federal law in the industrial sector, and which is widely observed in bargaining with public employees whether required by state law or not, may, however, constitute an obstacle to the development of faculty collective bargaining models suitable to the traditions and practices of higher education. Faculty organizations and procedures are usually designed and implemented to emphasize the right of the individual to have his full say and to vote his own position on all important educational issues, as well as on many other aspects of the institutional program. Indeed, in certain contexts it is readily and properly argued that this is an aspect of the faculty member's academic freedom. But where a single labor organization is certified to negotiate with the employer on a wide range of policy decisions that may be incorporated in an agreement, the faculty member who voted for another bargaining agent may feel he has lost his voice in institutional matters.

The faculty member may find some reassurance in the so-called doctrine of fair representation. Where the law imposes an exclusive bargaining agent, that agent is required to represent everyone in the unit fairly. This duty has been held to be particularly important in the processing of the grievances of individual workers. But in the negotiation of an agreement with the employer, the U.S. Supreme Court has observed that "the complete satisfaction of all who are represented is hardly to be expected. A wide range of reasonableness must be allowed a statutory bargaining representative . . . , subject always to complete good faith and honesty of purpose in the exercise of its discretion."[12]

Workers dissatisfied with the agreement negotiated at the table can criticize the way in which the bargaining agent has used its authority and purported to serve the interest of all the workers. They may get a chance to vote against the agreement, although the law does not re-

12. See Ford Motor Co. v. Huffman, 345 U.S. 330 (1953); Syres v. Oil Workers, 350 U.S. 892 (1955); and Vaca v. Sypes, 386 U.S. 171 (1967).

quire the bargaining agent to submit an agreement to the workers for their approval. Whether such a referendum is held or not, dissatisfied workers can put their hope in a new representation election at the earliest moment and work for the selection of another labor organization more sensitive to their interests and needs. But a labor organization once chosen is not easily supplanted, and minority elements in a work force must continue to do without direct representation on labor's side of the bargaining table. The duty of fair representation prevents the union from discriminating against dissenting or dissatisfied members of the unit, but it does not require the union to provide the minority employee with the kind of voice in union deliberations that the dissenting faculty member is permitted in faculty deliberations.

COLLECTIVE BARGAINING: AN ADVERSARY
OR COOPERATIVE RELATIONSHIP?

Collective bargaining, it is often said, should not be viewed as a process by which workers and managers join forces to operate an enterprise on a shared authority and responsibility basis. Instead, it must be viewed as an adversary relationship, even a political confrontation, between two opposing forces, within a single enterprise, which share certain limited goals but also have well-differentiated interests or needs: primarily increased profits for the employer and higher wages for workers.[13] The collective bargaining relationship is said to presume that each side has enough bargaining power to enable it to meet the other on sufficiently even terms that the resulting agreement will be balanced and fair—a reasonable "trade-off" will take place.

It is also said that in private industry the negotiable matters—
wages, hours, and conditions of employment—are confined to a rather
narrow range. The private enterprise is run for profit; the entrepreneurs

13. One labor relations lawyer, with collective bargaining experience in education, views collective bargaining as a power struggle within a political system: "Collective negotiations is itself a political system, and the leaders of a . . . negotiations structure—the negotiators, the executive boards, the departmental stewards—are themselves politicians. They are not enlisted in the service of reasonableness, rationality or the persuasive power of ideas. They are concerned with getting more, as management is with giving less. They understand that their ability to achieve this objective depends upon the effective mobilization and utilization of political power" (Donald H. Wollett, "The Status and Trends of Collective Negotiations for Faculty in Higher Education," 1971 *Wisconsin Law Review* [no. 1], 2, 32).

risk their capital to this end; the function of collective bargaining is to permit the employees to present their collective strength against the "boss" as a countervailing force against exploitation and oppression.[14]

Thus, the policy issues involving the purpose of the business—the design, manufacture, pricing, and marketing of the product or service—are properly the exclusive concern of management.

These views of collective bargaining may well fail to recognize the subtlety and complexity of the process, even as it is followed in industry where the employer-employee relationship is much simpler than it is at a college or a university. It can be argued that the process is often a mixed, ambiguous one—not fully adversary, not fully cooperative—and that the workers in industry do in fact frequently have a valid interest in corporate purposes and policies, an interest that can be encompassed by the "conditions of employment" language of the statutes. It is all very well to say: "If management's judgments are unsound, the business suffers the proper fate in the free enterprise scheme: it loses out to its competitors."[15] But workers increasingly have as good reason as does management—perhaps better reason—to want to avoid that kind of outcome. What passes for "management" in many a corporate enterprise today may have only minimal identification with ownership. Its interests and its destiny may be less closely identified with the continuing good health of the business than are those of many members of the work force. Certainly the workers have an increasingly important stake in those business decisions as to the making and marketing of the product that require intolerable assembly-line techniques or that bring the enterprise under social criticism as a polluter of the environment or a waster of scarce natural resources.

After four decades, collective bargaining may be viewed as part of the never-ending search for effective mechanisms to manage and control difficult or troublesome intrasocietal relationships in such a way that dysfunctional conditions are minimized. It is an example of a social mechanism that is partly public and partly private. The mechanism is established by statute and its use is supervised by public agencies, but the essential process and the results it produces depend

14. Doherty and Oberer, *Teachers, School Boards, and Collective Bargaining,* p. 90.
15. Ibid.

on voluntary and free choices by private parties.[16] At its best, it is a flexible mechanism. The purposes it is designed to facilitate can be sought through a relationship that is primarily adversary or primarily cooperative or a mixture of the two. Even if most bargaining in private industry is properly characterized as primarily adversary, the same relationship is not inevitable in higher education.

16. See Philip Selznick, *Law, Society, and Industrial Justice.* Selznick views collective bargaining as a system of industrial self-government and quotes with approval Dean Harry Shulman's reference to "the autonomous rule of law and reason which the collective labor agreement establishes" (p. 157).

CHAPTER TWO

The Emergence of
Faculty Collective Bargaining

FACULTY COLLECTIVE BARGAINING MADE ITS APPEARANCE AT FOUR-YEAR institutions on a scattered, somewhat spotty basis.[1] The starting point might be marked as September 1969, for on that date agreements took effect between the City University of New York (CUNY) and the two units into which its instructional staff had been divided for bargaining purposes. Although faculty bargaining at an institution is often said to begin with the selection or designation of a bargaining agent, the aim of bargaining is to reach an "agreement" with respect to wages, hours, and conditions of employment. Thus the date an agreement is signed may be regarded as the significant one, especially since the interval between the two events has, on occasion, been two or more years.

In actuality, two contracts were negotiated prior to 1969, both at four-year special-purpose institutions. At the United States Merchant Marine Academy, an agreement was signed in February 1968, with the American Federation of Teachers (AFT) as the bargaining agent. The academy is operated by the U.S. Department of Commerce, and the bargaining took shape under President Kennedy's Executive order of 1962, which permitted federal employees limited rights to organization and collective bargaining.

As early as the summer of 1967, an agreement was signed at Bryant College of Business Administration, a private institution in Rhode Island. Here, too, AFT was the bargaining agent. The Bryant case

1. This study concerns chiefly faculty collective bargaining at institutions above the two-year college level. Inasmuch as no single term applies to all such institutions, "four-year institution" is used to include both universities and undergraduate colleges granting a bachelor's degree. Where the context requires a particular emphasis, "college," "university," and "college and university" will also be used. Unless otherwise indicated, the references will be to institutions above the two-year college level.

17

provides an example of voluntary collective bargaining, for in 1967, the NLRB had not yet brought any private educational institutions within the jurisdiction of the National Labor Relations Act. Although Rhode Island had a "little Wagner Act," it was viewed as not applicable to private nonprofit colleges. In May 1967, the faculty voted, thirty-five to twenty, to support AFT Local 1769—previously organized by faculty leaders—and demanded that the administration and governing board bargain with it. A threat to withhold the grades of graduating seniors and also to acquaint the New England accrediting association with what at that time the faculty regarded as deplorable conditions apparently led the governing board to recognize the union as the faculty bargaining agent and to negotiate an agreement with this agent.[2]

In the summer of 1970, two state institutions—Southeastern Massachusetts University and Central Michigan University—and St. John's University, a private institution in New York, each negotiated a contract with its faculty.[3] Faculty bargaining had come to the two-year community colleges somewhat earlier. The agreement between the faculty at Henry Ford Community College and the school board in Dearborn, Michigan, in 1966 may have marked the formal beginning of collective bargaining in American higher education, although *de facto* bargaining was reported as occurring at that institution, and perhaps at one or two others, even earlier.

By June 1972, about fifteen four-year colleges and universities had signed agreements with their faculties.[4] Faculties of at least another twenty-seven institutions of this type had chosen bargaining agents and were engaging in the often time-consuming and difficult business

2. The present president of Bryant, Harry F. Evarts, appointed in 1970, was helpful in supplying information about the Bryant experience with collective bargaining. "The Bryant College Faculty Federation," which he made available with the approval of the author, John A. Ratichek, describes the conditions and events that led to the vote to support the union.

3. The representation election at St. John's was supervised by the New York State Labor Relations Board under a little Wagner Act, for the National Labor Relations Board had not yet authorized collective bargaining under federal law at private educational institutions.

4. Among the institutions having agreements were: Southeastern Massachusetts University, Boston State College, Bryant College, U.S. Merchant Marine Academy, City University of New York, State University of New York, St. John's University, Rutgers University, Monmouth College (New Jersey), the New Jersey state colleges, Central Michigan University, Oakland University, and University of Scranton.

of negotiating agreements.[5] Few outstanding public or private universities or colleges were yet to be found in either of these groups.[6] Several of the institutions with contracts were multicampus enterprises, such as the City University of New York, the State University of New York, and the New Jersey state colleges. If these were counted as separate units, the total of four-year institutions having written agreements was probably less than sixty. This was a significant, but not yet decisive, commitment by American higher education to collective bargaining as a desirable way of managing the employment relationship between governing board and faculty in four-year colleges and universities.[7]

Why did collective bargaining come to these particular institutions? Will it now spread more rapidly to institutions of all types and quality in all parts of the country and become an important part of the higher education scene for the indefinite future? Or is it possible that it is an experiment that will soon peak and then decline because of unimpressive results where tried and insufficient promise elsewhere? These are not easy questions, but some effort must be made to answer them.

Three conditions have usually been basic to the decision of any group of employees, including a college faculty, to engage in collective bargaining. The law must establish the right of the group to re-

5. In this list were seven Massachusetts state colleges (bargaining as individual institutions), the University of Rhode Island, Rhode Island State College, Long Island University—Brooklyn Center, Adelphi University, Bard College, Polytechnic Institute of Brooklyn, Dowling College, New York Institute of Technology, Pratt Institute, Fordham University Law School, Newark College of Engineering, College of Medicine and Dentistry of New Jersey, the Pennsylvania state colleges, the University of Delaware, Ashland College, Youngstown State University, Wayne State University, Saginaw Valley College, and the Nebraska state colleges.

6. For example, none of the forty-six members of the prestigious Association of American Universities was yet engaging in collective bargaining with its faculty. Contracts had been signed at the State University of New York and at Rutgers University, and bargaining agents selected at the University of Rhode Island and the University of Delaware.

7. There has been a tendency during the early years of faculty collective bargaining to overstate the extent of adoptions. For one thing, totals have often been presented of faculties said to be "engaging in collective bargaining" without any breakdown showing how many faculties have negotiated contracts and how many have taken the step of selecting bargaining agents but have not yet negotiated contracts. There has also been a failure to separate two-year and four-year institutions in stating numbers of institutions engaging in collective bargaining. Since faculty bargaining first appeared at two-year colleges and has been more widely adopted at such institutions, this combining of totals has frequently given a misleading impression of the extent to which faculty bargaining is occurring at four-year institutions.

quire their employer to bargain with them; there must be a substantial measure of dissatisfaction with existing conditions of employment; and someone must be making positive efforts to "organize" the work force—to persuade its members to support a "labor organization" (the law's term), or "union" (the popular term in industry) as the agency through which their collective strength can be brought to bear on their employer to win more satisfying employment conditions. How the law came to favor faculty bargaining will now be examined; the second condition will be examined in chapter three and the third condition in chapter five.

For the first three decades following the passage of the Wagner Act in 1935, the law did not encourage faculty collective bargaining; indeed, in large measure it prohibited such activity. Faculty members at *public* institutions were specifically excluded from the coverage of the federal labor relations statutes and nowhere did state laws authorize them to bargain. The employees of *private* colleges and universities were not expressly denied the right to bargain under the Wagner Act, but the National Labor Relations Board regularly declined to extend its jurisdiction to nonprofit organizations even where they were found to have a substantial impact on interstate commerce.

In passing the Taft-Hartley Act of 1947, Congress expressly acknowledged that collective bargaining was available to "professional employees," for it provided that they could elect to retain their identity in separate bargaining units. But no one seems to have thought that this provision might apply to faculty members at private institutions. In any event, the NLRB definitely closed out that possibility in 1951 by once more refusing to assert jurisdiction over nonprofit organizations. This ruling was made in a case involving Columbia University, where the issue of federal jurisdiction was raised by a CIO union that sought to represent the clerical employees in the university's libraries. There were no professional employees of any kind in the proposed unit.[8]

Conceivably a faculty at a private institution might have claimed the right to bargain collectively in one of the states where a little Wagner Act had been passed at some time after 1935. There is no record that any faculty ever made such a claim. This is not surprising, for as late as 1970 only eight states had statutes of this type which

8. 97 NLRB 424 (1951).

might have been regarded as applicable to faculties at private colleges and universities.[9] Collective bargaining between faculties and their institutions may also have taken place prior to 1965 on a voluntary basis, but if this happened anywhere history failed to record the fact.[10] This analysis suggests that where the applicable law does not establish a *right* to collective bargaining for such a professional work force as a college faculty, an essential condition to bargaining is indeed lacking.

State Laws Conducive to Faculty Collective Bargaining at Public Institutions

The first decisive change in the law affecting faculty collective bargaining took place in 1965 when Michigan and Massachusetts enacted statutes authorizing bargaining by public employees. By the end of 1972, thirty-seven states permitted some degree of discussion or agreement between management and labor in public employment. Only about two-thirds of these states, however, had enacted statutes extending the right of collective bargaining to public employees on a broad basis. Most of these statutes made no express reference to faculties; indeed, with few exceptions they appear to have been enacted with no thought in the legislative mind that they would prove applicable to faculties at state institutions. The evidence also shows that in most instances faculties, themselves, were not aware that the

9. In all, twelve states had passed little Wagner Acts by 1959. Eleven years later three additional states had brought the total to only fifteen. In the eight states with laws of this type that were applicable to faculties, the coverage has been called "inadequate." These statistics and the inadequacy judgment are derived from the opinion of the NLRB in its 1970 ruling in the Cornell University case (183 NLRB No. 41, 74 LRRM 1269 [1970]).

NLRB rulings are usually issued promptly in mimeographed form. Each ruling bears the number of the printed volume in which it will ultimately appear and also a case number. The permanent volumes are issued by the U.S. Government Printing Office a year or more later, and as yet none of the NLRB cases examined in this volume has been so published. Hence, the NLRB citations here are to the mimeographed rulings, and the exact pages of the permanent volume on which the quoted passages will appear are not yet available. Wherever possible LRRM citations are also given. The abbreviation refers to the *Labor Relations Reference Manual* (Washington: Bureau of National Affairs), a standard source of labor board rulings and similar materials, available in law libraries.

10. In the period in question it was uncertain whether the law allowed the governing boards at public institutions to bargain on a voluntary basis with their faculties. Moreover, voluntary collective bargaining is an inexact concept or process. It would be risky to assert that no faculty anywhere between 1935 and 1965 engaged in negotiations with its institution looking toward "agreement" on wages, hours, and conditions of employment.

statutes might apply to them. Only in an occasional state, such as New York, did such awareness lead faculty members to become active participants in the lobbying that helped bring about the enactment of a collective bargaining statute of general applicability.[11] Once such a statute had taken effect, however, it became apparent that it might cover faculties at public institutions.[12] As of the end of 1972, thirteen states had laws that were viewed as permitting faculties to claim full bargaining rights. In addition to Michigan and Massachusetts, these were Vermont, Rhode Island, New York, New Jersey, Pennsylvania, Delaware, Minnesota, Nebraska, Oregon, Alaska, and Hawaii.[13]

Why did state legislatures begin to enact laws authorizing collective bargaining by public employees in the mid-1960s? This question can be answered both by noting the waning of the old rationale that such laws were unnecessary and improper and by identifying some of the positive forces that led to the new legislation.[14] Prior to 1965, the belief was widely held that bargaining between a sovereign government and its employees was improper in principle—a contradiction in terms. Bargaining was also viewed as unnecessary in practice, on the ground that public employees could trust a responsible government in a

11. Among the groups that did lobby aggressively for such statutes were state civil service associations, organizations representing public school teachers such as the National Education Association and the American Federation of Teachers, and such labor unions as the American Federation of State, County and Municipal Employees (AFL-CIO) and the Teamsters Union.

12. There are some exceptions in both directions. Wisconsin was one of the first states to enact a law authorizing collective bargaining that can be classified as "generally applicable" to public employees. But its coverage is limited to employees in the "classified service." State university faculty members are not included in the classified service and are thus not eligible to engage in collective bargaining as a statutory right. It is also reported that when the bill was under consideration by the legislature, "nobody even thought of the university systems" (Thomas R. Wildman, "The Legislation Necessary to Effectively Govern Collective Bargaining in Public Higher Education," 1971 *Wisconsin Law Review* [no. 1], 275, 283). The Hawaii public employee collective bargaining statute, on the other hand, expressly authorizes bargaining by the faculties of the state university–community college system.

13. These data about state public employment relations laws are drawn from a paper by Alfred D. Sumberg presented at a conference, Collective Bargaining on Campus II, held by the Institute for Continuing Legal Education in Ann Arbor, Michigan, Nov. 11–12, 1972.

14. Arnold M. Zack, who has had much experience in mediating and arbitrating labor disputes in the private and public sectors, has identified some eight reasons for "a massive stirring of public employees" in the 1960s "as they began to object to decades of often paternalistic treatment" by their government employers. See his chapter, "Impasses, Strikes, and Resolutions," in *Public Workers and Public Unions*, pp. 101–2.

democratic society to treat them justly, since, among other things, it was not motivated by the businessman's wish to turn a profit. Also as an "article of faith," the interests of government workers were assumed to be more than adequately protected under federal and state civil service systems and thus collective bargaining for public employees was made unnecessary. Indeed, it was widely believed that the civil service concept and collective bargaining were fundamentally incompatible.[15] The argument that public workers could trust the government to treat them fairly was undermined as evidence accumulated that, in a pluralistic society, both elective and appointive officers who make public policy respond in varying, unpredictable, and highly political fashion to the wide range of conflicting social and economic pressures that are brought to bear on them. Recognizing this political fact of life, government workers did learn to lobby effectively on their own behalf in Washington and the state capitals. But so too did other groups with interests in tax policy or rival claims on public funds.

The incompatibility between the civil service concept and collective bargaining in public employment was gradually explained away by "study groups, legislative bodies, and labor relations practitioners."[16] The wall between the two systems began to collapse in 1962 when President Kennedy issued Executive Order 10988, granting a limited right to federal employees to join unions and to bargain collectively with the government. The coming of collective bargaining to the federal civil service undoubtedly prepared the way, albeit on a delayed basis, for the enactment of the state laws in 1965 and thereafter.

A general argument that undoubtedly carried great weight with state legislatures was the contention that government workers ought not to be denied a right that had come to be widely enjoyed by workers in the private sector of the American economy: all workers in a free society should possess a common right and opportunity to use their collective strength to improve their lot. Giving strength to this argument was the undeniable fact that, as the range of governmental activities and services was substantially broadened, the work of public employees increasingly resembled that of workers in private industry.

More pragmatic considerations were also at work, such as the desire

15. John W. Macy, Jr., "The Role of Bargaining in the Public Service," in *Public Workers and Public Unions*, pp. 5, 9. Macy is identifying the early prevalence of this belief, rather than endorsing it.
16. Ibid.

of state legislators to shift some of the burden of responding to the aggressive lobbying of public employees for annual wage increases away from themselves to "management" at the agency levels of government. But where such a motive was present, legislators stopped short of committing themselves to an automatic enactment of the tax and appropriations bills required to implement wage agreements reached through bargaining at the agency level. Indeed, there are indications that a countertrend may be developing in some states with public employee bargaining laws. According to an assertion beginning to be heard, because so much is at stake, collective bargaining with public employees must be brought back to the state capital from the agencies and institutions scattered about the state so that the legislature and the governor can take charge of the "management side" of the bargaining process. If that happens, the result could come to resemble the older arrangement by which state employees brought pressure on the governor and legislature at budget time through civil service associations and unions and through institutional spokesmen like university presidents. Lobbying and bargaining may yet prove to be similar or overlapping processes.

Prior to 1965, public employee strikes were everywhere viewed as unlawful. But now and then they did take place, particularly in attempts to compel public employers to allow their workers to organize and to bargain collectively. Legislatures may thus have had a further reason for enacting public employee bargaining laws: they hoped thereby to reduce the incidence of troublesome "organizational" strikes by public employees. A comparable desire to reduce the incidence of organizational strikes by workers in industry was expressly identified by Congress as one of the reasons for the passage of the National Industrial Recovery Act in 1933 and the Wagner Act in 1935. If such reasoning was a factor in the enactment of state public employee collective bargaining statutes, these laws have certainly not reduced the number of strikes in the public sector. Public employees in many states no longer need strike over the right to organize or to bargain, but many strikes now occur over impasses at the bargaining table. Public school teachers, in particular, now resort to the strike much more frequently than they did before the first public employee bargaining laws were passed. Strikes by such public employees as transit workers, firemen, policemen, and trash collectors have also become more numerous.

FEDERAL LAW CONDUCIVE TO FACULTY COLLECTIVE
BARGAINING AT PRIVATE INSTITUTIONS

The turnabout in the statutory situation affecting collective bargaining by college faculties was completed in June 1970 when the NLRB ruled that nonprofit private educational institutions could thereafter be required to bargain with their employees under federal law. The initial ruling was made in a case that involved certain nonacademic employees of Cornell University.[17] The case was unusual in several ways. For one thing, the petition to the NLRB to conduct a representation election among these employees came, not from the workers, but from Cornell University as the employer.[18] For another, the bargaining between Cornell University and its employees could have taken shape under state law, since New York is one of the few states with a little Wagner Act applicable to private educational institutions. In fact, Syracuse University joined Cornell in presenting a petition to the NLRB even though a representation election had already been conducted, over the university's protest, among its service and maintenance employees under the direction of the New York State Labor Relations Board.[19] The NLRB dismissed the petition from Syracuse, asserting that "it is well established that it will recognize the validity of State-conducted elections and certifications where that election procedure was free of irregularities and reflected the true desire of the employees."

Why did Cornell and Syracuse turn to the NLRB, asking it to reverse its 1951 ruling in the Columbia University case and bring private educational institutions under its jurisdiction? Recognizing that they

17. 183 NLRB No. 41, 74 LRRM 1269 (1970).
18. The National Labor Relations Act permits an employer to petition for such an election, "alleging that one or more individuals or labor organizations have presented to him a claim to be recognized as the [employees'] representative," and asking that the claim be established by a polling of his employees. In practice, petitions for representation elections come much more frequently from the employee side of the relationship. In its ruling in the Cornell case, the NLRB observed that "in the past it has been the nonprofit employer who has opposed Board assertion of its jurisidiction."
19. The joint employer brief submitted to the NLRB by Cornell and Syracuse stated, "Syracuse does not seek to nullify the results of the State Board election, nor does Syracuse seek a new election; rather, Syracuse merely requests that the National Labor Relations Board assert jurisdiction and issue the appropriate certification" (p. 3 of the brief).

were going to have to bargain with certain of their employees under
state law in any event, the two universities preferred to go forward
under federal law in the belief that this course offered them certain advantages, the principal one being that federal law prohibited unfair
labor practices on the part of unions as well as employers, whereas the
New York statute placed such restraints only on employers. In asking
the NLRB to take jurisdiction, the two universities made two points:
(1) the states had "notoriously failed [to meet the] investiture of trust,"
made in them by Congress in 1935, 1947, and 1959 and by the NLRB
in its ruling in the Columbia case, that they would enact adequate
labor legislation governing such enterprises as private colleges and
universities; and (2) their operations had substantial impact on interstate commerce warranting an assertion of federal jurisdiction.[20]

In any event, there is no indication in the brief submitted to the
NLRB by Cornell and Syracuse, or in the Board's ruling in the case,
that anyone recognized the way was being opened to collective bargaining under NLRB supervision by faculty members as "employees"
of private institutions. A number of other educational institutions were
permitted by the NLRB to submit amici curiae briefs in the Cornell
case on both sides of the question. Among those supporting NLRB
assertion of jurisdiction were Boston University, Colgate University,
Fordham University, New York University, Wheaton College, and
Yale University. Among the institutions that asked the Board to refuse
jurisdiction were Baylor University, California Institute of Technology,
Southern Methodist University, Texas Christian University, and the
University of Miami. Presumably each institution was influenced by
its estimate of its own collective bargaining problem, but there is no
indication that any one of these institutions was giving thought to the
possibility that it might one day be asked to bargain with its faculty.
Indeed, it appears that the entire higher education establishment was
unaware of the full import of Cornell's request to the NLRB that it

20. Employer's Brief, pp. 14, 19, 23. Tracy H. Ferguson, whose law firm
represented Cornell University at the time of the NLRB proceeding, later asserted
that in 1968 he had "raised the rhetorical question of whether it would not be
wise for a private university faced with an organizational campaign to ask the
NLRB to take jurisdiction." But he confirms that no one was then thinking about
collective bargaining by faculty members at private institutions. See his chapter,
"Private Institutions and the NLRB," in *Faculty Power: Collective Bargaining on
Campus,* ed. Terrence N. Tice, pp. 59–62.

assert jurisdiction over private institutions. Probably a faculty organization or faculty members at some private institution would, within the next year or two, have petitioned the NLRB to recognize its claim to bargain with its institution under federal law. But in that event the attention of the NLRB would necessarily have been sharply focused from the start on the special problems of the status and role of faculty members within the academic community and the suitability of fitting them into a standard employer-employee relationship under federal law.

The NLRB did recognize that, in reversing a ruling which had stood for nearly twenty years and in bringing private colleges and universities all over the country under its jurisdiction, it was (to use its words) entering into "a hitherto uncharted area." Two approaches were available to the Board in its effort to chart this area and to respond to the requests that soon came to it to apply federal labor law to the unique relationships existing between faculties and their institutions. The usual approach would be to proceed on a case-by-case basis and let the ruling in each instance depend substantially on the particular facts and issues of that case. The common law controlling faculty collective bargaining at private institutions would thereby take shape out of a careful consideration of the specific issues in particular situations. There was much to be said for this approach, particularly since it is the standard one used by administrative agencies and courts in this country. The danger inherent in the approach was that the first cases reaching the NLRB might come from atypical institutions, present unusual conditions or problems, be inadequately argued by the parties, and yet call for rulings on basic issues.

To avoid the danger that it might find itself making important rulings affecting all of private higher education on the basis of the particular facts and arguments that isolated cases might present, the Board, as its second approach, could have exercised its authority under the National Labor Relations Act and the Administrative Procedure Act to hold hearings and receive briefs from a variety of spokesmen for educational institutions and associations in an attempt to determine what, if any, general rules it might announce to guide everyone in the determination of so-called representation issues as faculty collective bargaining in the private sector developed. With one exception, the Board elected to use the first approach, that is, proceed on a case-by-case basis.[21]

The exception was made with respect to the issue of what constituted sufficient involvement of an educational institution in interstate commerce to warrant an assertion of federal jurisdiction over collective bargaining at that institution. The NLRB invited and received expert testimony and thereafter, late in 1970, announced, as noted earlier, that it would take jurisdiction over cases coming from any private institution having an annual gross revenue of at least $1 million for use in meeting operating expenses.[22] The Board estimated that this standard would bring 80 percent of all private colleges and universities under federal jurisdiction and "approximately 95 percent of all full and part-time non-professional personnel." Even at this point the Board made no specific reference to professors; indeed its own words seemed to suggest that only "non-professional personnel" would be affected by its assertion of jurisdiction over higher education.

ARE FACULTY MEMBERS MANAGEMENT OR LABOR?

Although the issue was never shaped so simply by the NLRB in its rulings, the question the Board had to answer in cases that followed the Cornell ruling was whether faculty members were managerial agents or professional employees of their institutions. If the former, the law denied them the right to bargain; if the latter, it permitted them to bargain. As it turned out, the issue of whether faculty members fell within the language of the federal statute was decided in three cases that came to the Board in quick succession from Long Island University, Fordham University, and Adelphi University. In these cases labor organizations petitioned the Board to be certified as bargaining agents for groups of employees largely consisting of instructional personnel. The contention that faculty members ought to be excluded from the employer-employee relationship as established in the National Labor Relations Act was much more carefully argued by

21. The NLRB has made sparing use of this rule-making authority, and thus some persons regard as misleading the suggestion that the Labor Board had two approaches available to it. But the difficulties of navigation it was likely to encounter in "the uncharted area" of higher education were so numerous that it can properly be argued that the NLRB should have used this second approach. Its authority to do so was undeniable. See David Shapiro, "The Choice of Rule-making or Adjudication in the Development of Administrative Policy," 78 *Harvard Law Review* 931 (1965).

22. 35 Fed. Reg. 18370 (Dec. 3, 1970).

the university in the Fordham and Adelphi cases than it was in the Long Island case, but the Board made its first and decisive ruling in the Long Island case.

The effort to organize the Long Island University faculties took shape as separate movements on two campuses—the Brooklyn Center and the C. W. Post Center. The NLRB thus had representation petitions to consider in two cases. Its rulings in these cases were announced simultaneously, the C. W. Post Center case being the more fully elaborated.[23]

In its ruling in the C. W. Post Center case, the NLRB specifically acknowledged that "this is the first case in which the Board has been called upon to make appropriate unit determinations in regard to university teaching staffs." The Board once again asserted that it was "mindful" that it was "to some extent entering into an uncharted area." But it nonetheless gave to the university's claim that NLRB jurisdiction "should not be applied to its professional personnel" the terse reply that "this contention is ... without merit." The Board also rejected the university's more specific argument that faculty members were "supervisors" and as such should be denied the right to bargain because the federal statute expressly excluded supervisors from a bargaining unit. Again the Board's explanation of its ruling was brief:

> ... we are of the view that the policymaking and quasi-supervisory authority which adheres to full-time faculty status but is exercised by them only as a group does not make them supervisors within the meaning of Section 2(11) of the Act, or managerial employees who must be separately represented. Accordingly, we find that full-time university faculty members qualify in every respect as professional employees under Section 2(12) of the Act, and are therefore entitled to all the benefits of collective bargaining if they so desire.

The Board thus moved, essentially without explanation, from its position in the Cornell case, which had concerned only nonprofessional

23. C. W. Post Center, 189 NLRB No. 109, 77 LRRM 1001 (1971); Brooklyn Center, 189 NLRB No. 110, 77 LRRM 1006 (1971). The petitions in both cases were first presented to the NLRB regional director for Region 29 and testimony was received by a so-called hearing officer. By order of the regional director, both proceedings were transferred to the NLRB "for decision pursuant to ... the Board's Rules and Regulations...." The rulings were then made by the full five-member Board after it had reviewed the records of the hearings and had received briefs from the parties. Essentially the same procedure was followed by the NLRB in all of the cases considered in this book except that later cases were heard by three-member panels.

employees, to one that brought a university's faculty within the "employee" category as defined in the National Labor Relations Act and also within the Board's discretionary exercise of jurisdiction. Faculty members are undeniably "professional employees" of a corporation, but they are also widely regarded as something more than that—as the principal policy-makers and operators of the corporation's business. The NLRB might reasonably have been expected to pause and give careful consideration to this unusual relationship between a university and its faculty in the first case coming to it from academe. In defense of the Board, it may be said that Long Island University failed to describe this unusual relationship with appropriate care. In later cases, particularly those involving Fordham and Adelphi Universities, the relationship was described and the argument made that faculty members and collective bargaining under federal law were not meant for each other. But by then the Board had already gone the other way in the Long Island University cases and it did not choose to repudiate its first ruling on the basic jurisdictional issue.

Any examination of the NLRB's responses to the arguments of the Fordham and Adelphi governing boards needs to take into consideration that certain difficulties of terminology—and of the realities behind terminology—were bound to prove troublesome to everyone concerned in these cases: faculties, trustees, labor unions, and labor boards. Four decades of experience with collective bargaining in the industrial sector have made it relatively easy to identify the opposing parties, or adversaries, there as "management" and "labor," or as "employer" and "employees." None of these terms is entirely suitable to the situation in higher education. Faculty members typically assert that they are not "employees" but "officers" of their institutions. They almost never think of themselves or identify themselves as "labor." "Management" is an even more ambiguous term in higher education than it is in industry. In industry, managers may or may not be "owners," and they may not have legal authority to act for the "corporation." Typically, such authority is vested in a board whose members are called "directors," of whom some may also be full-time salaried employees. In industry, however, there is usually significant overlap between "managers," "directors," and "owners." But who constitutes "management" at a college or university? At times some faculty members are tempted to say that "management" is "the administration." Administrators may speak for management in higher education, but in most situations the legal authority of management is vested in the governing board, even though trustees are seldom viewed as "managing" an institution.

A further difficulty is encountered in relating faculty members, administrators, and trustees to the "institution" with which they are all identified. What is the institution? Who speaks for it? Who exercises its authority? Who runs it? The administration, the governing board, or—as professors themselves frequently claim—the faculty? The point here is that such questions have never been satisfactorily answered in educational practice. In practice, trustees, administrators, and faculty members refrain from pushing for final answers and are content to settle, under the most favorable conditions, for a state of equilibrium in their relationships—a state difficult to describe and impossible to define. But collective bargaining statutes were not written with this equilibrium in mind. "Labor" and "management," "employer" and "employees" are the terms used in labor relations statutes, labor board rulings, and collective bargaining contracts. If faculties elect to make use of the formal process of collective bargaining and are permitted to do so by labor boards, it is impossible to avoid the use of these terms, even though the realities of educational life are thereby obscured and even distorted. There are inescapable difficulties, then, in applying to the world of higher education the terms and concepts originally intended to cover labor relations in private industry.

The Fordham and Adelphi University Cases

At Fordham University in November 1970, the American Association of University Professors chapter and the Law School Bargaining Committee filed petitions with the NLRB asking to be certified as bargaining agents for the general faculty and the Law School faculty respectively. The university's governing board decided to resist the coming of faculty collective bargaining to Fordham as vigorously as circumstances and the law permitted. Accordingly, it obtained the services of a former NLRB General Counsel as one of its attorneys and presented its case against federal jurisdiction with great care and at considerable length, both through oral arguments before an NLRB trial examiner and by means of a written brief to the NLRB. The governing board argued that the NLRB should dismiss the petitions on the ground that faculty members were not "employees" within the meaning of the federal statute. It further argued that, if the NLRB rejected this contention, the bargaining units called for in the petitions were not proper ones under the law. This later contention will be examined in the next chapter.

The governing board endeavored to show that at Fordham the faculty, or a considerable part of it, exercises managerial and supervisory authority. Among other things, it argued that the faculty, particularly through department chairmen and faculty committees ("the true power centers of the University"), makes and administers policy in important areas of the university's program and also exercises "effective" authority over the appointment, job assignment, promotion, and dismissal of individual faculty members and certain other university employees. In its brief, the governing board attempted to use against its faculty—and the AAUP as the faculty's potential bargaining agent— the basic argument that the latter had been making through the years that "a community of scholars is the essence of a university." The brief asserted:

> Fordham University is a community of scholars; the faculty members are not merely individuals who work at the University; they are the University. The University has no existence independent of its faculty. It is the faculty which determines the character and quality of the University, and which effectively controls its academic policies and activities. The suggestion of the Petitioners herein that the faculty are merely "employees" of the University as a separate and distinct "employer" is a startling and unfounded distortion of the fundamental facts of university life. . . .
>
> The relationship among peers in a University's assemblage of scholars is *sui generis*. Any effort to analyze the University's assemblage in terms of an employer-employee relationship will necessarily distort the true state of affairs beyond recognition. . . .
>
> The policy of the Board has thus far been to decline to assert its jurisdiction over the noncommercial activities of nonprofit corporations. The Board should continue to exercise self-restraint where the activities of a nonprofit university are noncommercial in nature and are intimately connected with its educational functions. The academic affairs of the University are clearly separable from the regular commercial functions and are not of a like nature to the commercial functions.[24]

Thus, concluded the governing board, if the faculty were allowed to bargain collectively with the university, it would in effect be sitting on both sides of the table as "management" and "labor."

24. Brief of Fordham University, pp. 8, 74, 76.

After the oral arguments in the Fordham case before the trial examiner had been made, but before the university's brief was submitted to the NLRB, the latter rendered its ruling in the C. W. Post Center case in which it essentially rejected the point the Fordham governing board was making. Fordham then asked that the case be set down for oral argument before the NLRB itself, but this request was denied. The Fordham governing board could not have been much surprised when it fared no better than had the Long Island board in persuading the NLRB that the petitions of the labor organizations should be dismissed, but it may well have expected that the NLRB would respond to its contention more carefully than it did to the less well developed but similar contention in the C. W. Post Center case. The NLRB, however, made almost no effort to go beyond its earlier rejection of the argument that faculty members are part of an institution's "management" and therefore should be denied the right to bargain collectively with the institution. The Board agreed that Fordham faculty members did possess policy-making authority in many areas and also exercised appointive powers over certain university employees. But it nonetheless "reject[ed] the Employer's contention that the faculty members are supervisors." The federal statute expressly defines supervisors as *individuals* who exercise certain types of "authority." In the Fordham case, the NLRB found that the faculty's "role in policy determination" is exercised "only as a group.... [T]his is insufficient to make the faculty members supervisors."[25] And, again, the role played by those faculty members who serve on committees and determine university policy is "one of participation in a group determination and does not make them individually supervisors." Thus, the conclusion:

25. 193 NLRB No. 23, 78 LRRM 1177 (1971). The "supervisor issue" is examined at this point only to the extent that it raises the possibility that an entire faculty, or a substantial part of a faculty, is ineligible for collective bargaining because its members are supervisory employees, excluded by statute from bargaining units. See chap. 4 for discussion of the inclusion in bargaining units of faculty members who are department chairmen or who serve on certain faculty committees whose work might be viewed as supervisory.

The Fordham governing board also argued that the AAUP petition should be rejected on the ground that AAUP was not "a labor organization" under the federal statute. The argument was largely based on evidence that AAUP itself claimed it was not a "labor union." But since the statute defines "labor organization" broadly, the NLRB disposed of this contention in a footnote, stating that "it is abundantly clear that AAUP meets the definition of 'labor organization' set forth in Section 2(25) of the Act."

we find that faculty members are not supervisors, but are professional employees within the meaning of Section 2(12) of the Act, and are entitled to all the benefits of collective bargaining if they so desire.

The National Labor Relations Act does not contain a satisfactory definition of an "employer" and it does not define "management" at all. It does state that "the term 'employer' includes any person acting as an agent of an employer, directly or indirectly," but the relevancy, if any, of this language to faculty collective bargaining has never been carefully examined by the NLRB. Here, too, the statute can be viewed as applicable only to an individual exercise of employer (managerial) authority, not to group exercise. Presumably this statutory language does require the exclusion of such university employees as the president, the provost, or the academic dean from a faculty bargaining unit. Presumably also, the governing board is clearly the employer, or management, in the context of university collective bargaining. That a governing board comprises a group is irrelevant, because the above definition of "employer," refers to "any person" acting as "an agent of an employer," but not to the employer himself or itself.

In March 1972, in the Adelphi University case, the NLRB again gave attention to the possibility that at such an institution faculty members are exercising types or degrees of authority on a collective or group basis that is substantially more managerial than is ordinarily viewed as consistent with "employee" status. The Board now for the first time conceded that some difficulty is encountered in applying the language of the federal statute to faculty members at such institutions as Long Island, Fordham, and Adelphi Universities:

> The difficulty . . . may have potentially deep roots, stemming from the fact that the concept of collegiality, wherein power and authority is vested in a body composed of all one's peers or colleagues, does not square with the traditional authority structures with which this Act was designed to cope in the typical organizations of the commercial world. . . .
> Because authority vested in one's peers, acting as a group, simply would not conform to the pattern for which the supervisory exclusion of our Act was designed, a genuine system of collegiality would tend to confound us.[26]

Although the Board conceded further that it was having to recognize and give "*some* effect" to the collegial principle, it concluded that

26. 195 NLRB No. 107, 79 LRRM 1545 (1972).

at these educational institutions "the ultimate authority does *not* rest with the peer group but rather with the board of trustees." Thus,

> We are not disposed to disenfranchise faculty members [from electing to exercise their statutory right to collective bargaining] merely because they have some measure of quasi-collegial authority either as an entire faculty or as representatives elected by the faculty.

The Faculty Role at a State Institution: The Eastern Michigan University Case

The cases thus far examined involve private educational institutions. A notable example of the same issue at a public university is found in the Eastern Michigan University case which was decided by the Michigan Employment Relations Commission (MERC) early in 1972. Three labor organizations sought designation as bargaining agent for a faculty unit at the university. Disagreement among them, and between them and the governing board, about the composition of the unit made necessary a proceeding before the commission. A trial examiner received briefs from the parties and heard arguments. Before the governing board indicated its position with respect to the composition of the unit, it made essentially the same attempt as the Fordham and Adelphi governing boards to persuade the labor board that it should dismiss the proceeding on the ground that collective bargaining between the governing board and faculty was not authorized by the Michigan statute. The trial examiner summarized the governing board's argument in his recommended decision to MERC, as follows:

> The University argues that unlike the normal employer-employee relationship, the academic community exercises the University's authority, and that the organizational and operational basis of the University is based upon "a community of power" with the faculty rather than the hierarchy of power found in the usual employment relationship. Thus, the Employer argues that the faculty of the University is the University, and that they participate in such matters as the selection of the University president and department heads, make up the curriculum and schedule, and engage in similar management-type matters which in other employment situations are decided by a central authority rather than by the persons affected. Therefore, the University argues that the imposition of rigid jurisdictional units upon the community of power as exercised in the major universities will destroy the university community as it has existed, and will intrude upon the constitutionally-sanctioned relationship between the University Board of Control and the academic community.

Having stated the nature of the university's reasoning so admirably, the trial examiner then largely ignored it. Instead, he seemed concerned only to show that faculty collective bargaining would not diminish the authority to run the university vested in the governing board by the state constitution. He disposed of the argument that faculty members help run the institution and are thus as much "management" as they are "labor" by noting that the NLRB "faced the same contention" in the Fordham case and "rejected it as being without merit." Thus, he advised:

> As the individuals involved herein have the usual incidents of the employer-employee relationship and are employees within the meaning of the Act, they are entitled to its benefits.

The full commission carefully considered other aspects of the trial examiner's recommendations and decided not to follow certain of them. But it accepted his recommendation on this basic issue without further discussion.[27]

The Faculty as "Management," a Dead Issue?

It is unlikely that any labor board will hereafter hesitate to let faculty members claim the right to bargain collectively, on the basis of a governing board's contention that the faculty is part of management and is thus not properly viewed as the worker half of the employer-employee relationship that collective bargaining statutes are concerned with. But the contention deserved much more serious consideration by the National Labor Relations Board and such a state board as the Michigan Employment Relations Commission than it was given—particularly where, as in the Fordham and Eastern Michigan cases, governing boards submitted impressive evidence documenting the substantial roles that the faculties were playing in the manage-

---

27. The recommended decision of the trial examiner and the MERC "decision and order" were available to us in mimeographed format. Two of the three labor organizations appeared before the commission as petitioners, the third as an intervenor. Each of the petitions received a case number (R70K-407 and R71A-2).

The trial examiner uses "university" as synonymous with "employer" and "governing board." In view of the frequent faculty contention that *it* is the university, this identification of the university as the employer is troublesome. In this book, the "employer" is usually identified as the governing board. But it is difficult to be entirely consistent on this point, in view of the common tendency of labor boards, the courts, and the parties to university collective bargaining themselves to use "university" and "employer" interchangeably.

ment of their institutions. These labor boards never seriously examined the distinction between "managerial employees" and "professional employees" and its relevance to the part played by faculty members in the operation of their institutions. In the end, the boards made their rulings pretty much on the basis of the meaning of the term "supervisor" as it is defined in labor statutes and administrative practice. In other words, "supervisor" is the legal dividing line between management and labor: the job role is what separates managerial employees (who cannot bargain) from professional employees (who can bargain). The precise definition and application of the supervisor concept will be examined in chapter four, as it has controlled the inclusion or exclusion of certain faculty members from faculty bargaining units. It is enough here to note that the NLRB took an easy way out of its dilemma by calling attention to the fact that the federal statute defines "supervisors" as "individuals." Thus, a faculty as a whole could not be denied the right to bargain because it collectively exercised many of the supervisory powers or duties expressly listed in the statute as identifying a "supervisor."

Just possibly the issue is not yet dead. A determined governing board, such as Fordham's, could carry the issue to the federal courts for review there, by refusing to bargain with its faculty and then defending itself against an unfair labor practice charge that it was not negotiating in good faith. The Fordham board did not face the decision whether to take this step, for the Fordham faculty voted against collective bargaining in the representation election ordered by the NLRB. (The law faculty, which the NLRB recognized as a separate unit, did select a bargaining agent, but it appears not to have bargained very aggressively with the governing board thereafter.)

One may also wonder how the NLRB will react to such an institutional bylaw as the following one at Oberlin College if the faculty of such a private institution seeks recognition as a bargaining unit:

> The General Faculty is intrusted with the management of the internal affairs of the College, but must obtain the concurrence of the Trustees in order to introduce any important change affecting the established methods or principles of administration.

Perhaps the NLRB will then recognize the "genuine system of collegiality" referred to in its ruling in the Adelphi University case and confess that it is indeed "confounded."

CHAPTER THREE

Faculty Dissatisfaction as a Cause
of Collective Bargaining

Six years after the enactment of the Michigan statute authorizing bargaining by state employees, only two faculties among the thirteen four-year public institutions had negotiated contracts. (Two others had chosen bargaining agents.) And in the entire private sector of American higher education, two years after the NLRB had cleared the legal way for faculty bargaining, the four-year institutions with faculty contracts could be counted on the fingers of one hand. Clearly, then, a faculty must have its own substantive reasons for taking the step that the law allows. Such reasons can be summed up as a dissatisfaction with things as they are and an expectation that things will get better under collective bargaining.

Samuel Gompers is remembered for his use of the word "more" to indicate what labor was seeking through unions and collective action. In Gompers' time, "more" essentially meant better wages. The language of the collective bargaining statutes, of a later date, suggests that labor's goal has become a more varied one of higher wages, shorter hours, job security, and better working conditions. Faculty members who have turned to collective bargaining have been motivated by a wish to improve their employment status in one or more of these four respects. In a rare instance, such as at Bryant College in Rhode Island, the contract that emerges from the negotiations reveals that compensation is the dominant or even the sole issue that motivates a faculty to resort to collective bargaining. But, as persons who claim to be "officers" of the nonprofit corporations with which they are identified, faculty members often hope to make gains out of collective bargaining running well beyond those that Gompers and his successors desired for industrial workers. What are these motives? Or, put specifically, what dissatisfactions are leading faculties to turn to bargaining as a way of trying to improve their lot?

DISSATISFACTION IN THE ACADEMIC PROFESSION IN 1969

In 1969, the Carnegie Commission on Higher Education undertook a series of surveys of students, faculty members, and administrators in the nation's colleges and universities. As part of this project, an elaborate questionnaire was sent to 100,315 faculty members at 78 universities, 168 four-year colleges, 43 junior colleges, and 14 predominantly black colleges. Selected from the nation's 2,433 colleges and universities, these 303 institutions were primarily those which had participated in the 1966 Cooperative Institutional Research Program of the American Council on Education. Usable returns were received from 60,028 faculty members, 59.8 percent of the group receiving the questionnaire.[1]

The questionnaire was designed to elicit factual data about the American academic profession, as well as about the attitudes of faculty members on a wide range of controversial issues. Among other things, the respondents were asked to indicate how they felt about collective bargaining, labor unions, and strikes in higher education, and also their levels of satisfaction with salaries, teaching loads, and institutional governance systems.

The collective bargaining item asked respondents to check one of four positions ("strongly agree," "agree with reservations," "disagree with reservations," "strongly disagree") on the following assertion: "Collective bargaining by faculty members has no place in a college or university." One could wish that the statement had been put in more positive and precise fashion, asking the faculty member to give his view of the desirability or probability of faculty collective bargaining at his own institution. But the response to the question does at least show how some 60,000 faculty members felt about the appropriateness of faculty collective bargaining in higher education in 1969. Moreover, by correlating the responses to this item with replies to several items designed to show the extent of faculty satisfaction and dissatisfaction with conditions at individual institutions, certain con-

1. The faculty questionnaire was designed and administered by the Survey Research Center at the University of California, Berkeley, and the Office of Research of the American Council on Education. The questionnaire, an explanation of the sampling and weighting techniques employed, and some preliminary summary data appear in Alan E. Bayer, *College and University Faculty: A Statistical Description.*

clusions may be entertained concerning the reasons why some faculties began turning to collective bargaining at the end of the 1960s.

As the assertion was worded—"bargaining has . . . no place"—an affirmative reply ("strongly agree" or "agree with reservations") meant that the respondent in effect was opposed to collective bargaining as an appropriate process "in a college or university." To simplify the analysis here, the reply percentages to the assertion as actually stated have been reversed. Thus, 59 percent of the 60,000 respondents strongly agreed, or agreed with reservations, that faculty collective bargaining "has [a] place" in American higher education. As shown in Table 1, the greatest support for collective bargaining was indicated by the faculties of predominantly black colleges and two-year colleges (more than two-thirds in each category), followed by public four-year colleges, private four-year colleges, private universities, and public universities.

A further analysis of the data shows that in all types of institutions nontenured faculty members supported collective bargaining more strongly than did their tenured colleagues, and younger faculty more than did older faculty. Thus, although less than half of the tenured faculty at the public and private universities favored bargaining (47.5 percent and 49.8 percent), support among nontenured faculty at these institutions (59.6 percent and 63.0 percent) and the numerical size of the nontenured groups were sufficient to produce an overall faculty majority at the two types of universities in favor of collective bargaining.

Opposition to collective bargaining was registered by more than half of the respondents only in the age category fifty-one and over: 55.8 percent at public universities, and 53.6 percent at private universi-

TABLE 1: *Percentage of Faculty Members Who Support Collective Bargaining, 1969 ("Strongly Agree" or "Agree with Reservations")*

Institutional Type	Age			All Respondents
	35 and Younger	36–50	51 and Older	
Public universities.................	60.4	52.6	44.2	53.2
Private universities................	65.4	56.8	46.4	56.6
Public four-year colleges...........	67.7	62.7	62.5	64.4
Private four-year colleges..........	68.9	59.8	50.3	60.3
Two-year colleges.................	74.7	66.7	65.8	69.4
Predominantly black colleges.......	77.1	67.4	64.8	70.0
All respondents..................	65.9	57.9	51.5	59.0

ties. Except at the public four-year colleges, where collective bargaining was supported with greater unanimity among all age groups and tenured and nontenured faculty members than in the other types of institutions, collective bargaining was an issue that divided faculties along the lines of age and tenure status.

Among the disciplines, only in engineering and law did less than a majority favor collective bargaining. The greatest support came from the faculties of psychology, social sciences, and medicine (see Table 2).

A number of items in the faculty questionnaire were designed to show the respondent's attitude toward his institution, his compensation, and the conditions under which he worked. We have analyzed the answers according to the type of institution at which the respondent was a faculty member, his age, and how he stood on collective bargaining. The exact assertions or queries to which respondents were asked to react and the range of possible answers were:

> In general, how do you feel about this institution? ("It is a very good place for me," "It is fairly good for me," "It is not the place for me.")

> Do you feel that there are circumstances in which a strike would be a legitimate means of collective action for faculty members? ("Definitely yes," "Probably yes," "Probably not," "Definitely not.")

> How would you rate faculty salary levels at your institution? ("Excellent," "Good," "Fair," "Poor.")

> Your own salary [is]: ("Excellent," "Good," "Fair," "Poor.")

> Teaching load at your institution [is]: ("Excellent," "Good," "Fair," "Poor.")

> A small group of senior professors has disproportionate power in decision-making in this institution. ("Strongly agree," "Agree with reservations," "Disagree with reservations," "Strongly disagree.")

TABLE 2: *Percentage of Faculty Members Supporting Collective Bargaining, by Discipline, 1969*

Discipline	Percentage	Discipline	Percentage
Engineering	38.8	Business	59.0
Law	49.0	Education	65.0
Biological sciences	53.5	Fine arts, humanities	65.6
Physical sciences,		Medicine	68.1
mathematics	53.9	Social sciences	68.7
All other disciplines	57.3	Psychology	69.8

The administration at your institution [is]: ("Excellent," "Good," "Fair," "Poor.")

Do you feel that the administration of your department is autocratic ("Very," "Somewhat") [or] democratic ("Somewhat," "Very")?

The effectiveness of your campus senate or faculty council [is]: ("Excellent," "Good," "Fair," "Poor.")

As shown in Table 3, although strong support for faculty collective bargaining was indicated by faculty members at two-year colleges,[2] these same respondents indicated greater satisfaction with their choice of college teaching as a career and with their present institutions than did faculty members at any other type of institution. In general, they did not indicate strong resentment of the power of senior professors, nor were they as critical of the administration of either their institutions or their departments as were faculty members elsewhere. They were slightly less satisfied with teaching loads, institutional salary schedules, and their own salaries than were respondents generally, but they were not more militant, and were only slightly more supportive of the faculty strike than their colleagues elsewhere.

At all types of institutions, faculty members who favored collective bargaining were more likely to indicate that a small group of senior professors had disproportionate power and, to a lesser degree, that their departments were autocratic, than were faculty members who opposed bargaining. They were more dissatisfied with the institutional salary schedules than with their own salaries, teaching loads, and the administration of the institutions, and they gave lower ratings to the effectiveness of faculty senates and councils. They were much more likely to feel that the faculty strike was a legitimate means of collective action than were those who opposed bargaining (see Table 3).

Faculty members at public four-year colleges, while supporting collective bargaining by roughly a two-to-one margin, indicated substantial satisfaction with both institutional salary schedules and their

2. The greatest support for bargaining (70.0 percent) was indicated by faculty members at the predominantly black colleges. They also indicated much greater dissatisfaction with their institutions, their salaries, their career choices, working conditions, and administrations, and a greater support for faculty militancy and the use of the strike, than faculties of the other types of institutions. Paradoxically, however, faculties at predominantly black institutions have not yet turned to collective bargaining, and there is thus no examination in this volume of the impact of faculty bargaining on these institutions. For the same reason, attention here is focused on universities and two- and four-year colleges, public and private, and not on a special category such as the predominantly black institution.

own salaries. However, the general satisfaction of the older faculty at these institutions inflated these percentages and disguised the wide difference of opinion between age groups at the public four-year colleges with respect to salaries, the administration of the institutions, and the power of senior professors, shown in Table 4.

The greatest divergence of opinion between those who favored bargaining and those who opposed it was over the issue of the faculty strike (Table 3). Among those who favored bargaining, support of the strike was greatest at private universities and least, surprisingly, at the two-year colleges. The strike was also the issue which divided all faculties most severely along age lines, with about 70 percent of faculty members at age thirty-five and below favoring the strike and less than half of those at age fifty-one and above favoring it (Table 4). There was little difference between types of institutions on this issue.

AAUP's SALARY SURVEYS:
A DECADE OF ECONOMIC PROGRESS IN ACADEME

If it is assumed that professors, like other employees, turn to collective bargaining to gain "more," we are faced with something of a paradox. The turn began in 1968 and 1969, at the end of a fifteen-year period during which academic salaries had shown a sharp improvement and almost certainly the greatest improvement during any similar period in the present century. This improvement resulted in large measure from a change in the supply-demand balance: the supply of academicians was not adequate to meet the demands of a higher education system that was enjoying great public favor and undergoing a period of unprecedented growth. But the possibility must also be considered that the annual faculty salary surveys conducted by the American Association of University Professors—the first made for the year 1958–59—in themselves constituted an effective mechanism for enabling the academic profession to capitalize on its improved market position.[3] These surveys may well have constituted a device for bring-

3. The surveys were conducted by AAUP's Committee Z on the Economic Status of the Profession. The first report was published in the *AAUP Bulletin* in June 1959. That these surveys may only have measured gains and not helped to cause them is suggested by AAUP's own findings of significant improvements in academic salaries as early as the 1955–57 biennium. It can be argued, however, that the continuing improvement in faculty salaries during the 1960s might not have been sustained in the absence of the AAUP surveys. See the AAUP report for 1969–70, "Rising Costs and the Public Institutions," 56 *AAUP Bulletin* (June 1970), 174–239, especially the graphs on pp. 176–77.

TABLE 3: *Faculty Satisfactions/Dissatisfactions, by Type of Institution and Respondents' Attitude toward Collective Bargaining*

(Percentage Distribution)

Respondents' Attitude[a] toward Bargaining, by Institutional Type	Collective bargaining by faculty members has [a] place on a college or university campus	Institution is a "very good" place for me	Faculty strike is legitimate in certain circumstances ("definitely yes," "probably yes")	Faculty salary levels are "excellent," or "good"	Faculty member's own salary is "excellent," or "good"	Institution's teaching load is "excellent," or "good"	Senior professors have disproportionate power in decision making ("strongly agree," "agree with reservations")	Administration of institution is "excellent," or "good"	Administration of department is autocratic ("very," "somewhat")	Effectiveness of faculty senate or council ("excellent," "good")	
All institutions											
Favor	59.0		63.6	42.4	50.0	47.8	47.0	45.7	33.1	34.8	1
Oppose	41.0		20.6	52.7	60.8	56.4	35.3	58.7	29.3	43.2	2
All respondents	100.0	47.9	46.0	46.6	54.5	51.3	42.3	51.0	31.5	38.3	3
Public universities											
Favor	53.2		62.9	41.3	51.5	53.8	50.0	42.4	38.2	32.0	4
Oppose	46.8		19.2	51.4	63.1	58.8	37.0	56.3	32.2	40.5	5
All respondents	100.0	47.0	42.6	46.0	56.9	56.1	43.9	48.8	35.4	35.9	6
Private universities											
Favor	56.6		66.0	44.7	48.5	59.5	53.6	50.5	39.4	37.8	7
Oppose	43.4		23.1	57.4	61.3	65.8	41.6	63.4	33.7	44.9	8
All respondents	100.0	49.9	47.0	50.3	54.2	62.3	48.3	56.2	36.9	41.1	9

	Public four-year colleges										
10	Favor.................	64.4		65.5	54.5	55.1	39.6	52.4	46.1	32.5	34.7	*10*
11	Oppose................	35.6		21.7	60.2	63.6	57.0	37.5	57.5	31.1	41.9	*11*
12	All respondents.......	100.0	42.3	49.7	56.6	58.2	42.5	47.1	50.2	32.0	37.3	*12*
	Private four-year colleges										
13	Favor.................	60.3		62.8	33.2	43.5	49.1	41.4	48.2	41.0	37.8	*13*
14	Oppose................	39.7		20.4	47.0	55.0	47.7	28.3	61.2	21.8	46.1	*14*
15	All respondents.......	100.0	48.7	45.6	38.8	48.2	52.3	38.4	55.2	33.2	41.2	*15*
	Two-year colleges										
16	Favor.................	69.3		60.5	44.2	53.2	37.3	32.4	50.0	24.5	39.4	*16*
17	Oppose................	30.7		18.2	56.4	61.1	49.1	24.1	64.1	21.2	53.7	*17*
18	All respondents.......	100.0	55.9	49.5	47.9	55.7	40.9	29.9	54.3	23.5	43.8	*18*
	Predominantly black colleges										
19	Favor.................	70.0		72.3	17.7	30.5	28.6	69.2	25.5	36.4	14.1	*19*
20	Oppose................	30.0		38.6	23.7	37.6	38.2	57.6	35.4	29.4	21.4	*20*
21	All respondents.......	100.0	29.9	62.2	19.5	32.6	31.4	65.7	28.5	34.3	16.3	*21*

a Favor = Those who "strongly agree" or "agree with reservations" that "collective bargaining by faculty members has [a] place in a college or university."
Oppose = Those who "strongly disagree" or "disagree with reservations" that "collective bargaining by faculty members has [a] place in a college or university."

TABLE 4: *Faculty Satisfactions/Dissatisfactions, by Type of Institution, Age of Respondents, and Attitude toward Collective Bargaining* [a]

(Percentage Distribution)

Respondents' Age by Institutional Type	Senior professors have disproportionate power in decision making ("strongly agree," "agree with reservations")			Administration of institution is "excellent" or "good"		
	Agree	Support Barg.	Oppose Barg.	Agree	Support Barg.	Oppose Barg.
All institutions						
1 All respondents	42.3	47.0	35.3	51.0	45.7	58.7
2 35 and under		54.8	44.8		39.0	50.9
3 36–50		44.4	34.2		46.9	58.2
4 51 and over		39.0	27.3		55.5	67.5
Public universities						
5 All respondents	43.9	50.0	37.0	48.8	42.4	56.3
6 35 and under		59.2	47.2		35.2	46.2
7 36–50		46.4	35.9		43.8	56.2
8 51 and over		39.6	27.9		53.5	67.3
Private universities						
9 All respondents	48.3	53.6	41.6	56.2	50.5	63.4
10 35 and under		60.4	52.1		44.8	59.3
11 36–50		52.3	41.9		51.7	61.4
12 51 and over		45.2	33.3		57.2	69.3
Public four-year colleges						
13 All respondents	47.1	52.4	37.5	50.2	46.1	57.5
14 35 and under		60.8	47.9		39.0	49.5
15 36–50		49.6	33.8		48.8	57.6
16 51 and over		42.6	29.5		53.7	69.1
Private four-year colleges						
17 All respondents	38.4	41.4	28.3	55.2	48.2	61.2
18 35 and under		50.5	37.1		45.0	56.4
19 36–50		38.7	26.5		47.2	59.2
20 51 and over		30.7	23.6		56.0	68.4
Two-year colleges						
21 All respondents	29.9	32.4	24.1	54.3	50.0	64.1
22 35 and under		35.0	30.5		41.4	60.5
23 36–50		29.3	26.1		51.3	64.8
24 51 and over		33.9	12.6		62.9	66.8
Predominantly black colleges						
25 All respondents	65.7	69.2	57.6	28.5	25.5	35.4
26 35 and under		77.8	64.9		15.0	20.0
27 36–50		66.3	54.7		25.9	38.3
28 51 and over		60.8	55.5		40.7	44.5

[a] Support bargaining = Those who "strongly agree" or "agree with reservations" that "collective bargaining by faculty members has [a] place in a college or university."
    Oppose bargaining = Those who "strongly disagree" or "disagree with reservations" that "collective bargaining by faculty members has [a] place in a college or university."

Respondents' Age by Institutional Type	Administration of department is autocratic ("very," "somewhat")			Effectiveness of faculty senate or council ("excellent," "good")		
	Agree	Support Barg.	Oppose Barg.	Agree	Support Barg.	Oppose Barg.
All institutions						
1 All respondents...............	31.5	33.1	29.3	38.3	34.8	43.2
2 35 and under................		38.3	36.0		30.2	37.8
3 36–50......................		31.1	29.5		35.1	41.8
4 51 and over.................		27.4	22.2		42.9	51.0
Public universities						
5 All respondents...............	35.4	38.2	32.2	35.9	32.0	40.5
6 35 and under................		43.0	38.4		27.4	33.9
7 36–50......................		36.3	32.6		32.0	38.2
8 51 and over.................		33.3	24.7		41.4	51.5
Private universities						
9 All respondents...............	36.9	39.4	33.7	41.1	37.8	44.9
10 35 and under................		45.8	39.5		34.3	42.0
11 36–50......................		39.5	35.8		37.8	42.1
12 51 and over.................		29.0	26.3		43.7	51.3
Public four-year colleges						
13 All respondents...............	32.0	32.5	31.1	37.3	34.7	41.9
14 35 and under................		40.3	42.3		31.6	39.5
15 36–50......................		29.3	30.3		34.8	40.3
16 51 and over.................		24.7	18.0		40.5	48.5
Private four-year colleges						
17 All respondents...............	33.2	41.0	21.8	41.2	37.8	46.1
18 35 and under................		45.1	24.7		35.3	41.0
19 36–50......................		43.2	23.2		37.0	45.0
20 51 and over.................		28.8	17.6		43.8	51.7
Two-year colleges						
21 All respondents...............	23.5	24.5	21.2	43.8	39.4	53.7
22 35 and under................		29.5	29.0		29.7	46.7
23 36–50......................		20.5	17.9		41.8	56.2
24 51 and over.................		23.5	18.4		52.2	57.1
Predominantly black colleges						
25 All respondents...............	34.3	36.4	29.4	16.3	14.1	21.4
26 35 and under................		46.5	36.8		12.4	10.5
27 36–50......................		34.0	27.1		11.4	26.5
28 51 and over.................		25.2	26.7		20.1	23.3

Continued on next page

47

TABLE 4: *Continued*

Respondents' Age by Institutional Type	Faculty strike is legitimate in certain circumstances ("definitely yes," "probably yes")			Faculty salary levels are "excellent" or "good"		
	Agree	Support Barg.	Oppose Barg.	Agree	Support Barg.	Oppose Barg.
All institutions						
1 All respondents..............	46.0	63.6	20.6	46.6	42.4	52.7
2 35 and under................		71.7	27.0		40.4	50.2
3 36–50......................		63.1	20.5		42.1	51.5
4 51 and over................		49.8	14.2		46.5	57.3
Public universities						
5 All respondents..............	42.6	62.9	19.2	46.0	41.3	51.4
6 35 and under................		71.8	26.0		39.7	49.1
7 36–50......................		60.7	20.2		41.6	50.3
8 51 and over................		50.0	13.2		43.7	55.7
Private universities						
9 All respondents..............	47.0	66.0	23.1	50.3	44.7	57.4
10 35 and under................		74.2	30.6		44.4	54.7
11 36–50......................		66.0	24.1		43.4	55.4
12 51 and over................		52.3	16.0		48.0	62.3
Public four-year colleges						
13 All respondents..............	49.7	65.5	21.7	56.6	54.5	60.2
14 35 and under................		72.3	25.0		50.6	59.5
15 36–50......................		65.6	23.4		53.6	59.9
16 51 and over................		52.9	17.7		63.4	61.9
Private four-year colleges						
17 All respondents..............	45.6	62.8	20.4	38.8	33.2	47.0
18 35 and under................		69.8	27.6		32.3	43.4
19 36–50......................		63.5	21.7		32.7	41.7
20 51 and over................		48.8	12.9		35.9	57.0
Two-year colleges						
21 All respondents..............	49.5	60.5	18.2	47.9	44.2	56.4
22 35 and under................		68.9	25.7		41.3	49.2
23 36–50......................		61.0	15.7		44.2	59.3
24 51 and over................		44.0	14.3		49.5	56.6
Predominantly black colleges						
25 All respondents..............	62.2	72.3	38.6	19.5	17.7	23.7
26 35 and under................		82.7	49.5		16.1	26.3
27 36–50......................		73.2	33.6		15.5	24.1
28 51 and over................		55.8	37.6		23.1	20.9

48

Respondents' Age by Institutional Type	Faculty member's own salary is "excellent" or "good"			Institution's teaching load is "excellent" or "good"		
	Agree	Support Barg.	Oppose Barg.	Agree	Support Barg.	Oppose Barg.
All institutions						
1 All respondents	54.5	50.0	60.8	51.3	47.8	56.4
2 35 and under		46.1	55.8		47.4	54.7
3 36–50		50.6	61.8		47.5	54.5
4 51 and over		56.1	64.4		49.2	61.4
Public universities						
5 All respondents	56.9	51.5	63.1	56.1	53.8	58.8
6 35 and under		48.4	58.3		54.2	58.0
7 36–50		53.2	64.3		53.8	57.8
8 51 and over		54.1	66.1		53.2	61.4
Private universities						
9 All respondents	54.2	48.5	61.3	62.3	59.5	65.8
10 35 and under		42.1	52.2		61.0	63.2
11 36–50		50.7	63.3		58.3	64.6
12 51 and over		54.6	65.4		59.7	69.7
Public four-year colleges						
13 All respondents	58.2	55.1	63.6	42.5	39.6	57.0
14 35 and under		51.7	58.5		40.6	54.5
15 36–50		52.7	63.4		37.5	53.2
16 51 and over		66.1	71.4		41.9	64.1
Private four-year colleges						
17 All respondents	48.2	43.5	55.0	52.3	49.1	47.7
18 35 and under		40.1	53.0		47.7	49.7
19 36–50		43.5	52.6		49.7	42.6
20 51 and over		49.4	59.7		50.3	55.3
Two-year colleges						
21 All respondents	55.7	53.2	61.1	40.9	37.3	49.1
22 35 and under		47.3	52.9		34.9	42.3
23 36–50		54.4	66.4		36.3	49.8
24 51 and over		61.7	60.9		43.8	55.6
Predominantly black colleges						
25 All respondents	32.6	30.5	37.6	31.4	28.6	38.2
26 35 and under		29.3	35.1		24.1	37.5
27 36–50		27.0	35.6		27.6	30.5
28 51 and over		37.6	42.4		36.5	49.1

ing pressure on individual institutions to seek higher rankings in these well-publicized annual reports by upgrading their salary scales. Although no scholarly study is available to confirm a direct relationship between the AAUP surveys and the improvement in academic compensation during the 1960s, many faculty members and administrators have testified to the existence of such a relationship at their institutions. And as many an administrator found, his institution's disappointing standing in the AAUP surveys strengthened his case with his trustees that the rate of improvement in faculty compensation must be substantially increased.

The AAUP surveys certainly helped gain national acceptance of the twin ideas that for a long time academicians had been members of a severely disadvantaged profession and that improvement in the profession's economic status should be forthcoming at the institutional level through significant increments year by year. Many other sections of the American work force also came during the 1960s to expect and enjoy annual improvement in their compensation, but the rate of improvement for college professors during the decade ran well above the increase in living costs as measured by the Consumer Price Index. Increases in "real faculty purchasing power" were enjoyed in every year from 1960–61 to 1968–69, ranging from a high of 5.9 percent in 1964–65 to a low of 1.7 percent in 1968–69.[4]

There was, of course, no abrupt decision by the academic profession either to abandon or to supplement the AAUP annual salary surveys by resorting to collective bargaining. The change in tactics was made slowly, institution by institution, and by mid-1972 could not yet be viewed as a far-reaching change in self-help efforts.[5] There had, however, been a significant slowing down in the annual rate of improvement in academic salaries at the end of the 1960s. The report of AAUP's Committee Z for the year 1970–71 revealed that average compensations for college professors had increased over the preceding year by only 6.2 percent, as against an increase in the Consumer Price Index of just under 6 percent. "The increase in *real* terms compared to

4. Ibid.
5. The AAUP, in becoming a more aggressive participant in collective bargaining, has recognized that its annual salary surveys may be endangered through refusal of some institutions to contribute salary data to an educational association that has decided to welcome the status of "labor organization" in the adversary relationship of collective bargaining.

the CPI was thus barely noticeable; this was, on average, a year of standstill" in the judgment of Committee Z.[6]

Dissatisfactions at Institutions Where Collective Bargaining Elections Have Been Held

Information concerning specific faculty dissatisfactions at those institutions where a proposal to engage in collective bargaining has been voted on can be sought in a variety of ways: in what is known generally about conditions at these institutions, in the literature circulated and from discussions held during the preelection campaign, and through interviews conducted on campus before or after the voting. The "yes-and-no" voting pattern in a representation election discloses little except as it may reveal a strong preference for one of the available options. (Many elections have failed to do that.) A secret ballot is used in these elections, and only the total votes cast for each option are announced. The difficulty of interpreting results is compounded where significant numbers of part-time teachers and nonteaching professionals have voted. It can be hypothesized that these latter groups often have more reason to be dissatisfied with their lot than do full-time faculty members and may thus provide higher percentages of the affirmative votes. But the hypothesis cannot be tested by analyzing the voting patterns in a variety of representation elections.

One exception is the election at Eastern Michigan University in March 1972, which does confirm the hypothesis. In this instance, on order of the Michigan Court of Appeals, the ballots in the first election were segregated into a faculty group and four nonteaching professional groups. The segregation was ordered because of pending litigation over the composition of the bargaining unit. The totals for the faculty group and the nonfaculty groups were announced separately as follows:

Faculty		Nonfaculty	
No bargaining	200	No bargaining	4
AFT	148	AFT	20
AAUP	146	AAUP	9
NEA	95	NEA	16
Challenged ballots	15	Challenged ballots	14

6. "At the Brink: Report on the Economic Status of the Profession, 1970–71," 57 *AAUP Bulletin* (June 1971), 223–85.

These results show that support for collective bargaining was much greater in the nonteaching professional group than in the teaching faculty. They show also that AAUP ran well behind AFT and NEA in votes cast by members of the nonfaculty group.[7]

Persons close to a bargaining election may have a good basis for making reasonable guesses about the voting patterns that shaped the outcome, although our interviews on campuses where representation elections have been held suggest that local interpretations of the outcome can vary greatly. Eventually, useful information may become available through opinion surveys of voters in faculty representation elections. There will be significant difficulties in designing and administering such surveys, and we know of none that has yet produced useful data.

Dissatisfaction with Compensation

Many of the faculties that have turned to collective bargaining since 1968 undoubtedly thought of themselves as disadvantaged units within the academic profession—as having failed to share adequately in the economic gains being enjoyed by their more fortunate colleagues elsewhere. General dissatisfaction with faculty compensation levels was clearly present at such institutions as Bryant College, CUNY, SUNY, Adelphi University, the Brooklyn Center of Long Island University, Central Michigan University, and Oakland University. The AAUP annual salary surveys show that in many instances the dissatisfaction was justified in the sense that compensation was below average. The 1968–69 survey revealed that the average compensation (salary plus fringe benefits) without regard to rank of some 229,125 faculty members at the 1,060 participating institutions was $12,892. Thirty-five of thirty-nine institutions and state systems that by June 1972 were engaging in collective bargaining with their faculties (see Table 5) participated in the 1968–69 survey. Of these, twelve reported compensation figures above $12,892 and twenty-three below (see Table 6).

7. In the representation proceeding, the Michigan Employment Relations Commission had ordered the nonteaching professionals included in the same bargaining unit with the teaching faculty, over the objection of the university. The university, as the employer, appealed this ruling of MERC to the Michigan courts. As of February 1973, a runoff election had not yet been held. The number of challenged ballots was sufficient to affect the second-place candidate (AFT or AAUP), and these ballots were under review by MERC. The issue under court review was also still undecided.

Even at CUNY, where compensation schedules at a number of the colleges already ranked among the best in the nation, there was a good deal of dissatisfaction. Faculty members were discontented with their compensation position vis-à-vis public school teachers and other city employees; teachers at the community colleges (who had been placed in the two CUNY instructional bargaining units) were dissatisfied vis-à-vis their counterparts at the senior colleges; and all CUNY teachers asserted that their superior compensation position nationally was more seeming than real when the high cost of living in New York City and other disadvantages of life there were taken into account.[8] Stated another way, the decision of the CUNY faculty to turn to collective bargaining in 1968 may show that precisely when things are getting better for a group, discontent manifests itself in new ways and expectations escalate sharply. Indeed, there is little evidence that the academic profession had become a happier or more contented collection of men and women by the end of the 1960s because of its improved economic status. The average professor would still have asserted that his profession had not yet risen to its proper level and was being less generously and fairly compensated than law, medicine, and engineering, where the requirements for training and certification were no more demanding than for the academic profession. A pertinent statistic is: only 46.6 percent of the respondents to the 1969 Carnegie faculty questionnaire rated their own salaries as "excellent" or "good."[9]

The adoption of collective bargaining requires majority support within a faculty, and probably all of the people who vote for it expect, one way or another, to receive improvement in their compensation. But expectations are often strongest among those faculty members who view themselves as grossly undercompensated by their institution or who harbor resentment toward colleagues who appear to have been the principal beneficiaries under a selective system of dispensing rewards on a special merit basis. The discontented are either impressed by the widely held notion that collective bargaining,

8. AAUP's Committee Z report for 1968–69 states that the annual cost of a higher living standard for a four-person family in New York in 1967 was 14 percent above the national average ("The Threat of Inflationary Erosion," 55 *AAUP Bulletin* [June 1969], 195).

9. Unfortunately, the questionnaire did not ask academicians to compare the economic status of their profession with that of law, medicine, or engineering. A good guess is that a large percentage of the respondents would have indicated a belief that their profession was a disadvantaged one in any such comparison.

TABLE 5: *Bargaining Agents Selected at Four-Year Colleges and Universities, through June 1972*

Institution	Control	Bargaining Agent			
		AAUP	AFT	NEA	Independent
Delaware					
Univ. of Delaware	Public	x	..	..	..
Massachusetts					
Boston State College	Public	..	x	..	..
Fitchburg State College	Public	..	..	x	..
Lowell State College	Public	..	x	..	..
Massachusetts College of Art	Public	..	x	..	..
North Adams State College	Public	..	..	x	..
Salem State College	Public	..	..	x	..
Southeastern Massachusetts Univ.	Public	..	x	..	..
Westfield State College	Public	..	x	..	..
Worcester State College	Public	..	x	..	..
Michigan					
Central Michigan Univ.	Public	..	..	x	..
Oakland Univ.	Public	x	..	..	..
Saginaw Valley College	Public	..	..	x	..
Wayne State Univ.	Public	x	..	..	..
Nebraska					
Nebraska state colleges	Public	..	..	x	..
New Jersey					
College of Medicine and Dentistry of New Jersey	Public	x	:	..	..
Monmouth College	Private	..	..	x	..
New Jersey state colleges	Public	..	..	x	..
Newark College of Engineering	Public	..	..	..	x
Rutgers Univ.	Public	x	..	..	..
New York					
Adelphi Univ.	Private	x	..	..	..
Bard College	Private	x	..	..	..
Brooklyn Center, Long Island Univ.	Private	..	x	..	..
City Univ. of New York[a,b]	Public	..	..	x	..
City Univ. of New York (lecturers, teaching assistants)[a,b]	Public	..	x	..	..
Dowling College	Private	x	..	..	..
Fordham Univ., Law School	Private	..	..	..	x
New York Institute of Technology	Private	x	..	..	..
Polytechnic Institute of Brooklyn	Private	x	..	..	..
Pratt Institute	Private	..	x	..	..
St. John's Univ.	Private	x[c]	..	..	..
State Univ. of New York[a,d]	Public	..	..	x	..
U.S. Merchant Marine Academy	Public	..	x	..	..
Ohio					
Ashland College	Private	x	..	..	..
Youngstown State Univ.[e]	Public	..	..	x	..
Pennsylvania					
Pennsylvania state colleges	Public	..	..	x	..
Univ. of Scranton[e]	Private	..	..	..	x
Rhode Island					
Bryant College	Private	..	x	..	..
Rhode Island College	Public	..	x	..	..
Univ. of Rhode Island	Public	x	..	..	..
Total		12	13	12	3
Public		9	6	11	1
Private		3	7	1	2

See footnotes on facing page.

whether in industry or education, has a "leveling" effect (upward for the disadvantaged) on salaries and fringe benefits, or they regard the turn to collective bargaining as providing a means by which merit increases will be determined by new people in accordance with new standards—either way, to their advantage. According to such reasoning, if control of the evaluation system can be shifted from faculty committees or a faculty senate to the bargaining agent, institutional policies will then change, to the advantage of some and the detriment of others.

Dissatisfaction with Governance Systems

The desire to improve working conditions other than compensation—in particular to alter their role in institutional governance—has influenced some faculties to turn to collective bargaining. Such noneconomic motivation has probably been predominant in Massachusetts, where the statute authorizing collective bargaining by state employees does not appear to make compensation a negotiable subject.[10] It is not surprising, then, that the faculty contracts at Southeastern Massachusetts University and Boston State College give considerably more attention to the faculty role in institutional governance than do many contracts in other states. At both institutions the faculties were unhappy with existing governance systems. A desire for reform was a strong factor in the decision to turn to bargaining.

10. The statute does not expressly forbid bargaining with respect to wages, but the usual "wages, hours, and conditions of employment" language is not used. Bargaining is authorized only with respect to "conditions of employment." The state legislature is presumably unwilling to commit itself to funding the salary increases for state employees that might be provided for in collective bargaining agreements at the agency or institutional level. However, the Massachusetts law authorizing collective bargaining by public school teachers goes to the other extreme and places town authorities under an inflexible legislative command to raise by taxes the funds necessary to implement contracts agreed to by school committees.

a Multiple-campus university.
b At CUNY, elections in the two instructional units approved by the New York Public Employment Relations Board were won in 1969 by AFT for the lecturer–teaching assistant unit and by the Legislative Conference (an independent faculty association) for the full-time instructional unit. About a year after the Legislative Conference negotiated a contract, it affiliated with the NEA, and in April 1972, it and the AFT local at CUNY (the United Federation of College Teachers) voted to merge. The new organization (Professional Staff Congress) has been designated as bargaining agent for the "instructional staff" and will negotiate a new contract with the university to replace the two original contracts, which expire August 31, 1972.
c Joint agent with the local faculty association.
d At SUNY the election was won by the Senate Professional Association (an independent faculty association), but by the time bargaining started, SPA had affiliated with NEA.
e These are examples of a collective bargaining relationship established on a voluntary basis. Bargaining at Youngstown State University cannot occur on a *de jure* basis, for Ohio has no statute authorizing collective bargaining by public employees. Whether bargaining at the University of Scranton, a private institution, is taking place outside the scope of relevant federal and state statutes is doubtful. See discussion, pp. 70, 164–65.

TABLE 6: *Comparison of 1968–69 Average Compensation of Full-Time Faculty Members at Institutions with and without a Faculty Bargaining Agent by June 30, 1972*

Rank Order in AAUP Salary Survey[a]	Institution[b]	Average Compensation, 9-Month Basis
1	*Harvard University*	*$19,800*
4	CUNY—City College	18,247
7	CUNY—Brooklyn College	18,121
11	*Massachusetts Institute of Technology*	*17,737*
13	CUNY—Hunter College	17,617
14	CUNY—Queensborough Community College[c]	17,423
15	*Yale University*	*17,414*
19	CUNY—Queens College	16,898
22	CUNY—Lehman College	16,740
24	*University of Michigan*	*16,729*
29	State University of N.Y. at Buffalo	16,240
33	State University of N.Y. at Binghamton	16,096
35	State University of N.Y. at Albany	15,711
36	*Haverford College*	*15,700*
41	*University of California*	*15,600*
42	State University of N.Y. at Stony Brook	15,483
47	Rutgers University	15,224
53	Newark College of Engineering	15,056
98	*University of Wisconsin*	*14,113*
101	Wayne State University	14,089
	SUNY—colleges of liberal arts[d]	13,738
156	*Boston University*	*13,502*
183	Pratt Institute	13,275
184	University of Rhode Island	13,274
186	CUNY—Manhattan Community College[c]	13,267
187	Oakland University	13,245
188	*University of Massachusetts (Amherst)*	*13,226*
191	Long Island University	13,125
195	U.S. Merchant Marine Academy	13,096
	New Jersey state colleges[e]	13,067
207	University of Delaware	13,024
	Average compensation for all ranks (229,125 full-time faculty members at 1,060 institutions)	12,892
249	Fordham University	12,726
258	St. John's University	12,633
272	Polytechnic Institute of Brooklyn	12,567
283	*Albion College*	*12,485*
303	Bard College	12,389
317	Ashland College (Ohio)	12,346
334	*Western Michigan University*	*12,262*
348	Bryant College	12,153
352	Rhode Island College	12,136
365	Adelphi University	12,076
386	Pace College	11,919
	Central Michigan University[f]	11,724
441	Youngstown State University	11,641
459	*University of Massachusetts (Boston)*	*11,528*
	Saginaw Valley College	11,413
	Southeastern Massachusetts University	11,289

56

TABLE 6: Continued

Rank Order in AAUP Salary Survey[a]	Institution[b]	Average Compensation, 9-Month Basis
	Pennsylvania state colleges[g]...........................	11,230
	University of Scranton..............................	11,042
	Monmouth College (N.J.)...........................	10,828
	Nebraska state colleges[h]..........................	10,616
	Salem State College................................	10,459
	Worcester State College............................	10,442
	Boston State College...............................	10,336
	North Adams State College.........................	10,105
	Lowell State College................................	9,970
	Westfield State College.............................	9,842

Source: "The Threat of Inflationary Erosion: The Annual Report on the Economic Status of the Profession, 1968–69," *55 AAUP Bulletin* (June 1969), 192–253.

[a] The survey was participated in by 1,060 institutions; rank order is assigned only to institutions paying compensations of more than $11,500.

[b] For comparison purposes, for certain institutions without bargaining agents, the listing is italicized.
    The following institutions, which had selected bargaining agents by June 1972, did not participate in the AAUP survey: Massachusetts College of Art, New York Institute of Technology, Fitchburg State College, College of Medicine and Dentistry of New Jersey, and Dowling College.
    Although both CUNY and SUNY have systemwide bargaining, participation in the AAUP survey was by individual campuses.

[c] Of the six community colleges in the CUNY system in 1968–69, only two are listed here: Queensborough Community College, with the highest average compensation, and Manhattan Community College, with the lowest average compensation.

[d] Combined figure for the ten liberal arts colleges in the SUNY system (Brockport, Buffalo, Cortland, Fredonia, Geneseo, New Paltz, Oneonta, Oswego, Plattsburgh, Potsdam).

[e] Combined figure for the six New Jersey state colleges (Glassboro, Jersey City, Montclair, Newark, Paterson, Trenton).

[f] Committee Z report failed to include Central Michigan University in its listing of 466 institutions with average compensation in excess of $11,500.

[g] Combined figure for eleven Pennsylvania state colleges (Bloomsburg, California, Cheyney, Clarion, East Stroudsburg, Kutztown, Mansfield, Millersville, Shippensburg, Slippery Rock, and Westchester). Edinboro and Lock Haven State Colleges did not participate in the 1968–69 survey.

[h] Figure is for Kearney State College. Chadron, Peru, and Wayne—the other three Nebraska state colleges—did not participate in the survey.

If the governance system is weak or nonexistent in terms of faculty participation, faculty members of all ages and viewpoints may unite in favoring collective bargaining as a means to counter the authority of trustees and administrators and to gain an appropriate faculty role in running the institution. Their dissatisfaction may, however, reflect conflict and tension within the faculty over the power structure that underlies an existing role in governance. Collective bargaining is then seen as a way of altering the status of, or equilibrium among, such governance agencies as the departments, faculty committees (in particular, those that handle faculty personnel and grievance matters), the faculty council or senate, and the new faculty "labor organization" necessitated by a turn to collective bargaining.

The Old Guard, Young Turk Conflict

Tension and conflict can take shape out of an Old Guard, Young Turk division within a faculty. For example, at a former teachers college, vocational school, or experimental college which had a limited purpose and program, but has been undergoing rapid growth and development into a college of arts and sciences or a regional university, a movement toward collective bargaining may be led by older faculty members who find themselves competing for salary increases and program support with aggressive young faculty members. This tension can be exacerbated where the young faculty members identify themselves with an enterprising new president (or vice versa), rather than with department chairmen and senior faculty members. In such a situation, the decision to turn to collective bargaining is not necessarily the work of young faculty members, although they may attempt to influence or even to gain control of the faculty's labor organization and the negotiations at the bargaining table, once their more conservative colleagues have supplied many of the votes making up the majority in favor of collective bargaining. Something like this condition can be discerned in the turn to collective bargaining by the faculties at Southeastern Massachusetts University, Boston State College, Central Michigan University, and Oakland University. Each of these institutions reveals a distinctive pattern, but all had experienced a fundamental change in character and purpose, accompanied by a sharp increase in the size of the faculty, the creation of new academic programs and departments, the appointment of a new president (at Boston State College, a sequence of new presidents and acting presidents), and the appearance of tensions between old and new faculty members and between part of the faculty and the president.[11]

Faculty Uncertainty over the Student Role in Governance

Disagreement within a faculty over the issue of student participation in institutional governance and decision making can also help set the stage for a turn to collective bargaining. The increased student involvement in institutional affairs of recent years has usually come into being with substantial faculty support. Many faculty members, however, have serious misgivings about this trend. They are particularly apprehensive about the consequences of student participation in decisions on faculty appointments, promotions, salary increases, and

11. The coming of collective bargaining to some of these institutions will be examined more fully in chap. 5.

tenure grants.[12] Collective bargaining in its traditional form is an adversary relationship between employer and employee. Hence there appears to be no direct role for students at the bargaining table. They are thereby excluded from the negotiation of a contract with respect to faculty wages, work loads, and other conditions of employment.

The Brooklyn Center of Long Island University is an exception. There, four student government officers asked to sit at the bargaining table as observers and consultants. According to reports, the administration promptly agreed, and AFT then gave approval. We have not talked with either negotiating team about how the presence of students affected the bargaining. A faculty member told us that the impression on campus was that things had gone well at the table: the students were allowed to answer questions put by the negotiators and to volunteer information; they were consulted; and they were pleased with the treatment they received. We were also told that the students had not leaked confidential information during the negotiations or otherwise rendered the bargaining process more difficult. What this example proves is difficult to say. The presence of students at the bargaining table is likely to complicate the situation in direct ratio to the degree of difficulty that management and labor encounter in discussing and reaching agreement on controversial issues. It is common practice in collective bargaining for each team to caucus privately at frequent intervals during the negotiations. Formal discussions are often suspended while representatives of the two teams meet together privately in attempts to develop solutions to problems that have produced dead-

12. The Carnegie Commission's faculty questionnaire revealed less faculty support for a student role in "faculty hiring and promotion" than in many other aspects of institutional decision making. Thus, only 5.8 percent of the respondents believed that students should have "control" or "voting power on committees" where faculty personnel decisions are being made. In some other areas, the respondents were more favorable to such student participation: admissions policy, 13.4 percent; curriculum planning, 14.8 percent; degree requirements, 13.8 percent; student discipline, 64.1 percent. In the areas shown below, each respondent was asked to check one of five positions regarding: "What role do you believe *undergraduates* should play in decisions on the following?":

	Control	Voting Power on Committees	Formal Consultation	Informal Consultation	Little or No Role
Faculty appointment and promotion	0.2	5.6	15.0	25.1	54.0
Provision and content of courses	0.3	14.5	35.2	36.6	13.4
Bachelor's degree requirements	0.2	13.6	30.0	24.7	31.5

locks at the table. It is unlikely that students will be welcome at such caucuses or private discussions away from the table.

Collective bargaining does not, however, necessarily exclude students from participation in the work of the agencies that are called on to administer a contract. Students cannot sit at the bargaining table as principals and help shape the institution's basic faculty personnel policies, but they can serve as members, with or without vote, on the agencies that apply these policies to individuals during the period that a contract is in effect.

There is little hard evidence that an antistudent motive has been a significant factor in influencing any faculty to vote for collective bargaining. But where collective bargaining exists, talk about excluding students from the faculty personnel decision process is sufficient to suggest the presence of that motive, just under the surface, in faculty deliberations and decisions with respect to collective bargaining. At CUNY, for example, the publications of the faculty bargaining agent, the Legislative Conference, during the years of the first contract (1969–72), revealed a thinly disguised distrust of student participation in faculty personnel actions. Also evident was a related fear that the CUNY administration was attempting to win students to its side in a continuing battle with the faculty in such matters as evaluation of faculty members for reappointment and tenure award, control of work loads, and the shaping of new educational programs.[13]

The *New York Times* has reported that at CUNY when the University Student Senate asked to have observers at the bargaining table during the 1972–73 negotiations "and to present testimony before the fact-finders, primarily on the need for more 'student input' in academic governance," the Board of Higher Education gave its permission but the faculty union, the Professional Staff Congress, refused. The *Times* account states:

13. For example, the Legislative Conference's newspaper, *The Reporter*, for May 1971 contained a page two article headlined "Students on P & B [Personnel and Budget Committees] Evaluations Opposed." The article, occasioned by the ongoing effort on the several CUNY college campuses to formulate "college governance plans," reflected an obvious distrust of the role of administrators in this effort. It stated: "In guidelines adopted by the LC Governing Board April 29, the Conference stressed that faculty fitness 'is to be judged only by peers on the criteria of professional competence and personal integrity'"; and "Exhorting the faculties not to surrender or compromise this principle, it recommended that college governance plans contain 'a clear, unambiguous statement of the faculty's exclusive responsibility for appointment, retention, promotion and the tenure of faculty.'"

The student leaders came away from the rebuff openly skeptical of the union's slogan, "Professors Want What Students Need." The union's president, Prof. Belle Zeller of Hunter College [sic], retorted, "All the students have to do is holler, and the administration quivers. We are fighting to preserve the power of the faculty through its own Faculty Senate."[14]

Is Faculty Bargaining Contagious?

Has there been a "domino effect" or a pattern-setting trend in faculty collective bargaining that influences additional faculties to take the step? The evidence is clearly affirmative, at least to the extent that a faculty which has reasons for contemplating the step to bargaining can be nudged toward action by what is happening at nearby institutions. For example, a considerable part of all collective bargaining at four-year institutions has taken shape within a hundred-mile radius of New York City during the three and one-half years since the faculty of CUNY voted to engage in collective bargaining in December 1968. As Table 5 shows, seventeen of the thirty-nine four-year institutions at which bargaining agents had been selected by June 1972 were located in either New York or New Jersey. Rhode Island, Pennsylvania, and Delaware brought the regional total to twenty-three institutions—well over half of the national total.

The faculties of CUNY were undoubtedly influenced to vote for collective bargaining in 1968 by the fact that the school teachers and most of the other public employees had been bargaining with the city for a number of years, to their obvious financial advantage. The university enjoyed a large measure of autonomy. Its governing board was relatively immune from political control by city officials. There may thus have been a temptation for faculty members to think that the university was above politics and that they could safely ignore the struggle of other city employees for "more." Moreover, the older colleges within the university were much admired and enjoyed strong alumni support. But the lesson that self-help did bring rewards was irresistible. As the city's budgetary difficulties became acute, CUNY faculty members saw continuing gains being made through collective bargaining by other segments of the public work force, and grew apprehensive that they would suffer unless they used the same means to

14. A. H. Raskin, "Unionism and the Content of Education: What Are the Bounds?" *New York Times,* Jan. 4, 1973, p. 70.

make their demands on the limited resources of the city (and the state). Much the same reasoning undoubtedly carried weight with the faculties and professional employees of the State University of New York when they voted to engage in collective bargaining at the end of 1970.

The interest in collective bargaining manifested at several private institutions in the New York City area did not, of course, have precisely the same roots as at CUNY. Many of the private institutions, however, had budgetary and educational problems that led their faculties to consider turning to collective bargaining, and the faculties could hardly remain insensitive to the aggressive and effective use of collective bargaining being made by organized labor in the New York City environment.

The progress of collective bargaining by teachers in Michigan provides a striking example of the domino effect. Public school teachers in Detroit and other nearby industrial communities began turning to collective bargaining in the mid-1960s. A 1965 statute had authorized them to bargain; their dissatisfaction with salaries and work conditions was acute; they had no strong sense that professional people do not join unions, bargain collectively, or strike; and they had long been observing the gains being won through collective bargaining by private industry workers in the southeastern industrial corner of the state. By February 1966, six months after the Michigan Public Employment Relations Act had gone into effect, bargaining agents had been designated in more than four hundred school districts in Michigan.[15]

Collective bargaining quickly moved from the public schools to the two-year community colleges, first in the Detroit area and then in all parts of Michigan. By 1969, agreements were in effect at twenty of the twenty-four public community colleges in the state. Some of these institutions were actually operated by public school authorities, but all of them had faculties with close career ties to public school teachers.

After the 1966 designations of bargaining agents in the school districts, about four years passed before faculty collective bargaining appeared at a four-year public institution in Michigan. Unlike the highly centralized but exceedingly diffuse State University of New York, the thirteen public institutions above the two-year college level in Michigan enjoy great autonomy. Each has its own governing board and each is said to enjoy a recognition in the state constitution that

15. Robert E. Doherty and Walter E. Oberer, *Teachers, School Boards, and Collective Bargaining*, p. 72.

gives it greater freedom from political or legislative control than is true in most states. The faculty at each of these thirteen institutions was clearly free to make its own decision concerning collective bargaining in its own way at its own time.

In 1969, the faculty at Central Michigan University led the way in voting to engage in collective bargaining. Central Michigan is well outside the Detroit area, but it is a former teachers college and it still has a strong college of education and a large faculty offering one of the state's principal teacher-training programs. The career tie to public school teachers thus probably helped provide a significant number of the affirmative faculty votes for bargaining.

The faculty at Oakland University in 1970 was the next one at a four-year institution to vote for collective bargaining. Oakland is on the edge of the Detroit metropolitan area and is close to several community colleges where faculty bargaining was taking place. The faculty at Wayne State University, which is in the heart of Detroit, began to consider collective bargaining in 1969. Several labor organizations competed for faculty support, and there were delays in the collection of signatures and the filing of petitions with the state labor commission. Disputed issues about the membership of the bargaining unit required extended hearings and an eventual ruling by the commission. When the election was finally held, the outcome was found to depend on how a number of challenged ballots were to be counted. All of this took time, and a bargaining agent was not certified until June 1972.[16] Our conversations with faculty members at both Oakland and Wayne confirmed the existence of the domino effect. We were told stories, for example, about faculty members' wives who were teaching at nearby community colleges and, because of collective bargaining, being paid higher salaries than were their husbands. The accuracy of these accounts and the adequacy of the explanation for the salary differences could not be checked. But there was no doubt that such stories were enjoying wide circulation on these campuses and were having an impact on faculty attitudes.

The faculty at Saginaw Valley College, which is less than one hundred miles from Detroit, in central Michigan, voted in January 1972

16. The faculty at Eastern Michigan University, in Ypsilanti, which is not far from Detroit, went through much the same series of steps as did the Wayne faculty, but as of June 1972 the analysis of the challenged ballots by the state labor commission had not been completed and no election result had been certified.

by the narrow margin of thirty-one to twenty-seven to engage in collective bargaining, with NEA as its agent. Saginaw Valley is only a few years old and has been strongly influenced from the beginning by its president, who helped bring the college into being. The faculty decision appears to have reflected local and personal factors more than it did external considerations or a statewide domino effect.

The faculty at Northern Michigan University, several hundred miles from Detroit, in the Upper Peninsula, voted to reject collective bargaining in 1971. The faculty at Western Michigan University, which is about one hundred miles west of Detroit and is perhaps academically the strongest of the state regional universities, was giving careful thought to collective bargaining but was proceeding in a leisurely way. Both of these faculties have demonstrated their short-run immunity to pattern setting as a force to lead them to collective bargaining. Presumably they will take the step only when they conclude that they have sufficient reasons of their own for doing so, or when they can no longer avoid the conclusion that they are losing ground in the competition for state funds or that their help is necessary to a collective effort by the faculties of all state institutions to force the governor and the legislature to provide additional funds for faculty compensation.

Much the same can be said of the faculties at the University of Michigan and Michigan State University, the two oldest and strongest institutions in the state system. The guess may be hazarded that if they turn to collective bargaining, it will be toward the end of the sequential development in the state. Efforts have been made for a year and more, principally by NEA, to collect enough signatures at Michigan State to force a representation election. The Michigan State Labor Commission finally set such an election for October 1972, apparently on the basis of a sufficient showing of interest by faculty members who signed either NEA or AAUP certification cards.[17] NEA has also been active on the University of Michigan campus but has not reached the point of collecting signatures.

17. The unit approved by MERC at Michigan State University encompassed essentially the entire faculty. At an election in October 1972, the faculty rejected collective bargaining by a margin of nearly two to one. The results were: No agent, 1,213; NEA, 438; AAUP, 280.

A faculty bargaining election was also held in October 1972 at Ferris State College in Michigan. The results were: No agent, 143; NEA, 137; AAUP, 133; challenged, 11. In the runoff election held in January 1973, NEA was established as bargaining agent by a vote of 221 to 161 for "No agent."

In the light of faculty representation elections held through February 1973, it is still difficult to identify and weigh the dissatisfactions that lead faculties to contemplate turning to collective bargaining. Unhappiness about compensation, chronic conflict with administrators and trustees, tensions and rivalries within a faculty, and proximity to other faculties that have already decided to engage in bargaining with their institutions are all likely to be influential. But the number of elections held thus far is still too small to support generalizations in which much confidence can be placed. The complex of factors and influences is seldom identical at any two institutions. Moreover, new considerations are becoming apparent. As the 1972–73 academic year comes to a close, the increasing need of many colleges and universities to limit the expansion of their faculties, or even to cut back from existing levels, may well become a dominant factor in persuading faculties to turn to collective bargaining as an effective means of protecting their interests, as they see them. This motive will almost certainly be powerful for faculty members on term appointments in institutions that have announced or are considering more stringent tenure patterns. The desperate financial outlook for many institutions may also lead some faculty members to vote against collective bargaining lest the resulting adversary relationship between the faculty and the governing board of an institution (and aggressive negotiations at the bargaining table) might exacerbate institutional difficulties to a point where no one's interests would be well served.

As faculty collective bargaining patterns take shape, the factors (dissatisfactions) influencing the voting in representation elections deserve, and undoubtedly will receive, the careful attention of scholars and the utilization of appropriate techniques for the measurement of faculty behavior patterns.

CHAPTER FOUR

Determining an "Appropriate" Bargaining Unit: What Happens to "the Faculty"?

COLLECTIVE BARGAINING STATUTES, EXCEPT IN HAWAII, DO NOT EXPRESSLY allow a faculty to claim the right to decide whether *it* wants to bargain collectively with its institution, and, if it does, to exclude other employees from *its* negotiations with management.[1] The statutes neither prohibit nor guarantee such an arrangement. At some institutions, collective bargaining under law has taken shape between the faculty, as defined professionally and traditionally, and the governing board. At other institutions where it is said that "the faculty" is engaging in collective bargaining, the employee group is in fact significantly different from the faculty, being either broader or narrower than the body commonly so defined. The membership of "faculty" bargaining units has been determined case by case, through a combination of attitudes and developments at each institution and a labor board's application of the law to each local situation. In the end, an "appropriate" bargaining unit is decided on. Certain employees generally regarded as faculty members may have been excluded on the ground that they are "agents of management" or "supervisors"; other employees not generally regarded as faculty members may have been included as falling within "the community of interests" that controls a unit's appropriateness.

The concept of "the faculty," as already noted, is inexact in higher education itself. Many faculties have themselves voluntarily admitted to their collective ranks, often with full voting power in faculty decision making, employees such as librarians, student counselors, registrars,

1. The Hawaii statute authorizing collective bargaining by state employees designates the "Faculty of the University of Hawaii and the Community College system" as an appropriate bargaining unit, but does not define "faculty." Several candidates for bargaining agent attempted to organize the faculty in 1971 and 1972, and considerable disagreement took shape concerning membership of the faculty unit. As of June 1972, the Hawaii Public Employment Relations Board had not resolved the unit issue or ordered an election. See chap. 5 for information about the outcome of the election at the University of Hawaii.

admissions officers, and even business officers, who do no teaching or scholarly research. Indeed, this extension of the right to participate in faculty affairs is now frequently extended to a limited number of students, who, of course, are not even employees of the institution. The erosion of the concept of *the faculty* at an institution as a company of teacher-scholars who have met exacting standards for admission to the academic profession has thus in part been a self-destruct process. On the other hand, rarely has a faculty excluded from its ranks certain persons, such as department chairmen, to whom labor boards upon occasion deny membership in a bargaining unit. This book will necessarily use such labels as "faculty collective bargaining" where some other language would more accurately describe a bargaining unit. It would take a tedious insistence on the use of detailed language to be precise in every instance. But the reader must constantly remember that the group of employees engaging in collective bargaining at a college or university, although referred to as the faculty, may be something more or less than the group of institutional employees traditionally regarded as "the faculty."

THREE STEPS REQUIRED IN FACULTY BARGAINING UNDER LAW

Before a faculty and the governing board of a college or university can engage in collective bargaining under the law, usually three things must take place:

1. The composition—membership—of the bargaining unit must be decided;
2. An election must be held in which a majority of the persons in the unit who vote decide that they want to require the management of their institution to bargain collectively with them;
3. A labor organization must be chosen to serve as the exclusive bargaining agent for all of the employees in the unit.

The procedures prescribed in collective bargaining statutes do not always permit a faculty to make these three decisions in a wholly rational way or satisfactory sequence. As already indicated, a faculty may well discover that it has less control over composition of the bargaining unit than it had expected. And it will discover that it must take the second and third steps simultaneously, even though, logically, a bargaining agent should be selected only after the decision has been made to bargain collectively. There are instances where members of a faculty have debated the issues more or less in accordance with good academic practice, have decided in favor of collective bargaining, have selected a bargaining agent that faculty people have organized and control, and have thereafter negotiated a contract that speaks to the needs of the unique employer-employee relationship between the faculty and the governing board of an educational institution. Such a happy result usually occurs where only one labor organization offers itself as a candidate for bargaining agent and supplies evidence that it has the support of a majority of the employees in the unit, and the governing board offers no objection to the bargaining unit within which the labor organization has chosen to solicit support. Under these circumstances, the public labor board is almost always prepared to accept the unit agreed upon by the employer and employees as a proper one.

Rutgers University, even though a multicampus state university, provides an example where the parties encountered no difficulty in reaching agreement on the membership of the faculty bargaining unit. The Council of AAUP Chapters at the several campuses of the university was the only candidate for bargaining agent. Both sides agreed that the unit should consist of "all Rutgers University faculty members," defined as persons "discharg[ing] at least one-half (50 percent) of a full-time academic job assignment" and possessing a standard faculty rank or an appointment on the research, library, and extension staffs with an equivalent rank to the specified faculty categories. This harmonious result probably depended on two considerations: as the only candidate, the local AAUP leaders chose to regard the proper unit as one made up of Rutgers employees who in general were eligible for membership in the national AAUP under the latter's existing regulations; and the administration and governing board of the university chose not to resist the coming of faculty collective bargaining to the institution and regarded AAUP as a desirable bargaining agent.[2]

In many other instances, making the three determinations has proved to be a lengthy, complicated business in which faculty members find that bargaining resembles the industrial model of employer-employee relations as much as it does any traditional way of running a university.

2. In 1972 the national AAUP amended its constitution to broaden eligibility for active membership well beyond its traditional requirement that applicants must hold at least a one-year appointment at an approved institution with the rank of instructor or higher "or other acceptable evidence of faculty status" and engage in at least half-time teaching or research.

As interest in the possibility of collective bargaining takes shape on a campus, the local unit of one or more "labor organizations"—the American Association of University Professors (AAUP), the American Federation of Teachers (AFT), the National Education Association (NEA), a state civil service association, and perhaps an independent "faculty association"—invites members of the faculty to sign "authorization cards" indicating that they favor having a particular organization serve as the faculty's agent in collective bargaining. Such card signing is a serious business—more serious than is sometimes realized—for as soon as any of the labor organizations collecting signatures has the apparent support of 30 percent of the employees in the unit it views as the proper one, it is entitled to petition the government labor board with jurisdiction to conduct a "representation election." If it has the support of a clear majority of the persons in the unit, it can ask the employer to recognize it, or the labor board to certify it, without an election. Once a petition has been filed with the labor board, other labor organizations can either meet the 30 percent requirement too, or file as "intervenors" with 10 percent of the signatures of the unit members. If there is disagreement about the membership of the bargaining unit, the petitioners and intervenors are thereafter entitled to defend their positions on this issue, as is also the governing board of the institution. The labor board will then make a ruling determining composition of the unit, and order a "representation election" in which all of the petitioning and intervening organizations become candidates for bargaining agent. The ballot also offers a "no bargaining" or "no agent" option.

In the representation election, a faculty may find that it cannot vote a simple choice between whether or not *it* wishes to bargain collectively. For one thing, the bargaining unit defined by the labor board may include significant numbers of employees not traditionally considered "faculty members," such as nonteaching professionals and part-time teachers. There is a more serious difficulty: faculty members are able to make a clear choice between supporting collective bargaining and voting for "no bargaining" only when the representation election offers a ballot with a "no bargaining" option and only one labor organization as candidate for bargaining agent. In many of the faculty elections thus far held, two or more organizations have appeared on the ballot, with the result that "no bargaining" becomes one of three or more options, each with equal status and potential. Labor laws do provide that if no one of these options receives a majority of all the votes cast on the first ballot, a runoff election shall be held between the two top choices. But a runoff does not help a faculty make independent decisions on the two separate issues of (1) whether it wants to engage in collective bargaining at all, and (2) if it does, what organization it wants as bargaining agent. This dilemma is illustrated by remarks of faculty members, repeated to us with variations at a number of institutions where faculty collective bargaining was under consideration: "I am not in favor of collective bargaining, but it may be inevitable here. That being so, I feel I must vote for X as bargaining agent, rather than for the 'no bargaining' option. I am afraid to run the risk that Y and Z will be contenders in a runoff election. If we must have bargaining, I want X. But my preference is for no bargaining at all."

To the typical faculty, a much more sensible and appropriate procedure would be to hold a preliminary election in which the sole question would be, "Do we want to engage in collective bargaining?" If that proposition carried by a majority vote, the faculty would then proceed to the selection of a bargaining agent, with a runoff election (third in the sequence of elections) if necessary to produce a majority choice.

The logic of such a way of proceeding was illustrated in 1972 at Youngstown State University, a public institution. Ohio has no statute authorizing collective bargaining by state employees. The governing board, however, accepted a recommendation from the university's administration that collective bargaining take place on a voluntary basis if a majority of faculty members eligible to vote indicated their support for bargaining. Since the parties were not subject to a state labor statute or board, the governing board was free to propose, as it did, that the faculty vote first on the simple issue, "Shall we engage in collective bargaining?" and then, if that proposition carried, select a bargaining agent. The governing board also reached an agreement with the two candidates for bargaining agent—AAUP and NEA—that the unit should consist of the "full service nine months teaching faculty holding regular appointments for the 1971–72 academic year." In the first election, the faculty voted by a margin of 279 to 81 to engage in collective bargaining, and in a second election it chose NEA over AAUP as its bargaining agent by a vote of 195 to 141.

What Is the Faculty?

There is probably no aspect of the total process of collective bargaining that poses a greater risk to the long-term interests of a faculty, as members of a profession with exacting entrance and performance standards and also as members of a local "company of scholars," than does this determination of the membership of the bargaining unit. And yet the faculty, as such, is not usually entitled to be heard before the labor board ruling is made. That privilege is reserved to the candidates for bargaining agent and to the institution's governing board. A faculty in its official institutional sense might be allowed to submit an amicus brief stating its position to a labor board during the course of a unit determination proceeding. But we know of no instance where this has yet occurred.

If a faculty were allowed to state its position at a labor board hearing on the unit composition issue, it might endeavor to show the labor board that its members are persons holding a standard academic appointment in the instructor-professor range and engaging in essentially full-time research and teaching. It could, if it wished, also identify as its members a small group of the institution's professional employees who supply student services, operate the library and the computer center, or are in other significant ways supportive of the instructional and research programs, and whom the faculty itself has already welcomed to its ranks as voting members. In other words, the faculty could argue the case that there is such a thing as "the academic profession," with everything therein implied with respect to training, certification, work standards, service ideals, and measurement of individual performance. The faculty might claim that such professional goals and ideals can be fulfilled only where the cohesion and integrity of the academic group of employees is protected against the addition of other employees who are not properly viewed as part of the academic profession or against the subtraction of still other employees who are most assuredly part of the company of teacher-scholars.

As things are, a "faculty" is dependent on the representatives of the labor organizations that seek designation as the faculty's bargaining agent to explain and defend faculty traditions and preferences at a labor board unit determination proceeding. Labor organizations have frequently served faculty interests quite poorly in this respect. In some instances, an institution's management has presented the case for faculty cohesion and community of interests more faithfully than have the labor organizations.

The labor organization that takes the initiative in attempting to organize a faculty gains first chance to decide what the composition of the bargaining unit ought to be, for it circulates authorization cards to the persons it views as constituting an appropriate unit. The three national organizations that seek to represent faculties through their local affiliates have all taken stands in this respect through the years. In general, AAUP and AFT are teacher organizations, and thus might be expected to favor units limited to faculty members in a strict professional sense. NEA long welcomed administrators as well as teachers to its ranks and might thus be expected to favor units open to all of an institution's professional employees. In practice, the local affiliates of all three organizations have usually been influenced in their decisions to circulate cards on a narrow or broad basis by their estimates of the support they can hope to receive from persons in each segment of a possible bargaining unit. No one of the three organizations yet has a very good record for consistency or firm adherence to its own traditions or commitments.

THE LAW'S VIEW OF AN APPROPRIATE UNIT

A labor organization, in planning its strategy for attempting to organize a faculty, must bear in mind the rulings of the labor board on certain flexible issues, as made in earlier unit determination cases. A collective bargaining statute, while stating some requirements or limitations with respect to bargaining units, usually grants the labor board enforcing the statute a large measure of discretionary authority to determine appropriate bargaining units. Federal law, for example, permits the NLRB to determine whether the unit shall be industry-wide, companywide, or limited to a single plant or department. It also authorizes craft units (for example, electricians, carpenters, masons, plumbers), and all employers using members of the craft union in a particular locale can be required to bargain with that union and reach a "master agreement" controlling conditions of employment in their businesses in the area.

Through the years the NLRB has developed its own series of tests for determining the appropriate bargaining unit in an individual case. For one thing, it follows a rule that a unit need only be "appropriate," and not the *best* or the *most* appropriate unit. This rule may be viewed as desirable in the sense that it allows considerable freedom to employers and employees to work out unit determinations deemed suitable in practice to the conditions in a particular industry, plant, or locality. The disadvantage is that the resulting lack of uniformity and consistency may operate to the detriment of one side or the other in certain situations.

In general it may be assumed that statutes and labor board rulings together require that the members of a bargaining unit have a "community of interests" or constitute "an identifiable, homogeneous group." Among other factors that the NLRB says it will consider in determining appropriate bargaining units are: the similarity of duties, skills, wages, and working conditions of the employees in question; past bargaining history or patterns in the industry or company or plant in question; the extent and type of existing union organization of the employees involved; the appropriateness of the unit in relation to the organization of the company; and, finally, where there is a question of professional status or craft cohesion, the employees' wishes.[3] Some of these rules may seem to encourage faculties, in the restricted sense of companies of teacher-scholars, to believe that the NLRB and state labor boards observing similar standards will support them in their efforts to resist being absorbed into larger units that include nonteaching and nonresearch employees of their institutions. This encouragement is not always borne out in practice. Among other things, faculties have to adjust to a strong labor board preference (not usually articulated as a "rule") for large units—units as broadly inclusive of employees as the conditions of a case will permit.

The labor organization that takes the initiative in attempting to organize a faculty must make guesses about the attitudes of management and of the other labor organizations that may also seek to become petitioners or intervenors. Will they go along with the approach used by the first organization and accept its view of the appropriate unit? Or will they take different positions on this highly important issue? If they do, will an election be delayed? If so, whose interests will be served by delay? What will be the cost of a lengthy proceeding before the labor board?

3. This summary is taken from the *Primer of Labor Relations,* 18th ed., pp. 24–26.

What are the variables of inclusion or exclusion that may have to be considered and settled as a faculty bargaining unit takes shape? The principal issues that have proved troublesome are the following:

1. *The multiple campus issue:* Shall the faculties on the several campuses of a university or a state college system be organized into separate units or be placed in a single unit coterminous with the university or system?

2. *The part-time teacher issue:* Shall part-time teachers be included on the ground that they have an essential "community of interests" with full-time teachers, or be excluded on a variety of grounds, such as they do not have to meet the same standards for admission to college teaching as do their full-time colleagues, are not paid in the same way, are not eligible for tenure, are not voting members of the faculty, may hold other jobs to which they give their first attention and loyalty? If some but not all of an institution's part-time teachers are to be included in a faculty bargaining unit, how shall the line be drawn between the two segments of the part-time group?

3. *The nonteaching professional issue:* Shall the teaching-research faculty and the institution's other "professional" employees, who do no teaching or research but whose work is called "supportive" of the teaching-research function, be placed in a single unit or in separate units?

4. *The faculty fragmentation issue:* Must a university faculty bargain as a unit, or can segments, such as law and medical faculties, ask to be recognized as separate bargaining units or to be excluded from a general faculty unit?

5. *The department chairman issue:* Shall chairmen be included, as their faculty peers' principal spokesmen to the administration, or excluded on the ground that they are supervisors or agents of management, as these categories are defined in labor-management law?

6. *The faculty committee issue:* Must faculty members who serve on certain faculty committees, such as those that pass on questions of faculty appointments, promotions, and the like, or that help adjust faculty grievances, be excluded on the ground that they, too, fall within a statutory ban on supervisors?

As already mentioned, none of these issues may prove troublesome at an institution, particularly where the single candidate for labor organization and the administration and governing board can agree on the composition of the unit before the labor board is asked to conduct a representation election or certify a bargaining agent. In such cases, the proposed unit usually coincides quite closely with the voting members of "the faculty" at the institution. A consideration of collective bargaining where problems of unit determination have arisen may help illuminate the problems.

THE MULTIPLE CAMPUS ISSUE

City and State Universities of New York

The two great multicampus universities in the state of New York, the City University of New York (CUNY) and the State University of New York (SUNY), provide good examples of unit determination problems in faculty collective bargaining. Disputed issues were sufficiently serious to require lengthy proceedings before the director of representation of the New York State Public Employment Relations Board (PERB). In the CUNY case, six days of hearings were held in February and March 1968, and an opinion was rendered by the director on May 1. PERB then considered the record and the director's finding and on August 9, by a two-to-one vote, affirmed his finding. In the SUNY case, extensive hearings were held between July 1968 and March 1969. The ruling by PERB's director of representation was made in August 1969, and that of the full board in October 1969.[4]

4. The PERB ruling in the CUNY proceeding is cited as Case No. C-0008 (1968). There are two PERB documents in the CUNY and SUNY cases. The director's ruling in the CUNY case was appealed to the full board by the university's governing board, and in the SUNY case by AFT. In both instances PERB affirmed the initial rulings. The rulings in the SUNY case are cited as Cases Nos. 0253, 0260, 0262, 0263, 0264, and 0351 (1969).

We had the benefit of extensive interviews at CUNY, including sessions with officers of the Legislative Conference and the chancellor (Albert H. Bowker) and several vice-chancellors. Several articles in 1971 *Wisconsin Law Review*, no. 1, provided useful information about the CUNY and SUNY cases; see especially the article by the vice-chancellor for administration at CUNY, Bernard Mintz, "The CUNY Experience," p. 122. We also had access to case studies prepared for the Institute for Educational Management at the Harvard Graduate School of Business Administration, and similar case studies of the coming of faculty bargaining at Central Michigan University and Southeastern Massachusetts University. The institute studies are usually presented under fictitious names and some facts revised to enhance the value of the case for student consideration; however, much of the record is accurately presented and the documents have been useful in checking other sources of the events at CUNY, CMU, and SMU.

Between them, these two university systems account for almost all public higher education in New York State. Each is a university system that includes liberal arts and special-purpose colleges at the undergraduate level, as well as university centers offering graduate and professional programs. Each system is centralized, having a single governing board, a set of universitywide administrators, and an integrated budget. But the individual units are widely dispersed geographically, differ in their traditions and purposes, have their own faculties, administrators, and student bodies, and enjoy significant autonomy in shaping and operating their educational programs.

In the CUNY proceeding, the two candidates for bargaining agent were the Legislative Conference, an independent faculty association, and the United Federation of College Teachers (UFCT), Local No. 1460 of the American Federation of Teachers (AFT). Both labor organizations and the Board of Higher Education of the City of New York (the governing board of the university) were in agreement from the start that if faculty collective bargaining took place, it should be conducted on a universitywide basis, rather than by separate campuses. At the time of the proceeding the university consisted of sixteen units, some old and some new, ranging all the way from two-year community colleges to a graduate center. Moreover, the oldest units, such as City College and Hunter College, had once enjoyed substantial autonomy and had acquired high respect and standing in their own right in the world of higher education. Thus, the unanimity of opinion that faculty bargaining should take place on a universitywide basis was somewhat surprising. Presumably the unanimity reflected the fact that the two labor organizations had themselves taken shape on a universitywide basis many years earlier and had been endeavoring to serve the interests of the entire university faculty, both through informal negotiations with the Board of Higher Education and lobbying in the city and state legislative arenas. The BHE presumably had obvious reasons for preferring to bargain on a centralized basis, should the faculty vote to claim its right to bargain under the New York public employee labor relations statute, known as the Taylor Law. PERB readily accepted the proposal that faculty bargaining at CUNY should be systemwide.

The inclusion of the community college instructional staffs in the centralized bargaining was significant, particularly since, as it turned out, they made the most substantial economic gains that came to any of the participants in the bargaining process. With the exception of the faculty bargaining unit established by statute in Hawaii, in no other instance have two-year college teachers been placed in the same unit with four-year college teachers. It is not clear whether they were included at CUNY because the units followed the institutional arrangement automatically or for reasons of conscious intent.

At the time of the PERB proceeding, the State University of New York was a vast conglomeration of some sixty-one units, located throughout the state except New York City, and ranging in purpose from community colleges to university centers. By stipulation of all the parties, the thirty-one community colleges and the four contract colleges at Cornell University were to be omitted from whatever negotiating unit or units might be approved by PERB. The twenty-six campuses to be included were: four university centers, two medical centers, eleven four-year colleges, six two-year agricultural and technical colleges, a forestry college, a maritime college, and a ceramics college. Several of these campuses had existed as independent and even private institutions before being absorbed into SUNY sometime after its establishment in 1948. Others were new units, created to round out the SUNY system, functionally and geographically.

In the SUNY case there was much disagreement among the parties concerning the makeup of the bargaining unit, both functionally and geographically. Five AFT locals filed the first petitions with PERB in May 1968, each seeking certification as the negotiating representative of the professional employees on a single campus. In January 1969, the University Faculty Senate also filed a petition seeking certification as the representative of all of the university's professional employees in a single systemwide unit. Thereafter, two other candidates—AAUP and the Civil Service Employees Association (CSEA)—filed intervening petitions in which they, too, favored a unit for the entire university, although they differed on the employees to be included. As in the CUNY case, the university governing board favored bargaining with a single, systemwide unit containing all of the professional employees. AFT thereafter amended its original petition and "sought a 'dual unit' bargaining structure wherein each campus of SUNY would select its negotiating representative to deal with local issues and a council of local representatives would represent the subject employees on statewide issues." The PERB director of representation ruled in favor of a single unit for the entire SUNY system, noting that the university and all other candidates for bargaining agent "vigorously opposed" the dual unit proposed by AFT. He reported,

> They argue . . . that a negotiating structure which encompasses campus-wide units will be ineffective since it will not reflect the power structure of the University which is centralized in one Board of Trustees, and chaotic since it would balkanize SUNY into campus or regional power groups, encourage factional conflicts, and ultimately result in the destruction of SUNY's unified structure.

AFT appealed the director's ruling to the entire board, which also ruled in favor of a single statewide unit containing all of the university's professional employees. The board observed,

> the route urged upon us by [AFT] would seem to lack the stability and responsibility necessary in the negotiating relationship. We feel on the record before us that a single state unit can provide meaningful and effective representation for the employees involved on both statewide and local issues.

Four Michigan Universities

In Michigan, where the thirteen state institutions above the community college level have more autonomy than do the SUNY and CUNY components, all units approved thus far have been at the campus level. The units at Central Michigan and Oakland Universities, the first senior institutions to sign contracts with their faculties, were fixed with little difficulty, for at each institution the governing board and the single candidate for bargaining agent were in basic agreement. Local units have also been recognized at Saginaw Valley College, Eastern Michigan University, and Wayne State University, although (as will be discussed below) there was substantial disagreement at the last two institutions concerning the composition of the units, which was resolved by the Michigan Employment Relations Commission (MERC) after extended hearings on the disputed points.

Four State College Systems

Faculty bargaining is taking shape at the campus level at the eleven institutions in the Massachusetts state college system—which are, however, controlled by a single state board of trustees—and bargaining agents have been chosen at seven—AFT at five and NEA at two. In Pennsylvania, the opposite route was taken of bargaining on a systemwide basis through NEA as the single bargaining agent, even though each of the thirteen colleges has its own board of trustees. In Nebraska, NEA is also the bargaining agent on a systemwide basis for the four state colleges.

A somewhat unusual situation took shape in New Jersey. There the six four-year state colleges have separate governing boards, although there is a State Board of Higher Education with some authority over these colleges. Presented with separate petitions from each campus, the Public Employment Relations Commission ruled that representation elections should be held at each institution. In the elections that followed, the State Faculty Association, an NEA affiliate, won the bargaining agent designation at all six institutions. It then entered into negotiations on a statewide basis with the Board of Higher Education and arrived at a single contract for all six institutions.

Does it make a difference whether bargaining at state colleges takes place on a system or campus basis? It is too early to tell. The negotiation of separate contracts for each college in Massachusetts will permit experimentation with different models and the making of adjustments in the light of local problems and institutional differences. But the existence of a single "management" will tend to make for uniformity in the contracts, for the governing board will find it hard to make significant concessions in some instances and deny them in others. On the other hand, AFT and NEA may each elect to go after different gains or concessions in an attempt to show that it is the more effective bargaining agent.

THE PART-TIME TEACHER ISSUE

Whether to put full-time and part-time teachers in the same or separate bargaining units is an issue that labor boards have found hard to resolve consistently. In industry bargaining, the NLRB and many state labor boards have usually followed a rule that those part-time employees who, because of regularity of employment or for other reasons, have a substantial community of interests with full-time employees shall be regarded as "regular part-time employees" and included in a bargaining unit. Other part-time people are to be regarded as irregular or casual employees and must be excluded from units. But drawing the line between these two types of part-time employees in faculty cases is often a complex matter. If all parties to a unit determination proceeding are in agreement on what to do about part-time personnel, the labor board will usually go along with them. But if they are in disagreement, the board must make the determination. In actual fact there has been considerable disagreement among the parties to representation proceedings on this issue. University managements and faculty bargaining agent candidates have not been consistent in the positions they take from case to case. A search can be made for reasoned positions, or, as noted earlier, allowance can be made for the possibility that each party takes its stand on its estimate of how the persons in the disputed group will vote if they are included in the bargaining unit. Both explanations appear to be valid.

The labor board rulings that have become necessary where the parties are in disagreement have not been wholly satisfactory. Boards appear to have been influenced more by the number of courses or hours of instruction given by part-time teachers than by such important considerations as the extent to which part-time teachers share with full-time faculty members the same professional qualifications, methods of appointment, compensation, teaching roles, and power to determine educational policy and participate in institutional governance. Boards may have thought the latter factors too subtle to be easily measured; the former, an easy measurement to fix and apply, and one that tends to bear out boards' preferences for large employee units.

Part-Time Teachers in the CUNY and SUNY Cases

In the CUNY case, both labor organizations took the position that the instructional staff of the university should be divided into two units for bargaining purposes, although they differed on the exact membership of the two units. The university's governing board—the Board of Higher Education of the City of New York—asked PERB to approve a single bargaining unit made up of the entire "instructional staff," contending this approach would be more consistent with the institution's existing administrative and educational practices and needs. The PERB proceedings on the unit composition issue occupied a nine-month period from November 1967 to August 1968.

The first ruling on the nature of the unit, made by PERB's director of representation, favored the two-unit approach and accepted the Legislative Conference's proposal for the specific membership of these units. The LC petition had proposed that persons with the rank of lecturer or teaching assistant be placed in one unit and all other members of the instructional staff above these ranks in another unit. The latter unit was seen by LC as containing all of the instructional employees who were essentially full time and who occupied posts that offered the possibility of tenure or were considered to be of a career nature. The lecturers and teaching assistants in the other unit were thought of as essentially temporary and part time. Neither the full-time, part-time distinction nor the tenure-temporary one was entirely valid originally, and, as time has gone by, these distinctions have become increasingly confused. The United Federation of College Teachers (AFT), under a very different plan, would have placed the science and engineering technicians in one unit and all other members of the instructional staff in a second unit.

The director of representation carefully examined the similarities and differences in the employment conditions of the two groups proposed by LC and concluded that

> Despite . . . common interests, the major differences between the permanent staff and the . . . lecturers in important terms and conditions of employment such as tenure, fringe benefits and the method of determining salaries, create a sharp conflict of interest which mandates separate representation.

The BHE appealed the PERB director's two-unit ruling to the full three-member board, which upheld the ruling by a two-to-one vote. In its decision, PERB noted that at CUNY the nontenured, part-time staff approached the full-time faculty in number, and that many of these part-time employees held other jobs to which they gave their primary professional loyalties. PERB seemed anxious to protect the integrity of the full-time faculty, observing:

> The faculty-rank-status personnel are the heart of the University. It might be compromising to their independence and to the very stability of the University for non-tenured instructional personnel, in numbers almost equal to that of faculty-rank-status personnel to be included in the unit of faculty-rank-status personnel.

A count made by the director of representation had showed that at CUNY there were 4,747 "permanent staff" instructional employees in posts viewed as "tenured or leading to tenure," and 4,258 "temporary staff" employees in nontenured posts. CUNY was thus clearly an institution that made heavy use of temporary or part-time teaching personnel, and this situation unquestionably influenced the two bargaining agent candidates and the labor board to favor separate bargaining units for the two classes of employees. The surprising stand was that of the BHE. Its wish to concentrate collective negotiations in one unit "consisting of all instructional personnel" was perhaps understandable but questionable in terms of sound personnel management practices in industry. But it might also have been expected to foresee that such an arrangement would create pressures in the negotiations at the bargaining table to bring the large number of "have-nots" up to the level of the "haves" with respect to compensation and other conditions of employment. Three years later in 1972, as the three-year contracts in the two units were expiring, the Legislative Conference (which had already combined forces with NEA a year previously) and the AFT local at CUNY merged and demanded that the resulting organization, the Professional Staff Congress, be recognized as the bargaining agent for the entire instructional staff of the university. The BHE had now reversed its position and attempted to persuade PERB to approve three bargaining units: one for the full-time faculty eligible for tenure, one for the part-time or temporary faculty, and one for the nonteaching professional employees. PERB resolved this dilemma by ordering an election in which all of the employees in the two existing units were allowed to make simultaneous determinations whether they wanted to constitute a single bargaining unit and whether they wished the PSC to be their bargaining agent. The vote in favor of a single unit was 8,258 to 942, and in favor of PSC was 8,789 to 538. Thus, by the summer of 1972 the CUNY "instructional staff" had been recognized as a single bargaining unit, represented by a labor union formed out of three organizations that had once been aggressive rivals: LC, NEA, and AFT. The new union claimed to represent 16,000 professional employees at CUNY, among whom the traditional tenure-eligible classroom teachers were a definite minority!

In the SUNY case, PERB approved a single unit for the university's entire professional staff—full time and part time—of some 16,000 persons. Indeed, it ordered some 2,000 part-time employees included in the unit, without any explanation of its ruling, and even though none of the parties to the PERB proceedings had argued for this outcome. The SUNY ruling provides a good example of the preference labor boards show for all-inclusive bargaining units, in the face of other considerations in favor of breaking up a work force into two or more units.

The Part-Time Issue at Other State Institutions

At most of the other state institutions considered above in connection with the multiple campus issue, the part-time issue was not troublesome because management and labor reached agreement at the campus level. Thus, the Southeastern Massachusetts University faculty unit is confined to the full-time instructional staff. The same is true at all of the seven Massachusetts state colleges where units have been determined and agents chosen. At Boston State College, the first of the state colleges to sign a contract with its faculty, the unit is narrowly confined to persons holding full-time appointments by the board of trustees in one of the four faculty ranks from instructor to professor or in one of several librarian categories. The units at Central Michigan and Oakland Universities are also confined to full-time professional employees.

Eastern Michigan and Wayne State Universities

The part-time issue was more troublesome in two representation proceedings before the Michigan Employment Relations Commission early in 1972.[5] The cases were similar. There had been much discussion within faculty circles on both campuses about collective bargaining during 1970. At the end of the year at Eastern Michigan, both AAUP and AFT submitted sufficient faculty signatures to MERC to qualify as petitioners. NEA entered the case as an intervenor. At Wayne there were four petitions—AFT, AAUP, the Wayne Medical Faculty Association, and the Wayne State University Professional and Administrative Association. A Faculty Association filed as an intervenor. The Professional and Administrative Association, which was already petitioning for recognition as the bargaining agent for certain professional and administrative employees of the university, sought to have the "academic staff" (nonteaching professionals) added to its unit.

Three days of hearings were held in the Eastern Michigan case in January and February 1971, before a MERC trial examiner; the Wayne case required fourteen days of hearings before the same examiner between February and April. Briefs were submitted in both cases after the hearings had been completed. The trial examiner submitted pro-

5. The Eastern Michigan case carries MERC case numbers R70K-407 and R71A-2 (1972). The Wayne case numbers are R71B-58, R71B-75, R71B-79, and R71C-137 (1972).

posed decisions in both cases to MERC in early December. MERC heard further oral arguments in both cases in late December and rendered its final decisions in February 1972. The two cases thus illustrate the substantial delays that can be encountered when the parties are in disagreement about the composition of the bargaining units.

In the Eastern Michigan case the governing board wanted all part-time teachers excluded from the faculty unit; all of the labor organizations asked for the inclusion of "lecturers employed to teach six hours or more for two or more consecutive semesters." (This description of what might be called "regular part-time teachers" coincided closely with AAUP's membership requirement for "active members" of the association.) The examiner stated that "the question is whether [the lecturers'] relationship to the University and to the bargaining unit is sufficiently regular and permanent so as to give them a community of interest with other faculty members and justify allowing them to vote in an election." He noted that at the time of the hearing there were just over 200 lecturers at Eastern Michigan and a permanent faculty of approximately 675. He found that these part-time teachers have limited responsibilities to the university in that they teach but do not take part in faculty committee work, help shape educational policy, or advise students; are paid on a different basis from the faculty; and are not eligible for tenure. He concluded that "their employment is temporary and casual in nature, and [that] they do not share employment interests with the permanent teaching staff" and recommended that they be excluded. This recommendation was rejected by MERC. In including the part-time teachers in the unit, MERC asserted:

> Lecturers have common intellectual interests with faculty members whose teaching work they supplement. Certainly they share a community of interests toward the student's development. Since the functions of the lecturers are not dissimilar in terms of the educational process, from those of the faculty members and staff counselors, we conclude that the similarities of functions require inclusion of the lecturers in the bargaining unit.

In the Wayne case, all of the parties had agreed by stipulation that "adjunct faculty" ("who may teach one course in the evening") should be excluded, but that a small number of "regular faculty" referred to as "fractional-time teaching faculty" who teach more than half time should be included. The examiner and MERC both accepted this stipulation.

Who was right about what to do with part-time teachers at Eastern Michigan: the trial examiner or the full labor commission? One takes his choice, depending on whether one views "the academic profession" and "the faculty" as precise terms that should be narrowly applied to persons who meet exacting standards having historical and professional validity, or as broad terms that may be loosely applied to any and all persons who help sustain the teaching program of an educational institution. The EMU case does clearly indicate that, in interpreting and applying relevant statutes, the professionals who staff a labor board operation can be in sharp disagreement on how to settle a disputed issue.

THE PART-TIME TEACHER ISSUE IN NLRB CASES

Long Island University

In the first faculty collective bargaining cases to reach the National Labor Relations Board from the private sector of higher education early in 1971, the issue of what to do about part-time teachers proved troublesome. This board, too, revealed a strong bias in favor of the all-inclusive unit. In the Long Island University Brooklyn Center and C. W. Post Center cases, the Board found the parties in substantial disagreement on the issue. In the Brooklyn Center case, both candidates for bargaining agent, AFT and AAUP, supported a unit made up of professional employees directly or indirectly engaged in instruction, including part-time teachers. The university's governing board took the stand that, if an election was to be held, full-time faculty should be represented in one unit and other employees in separate units. In the C. W. Post Center case, AFT was the only candidate for bargaining agent. It again argued for the inclusion of part-time teachers, and the LIU governing board again argued for their exclusion.

The NLRB, in its rulings in the two Long Island University cases, directed that the part-time teachers be included in the units with the full-time faculty.[6] In the C. W. Post Center case the Board approved a unit consisting of 335 full-time teachers, 206 part-time teachers, 27 librarians, one research associate, and two guidance counselors. In the Brooklyn Center case, the approved unit consisted, for the first semes-

6. C. W. Post Center, 189 NLRB No. 109, 77 LRRM 1001 (1971); Brooklyn Center, 189 NLRB No. 110, 77 LRRM 1006 (1971).

ter of the academic year, of 361 full-time teachers, 96 part-time teachers, and one guidance counselor. The Board acknowledged that the status of part-time teachers was different from that of full-time faculty members in many ways: part-time people were not eligible for tenure, were appointed for different periods of time and paid on a different basis, did not enjoy the usual fringe benefits, and did not have the power to vote at faculty meetings (although the Board asserted, without citing evidence, that "on occasion they have voted"). The Board also noted that many part-time people taught only in night programs and that some held positions at other colleges and universities. In the face of these findings, the Board reached the wholly undocumented conclusion that "these employees have the same educational background as their full-time faculty counterparts and engage in exactly the same teaching activities." The Board found "that the full-time and adjunct faculty were professional employees *with common interest* who together constitute a unit appropriate for collective bargaining" (emphasis added).

The Board was clearly anxious to follow the precedents it had set through the years in unit determination rulings in the industrial sector. It spoke of "well-settled principles" in earlier rulings, stated that it was unable to discover "any clear-cut pattern or practice of collective bargaining in the academic field which requires the Board to modify its ordinary unit-determination rules," and rejected the employer's contention that faculties are different from "other types of employees," stating that it was

> not persuaded that [the principles it had been applying to such other employees would] prove to be less reliable guides to stable collective bargaining in the [educational] field than they have proven to be in others. . . . [So] we shall apply them in this case.

The Board found that the part-time teachers at both of the Long Island campuses met its standard of "regular part-time professional employees" (rather than irregular or casual employees) and were properly included in the faculty unit. It supported this finding by the conclusion that the "qualifications and chief function, teaching," of these part-time employees were "identical with those of the full-time faculty." However, the Board left it to later cases to formulate a rule or standard that might separate "regular part-time" teachers from irregular or casual teachers in terms of work loads.

The statistics on faculty at the two Long Island University campuses, noted by the NLRB, show that the university is an institution that, either because of the nature of its teaching programs or for reasons of financial exigency, makes substantial use of part-time teachers. In defense of the NLRB and state labor boards, which must decide what to do with large numbers of part-time personnel at such institutions, it can be said that the issue would not arise if all educational institutions adhered to high standards in the maintenance of full-time faculties. On the other hand, urban institutions offering a wide variety of vocational, adult, extension, and continuing education programs often find it essential for budgetary reasons and even desirable for educational reasons to staff these programs with part-time teachers who possess special qualifications to teach them and who would not be available for full-time appointments. But the other side of this argument is that the two parts of the faculty may well be so different in qualifications, teaching roles, outside commitments, methods of compensation, and involvement in institutional governance, that they should be separated into different units for bargaining purposes.

Fordham University

Not long thereafter, in the Fordham University case, the NLRB adhered to its position that "regular part-time" teachers should be included in a faculty unit, even though the evidence showed that at Fordham most part-time teachers had full-time jobs outside the university, many as faculty members elsewhere, that they were not eligible for tenure, and that they did not participate in faculty policy making.[7] Not counting the law faculty, the Fordham faculty consisted of 480 full-time and 235 part-time teachers. The Board did indicate that it would not have insisted on including the part-time people in the unit, had there been agreement among the parties to exclude them. AAUP, the candidate for bargaining agent, had asked that they be included, but the university governing board had asked that they be excluded.

The NLRB and state labor boards ordinarily permit the opposing parties in a litigated case to reach an agreement on a disputed representation issue through a stipulation, even though the agreement differs from the ruling the board would make, based on its precedents and inclinations, if the parties remained in disagreement. In its ruling in a unit determination case at the University of New Haven, where

7. 193 NLRB No. 23, 78 LRRM 1177 (1971).

the parties were in disagreement, the NLRB had ordered "regular, part-time professional employees whose qualifications and work functions are identical with those of the full-time faculty" included in a faculty unit. In a footnote, however, the Board called attention to its "policy to exclude regular part-time employees from a unit where the parties have stipulated to their exclusion." It cited as the authority for this policy the Uxbridge Mill case, a Board ruling in the industrial sector.[8] In its Fordham ruling, the NLRB directed AAUP and the university to reach agreement on where to draw the line between "regular part-time" teachers and those whose work at Fordham was so irregular or marginal that they ought to be excluded. Eventually the two parties did agree on criteria by which *all* the part-time people were excluded.

The University of Detroit

In the University of Detroit case, the NLRB itself set the standard for the inclusion of "eligible" part-time teachers in the unit. In this case AAUP, the petitioning labor organization, wanted part-time teachers excluded, and the university's governing board wanted them included. AAUP asked that if the Board did decide to include them, it establish a test to ensure that only those part-time teachers who had a substantial and continuing interest in the wages, hours, and working conditions of unit employees would be eligible to vote. The Board established such a test, although it rejected the standard proposed by AAUP. Instead, having carefully reviewed a detailed statistical analysis of the faculty staffing arrangements in all of the schools within the university, it applied a "4-to-1 full-time-to-part-time-hours-taught-ratio...." This meant that, in all schools except those of law and dentistry, part-time faculty members teaching three hours or more per semester were declared eligible to vote. The formula produced somewhat different results in the law and dentistry schools.[9]

THE NONTEACHING PROFESSIONAL ISSUE

"Nonteaching professionals" is a way of describing those employees of an educational institution who do no teaching, but function in such positions as librarians, data processing personnel, registrars, student

8. University of New Haven, 190 NLRB No. 102, 77 LRRM 1273 (1971); Uxbridge Mill, 109 NLRB 868, fn. 9 at 870.
9. 193 NLRB No. 95, 78 LRRM 1273 (1971).

counselors, health officers, and placement office directors, and thereby render services supportive of teaching and research. Such employees are usually called "professionals," although they often possess no graduate degree qualifying them to teach in a particular discipline and may or may not have had graduate training in a field requiring specialized intellectual instruction or in the field in which they work. Where their inclusion in a faculty bargaining unit is in dispute, a labor board usually finds itself weighing many of the same considerations as for part-time teachers: Are the qualifications, methods of appointment and compensation, job duties, and working conditions of these employees such as to give them a "community of interests" with the teaching faculty?

The Status of Professional Employees under Federal Law

Before examining the resolution of this issue at institutions where faculty bargaining is taking place, it should be noted once more that the National Labor Relations Act and some state laws forbid the placing of professional employees in a bargaining unit with nonprofessional workers unless a majority of the former vote for inclusion. The federal statute defines "professional employee"—with considerable precision and in exacting terms, as follows:

> The term "professional employee" means—
> (a) any employee engaged in work (i) predominantly intellectual and varied in character as opposed to routine mental, manual, mechanical, or physical work; (ii) involving the consistent exercise of discretion and judgment in its performance; (iii) of such a character that the output produced or the result accomplished cannot be standardized in relation to a given period of time; (iv) requiring knowledge of an advanced type in a field of science or learning customarily acquired by a prolonged course of specialized intellectual instruction and study in an institution of higher learning or a hospital, as distinguished from a general academic education or from an apprenticeship or from training in the performance of routine mental, manual, or physical processes.[10]

This is a remarkable definition, one which, taken seriously (or merely literally), might well lead the NLRB to exclude a good many white-collar workers from a bargaining unit containing other admittedly professional employees, on the ground that the former, while

10. §§ 2(12) and 9(b)(1). 49 Stat. 449 (1935), as amended by Pub. L. No. 101 (1947) and Pub. L. No. 257 (1959); 29 U.S.C. §§ 151–68 (1970).

performing work well above "routine mental, manual, mechanical, or physical" tasks, nonetheless fail to meet all of the statute's rigorous requirements for professional status.

Long Island University, C. W. Post Center

In the C. W. Post Center case, AFT as the petitioner asked that a number of nonteaching employees be included in the faculty unit; the university governing board asked that they be excluded. In this and similar cases, the NLRB has shown an inclination to favor units containing all of an educational institution's professional employees, teaching and nonteaching alike. But, unlike some state labor boards, it does attempt to satisfy itself that the evidence in a disputed representation proceeding does show that the nonteaching employees are "professional" within the statute's definition before including them. At C. W. Post, it included twenty-seven librarians in the faculty unit, finding, among other things, that they all possessed master's degrees in library science. It excluded a chemistry laboratory assistant and a biology technical assistant on the ground that their work did not require them to have advanced degrees in their fields. Guidance counselors were included on a finding that they "are required to have advanced knowledge and are performing the intellectual and varied functions contemplated . . . in Section 2(12) of the Act." Admissions counselors and academic counselors were excluded because they "are not required to have knowledge of the advanced type, and are not performing . . . intellectual and varied tasks."

CUNY and SUNY

Most states follow federal practice in making it possible for professional employees to form separate bargaining units, although state statutes do not always expressly provide for this. In Oregon, for example, it is reported "that no provision is made for separate representation of professional employees, and the practice . . . has been to include them in the same unit with nonprofessionals."[11] There is no

11. J. G. Grodin and M. A. Hardin, "Public Employee Bargaining in Oregon," 51 *Oregon Law Review* (Fall 1971), 7, 19. Inasmuch as there has been no faculty bargaining in Oregon, the quoted passage refers to other types of public employee bargaining units. The same issue of the *Oregon Law Review* contains a useful article, Lee C. Shaw and Theodore R. Clark, Jr., "Determination of Appropriate Bargaining Units in the Public Sector: Legal and Practical Problems," pp. 152–76; see especially pp. 172 ff.

provision in the New York Taylor Law for separate units of professional employees and no definition of such employees, but the CUNY and SUNY representation cases were decided by the Public Employment Relations Board as though the units in both cases would contain only employees of professional standing. In the original CUNY case, PERB described the two units as encompassing the institution's "instructional staff" (which was the descriptive term used by the university itself), divided primarily between full time and part time. Yet a little-noted fact was that a significant number of nonteaching professionals, or "satellite personnel," such as science technicians, physicians, clinical assistants, dentists, business managers, fiscal officers, and registrars, were placed in the full-time unit. This group appeared to include between 400 and 500 employees. The director of representation found that although they

> are not primarily concerned with the instruction of students, they share with the rest of the permanent staff a community of professional interest inasmuch as they are engaged in directly supportive activities that are clearly and closely associated with the function of teaching. . . . All are professionals, and their functions dovetail.

At SUNY, the single unit, as already noted, consisted of the institution's total professional staff of nearly 16,000 persons. It is estimated that some 11,000 were instructional personnel and 5,000 were nonteaching professional employees, who are explicitly described in the contract as "non-academic." The PERB written opinions accompanying its rulings do not state what criteria, if any, were used in determining the professional standing of certain members of the units. At CUNY, for example, the credentials of an "assistant to fiscal officer," a "registrar's assistant," and an "assistant to higher education officer" remained unexamined, but presumably the persons holding these offices could not meet the exacting test found in the federal statute.

In 1972, as we have seen, all of the so-called instructional employees at CUNY—full-time and part-time teachers and nonteaching "professional" employees—became part of one all-inclusive unit in the SUNY pattern. The unit numbers some 16,000 employees and is represented by the Professional Staff Congress. PERB made no apparent attempt to satisfy itself that all of these employees had professional competence or functions in the sense required where the federal statute is controlling.

Eastern Michigan and Wayne State Universities

The nonteaching professional issue was raised in both the Eastern Michigan and Wayne State cases. The Michigan statute does not define "professional employees" or guarantee them the right to form separate bargaining units, although the trial examiner in the Eastern Michigan case wrote in his recommended decision that "the Commission has generally recognized ... units 'limited to those of a common professional pursuit.'" In the Eastern Michigan case, the university governing board favored exclusion of academic advisers, student counselors, and residence hall advisers; all of the bargaining agent candidates wanted them included. At Wayne, the governing board divided its employees into six classifications, ranging from "teaching faculty" to "skilled and operational personnel," for administrative purposes. The board asked that the second category of "academic staff" (essentially academic counselors, student advisers, etc.) be joined with the third category of "professional and administrative staff," for which group the Professional and Administrative Association (P&A) was petitioning to be recognized as the bargaining agent. AFT asked that these nonteaching professionals be placed in the faculty unit; AAUP asked for a unit limited to faculty "eligible for tenure."

The MERC trial examiner recommended that at both institutions the nonteaching professionals be excluded from the faculty unit. At Eastern Michigan he found that the members of the teaching faculty "represent a clearly identifiable unit with common interests and working conditions" which "in the main" were not shared by members of "the rather extensive supporting professional staff." He concluded that

> the addition of supportive personnel to a basic teaching faculty unit would add employees to the unit whose duties are more dissimilar than similar to the duties and working conditions of the teaching faculty.

The trial examiner recognized that he was departing from the NLRB's C. W. Post ruling on this issue and asserted that

> a more functional approach to the definition of a bargaining unit in a major university, sought by the Employer herein, is better suited to the faculty realities of such institutions than the strictly professional approach used by the NLRB.

The examiner recommended that at Wayne the question of the inclusion of nonteaching professionals in a unit to be represented by P&A

"be handled through the collective bargaining process" if P&A "should prevail in any election ordered by the Commission."

MERC rejected the examiner's recommendations in both cases and placed the nonteaching professionals in the faculty unit. It dealt with the issue at some length in its Eastern Michigan decision:

> The supporting staff and faculty are functionally integrated groups by virtue of their synergistic efforts aimed at the education of University students.

And again:

> The record disclosed that a primary purpose of the University is to educate and prepare students for the eventual roles that they will lead in life. This educational process is the central focus of the activities of *both* the faculty and the several classes of advisers and counselors. Upon matriculation at the University, the student-client subscribes to the services of both the faculty and the counselors. The community of interest is determined by the interrelationship of the several skills which are brought to bear on the student-client.

MERC also observed that:

> Separation of these groups as proposed by the University would create fragmented bargaining units which we have consistently sought to avoid.

MERC responded to the university's concern that the inclusion of nonteaching professionals in the unit "would dilute the 'community of power' concept" with the sweeping observation, "The University need have no concern." The presence of nonteaching professionals in the unit, it stated,

> need not deprive the teaching personnel from [sic] the same type of participation in educational decision making as they have had in the past. This decision making . . . is not the process of collective bargaining.

In making this last assertion, MERC ignored the fact that "the process" of bargaining at other institutions was already beginning to encompass the wide range of institutional relationships, processes, and problems in which a faculty has an interest. "Everything is bargainable" is an observation frequently made about faculty collective bargaining. It is true that collective bargaining requires only that both sides bargain in good faith; neither side is compelled to agree to the inclusion in a contract of any particular provision. Presumably the governing board at Eastern Michigan would be free in its bargaining to refuse to accept any agreement that would threaten or undermine the position of "the faculty" as the dominant intellectual force in shaping the purpose and life of the university community.

In such a situation, however, a real danger is created that "the faculty," in any traditional or professional sense, will no longer be in a position to argue or defend its interests from its side of the bargaining table. Numbers become important. Any bargaining agent must reflect the interests, demands, and concerns of unit members as these are asserted on a majority basis. The threat, of course, is great that the diversity within the unit will lead to a leveling downward, or compromising, of faculty interests, as the agent attempts to represent and serve the interests of large numbers of unit members whose training, outlook, standards, and duties *are* different in many ways from those of the professional college teacher-scholar. In any event, MERC's failure to follow its trial examiner's recommendation on the issue of the integrity of a teaching faculty is appalling from the point of view of the interests of the academic profession. To hold, as MERC did, that any university employee who helps "prepare students for the eventual roles they will lead in life" contributes to "the educational process" and that this justifies placing all such employees in the same bargaining unit is to withdraw society's recognition of "the company of teacher-scholars" as an ancient profession responsible for the instructional program of a university. It substitutes mere job duty or orientation for exacting professional training and observance of professional standards as the test for membership in the academic community.

THE FACULTY FRAGMENTATION ISSUE

The danger that the unit determination element in collective bargaining will weaken the cohesion and integrity of a college or university faculty has thus far been greater on the side of the inclusion of employees who are at best peripheral members of the academic profession. But there are risks in the other direction: on the exclusion from general faculty units of employees or groups of employees who are integral to the central teaching-research function of an educational institution. In most instances these risks have not become realities, but there are some disturbing indications that such a trend may yet develop.

Labor boards may be expected to reject petitions coming from bargaining agent candidates seeking to represent the faculty members of individual academic departments or of separate undergraduate colleges within a university. Thus, in 1970, the NLRB rejected the petition of a labor organization that sought to represent a group of non-academic employees identified with the department of public health at the Yale School of Medicine. The Board held that the unit was inappropriate inasmuch as the department was one of seventeen in the medical school and one of sixty-eight in the university as a whole.[12] Also in 1970, in a Michigan State University case, the Michigan labor board rejected a petition coming from an NEA unit asking to be certified as the bargaining agent for the faculty of the University College, an undergraduate unit. The governing board opposed the petition on the ground that, if bargaining were to take place, the entire university faculty would be the appropriate unit.[13]

A GRADUATE OR PROFESSIONAL FACULTY AS A SEPARATE UNIT
Law Faculty at Fordham University

There is a greater likelihood that university faculties may be fragmented for bargaining purposes by labor board rulings permitting professional or graduate school faculties to be excluded from general faculty units, or to organize as separate units if they care to do so. Some law faculties, with encouragement and advice from the Association of American Law Schools, have argued that their professional activities and responsibilities are so special that they ought not to be included, against their wish, in a bargaining unit with the rest of a university faculty. This argument prevailed at St. John's University, where the New York Labor Relations Board approved a unit from which the law faculty had, at its request, been omitted, and at Fordham University in 1971, when the NLRB, in approving AAUP's petition that an election be held to select a bargaining agent, agreed with AAUP and the law faculty that the latter should constitute a separate unit.[14] The Fordham governing board had opposed this fragmentation of the faculty in its arguments before the NLRB.

In this case, the brief submitted by the Association of American Law

12. Yale University and Yale Non-Faculty Action Committee Unit No. 1, 184 NLRB No. 101, 74 LRRM 1637 (1970).
13. 1970 MERC Lab. Op. 1029.
14. 193 NLRB No. 23, 78 LRRM 1177 (1971).

Schools is a remarkable document. Prepared by three eminent law professors at institutions other than Fordham, it is, as might be expected, effectively argued. But the picture it offers of law professors' view of themselves as a discrete part of the academic profession is somewhat startling and even disturbing. The law professors clearly distrust the leveling effect of collective bargaining and are anxious to protect their special status in higher education, including their well-above-average salaries. Thus the brief states:

> The law teacher has a characteristically different type of academic background, is recruited from a different manpower source, has a different orientation to the non-academic world, is compensated at a different level, and advances through the academic ranks at a different pace.

> Law faculties are generally recruited from amongst the practicing profession rather than directly out of the academic environment.

> ...whereas 52.7 percent of all full-time university teachers hold re-research doctorate degrees, only 8.8 percent of the full-time teachers in our random sample of accredited law schools hold the research doctorate.

> Law faculty can choose between teaching and practicing their profession. For this reason, their salaries are influenced by the larger market place. And, because law is a well compensated profession, law teachers are paid markedly above the general university compensation levels.

Perhaps the most remarkable argument in support of the brief's claim that law faculty are a separate breed is that law school students have "a distinctive set of attitudes and values" that set them apart from other students:

> Studies show that, to a distinguishing degree, law students identify with making money, helping others and being socially useful. In contrast with other university students, the law student tends to reject originality, creativity and a gradual, secure road to success. In addition, those who have studied law students in comparison with other students report that law students feel an exceptionally strong need to find order in our social system and to shape aggressive drives. Moreover, it is reported that law students have had particular childhood relations with their parents and others, distinguishable from the childhood experiences of those enrolled in other sorts of professional programs.[15]

15. The quoted passages appear on pp. 8, 9, 11, and 19 of the brief.

In finding that "the law school faculty constitutes a distinct group of employees whose separate community of interests is not irrevocably submerged in the broader community of interest which they share with other faculty members," the NLRB took notice of evidence showing that members of the Fordham law faculty were housed in a separate building, had their own academic calendar, determined their own educational program, enjoyed higher salaries and ranks than the general faculty, and were eligible for tenure after a shorter period of service. The Board also noted that a law faculty has certain legal or professional obligations to agencies external to the university, such as the state bar association and the courts.

Expressing some reluctance to depart from its long-established practice of stretching the "community of interests" doctrine to create the broadest possible employee unit, the Board noted that in this instance there was no prior bargaining history on an all-faculty basis and that no labor organization sought to include the law faculty in such a broad unit. The Board relegated to a footnote an indication of its awareness that many of the factors set forth might have been equally applicable to the university's other professional faculties, had any of them asked to be separately represented.

The NLRB ruling in the Fordham case increases the likelihood that faculty bargaining in private broad-purpose universities will take shape henceforth on a fragmented basis. It is hard to see how the Board, unless it reverses its Fordham ruling quite decisively in some new university case, can refuse to approve petitions from labor organizations representing faculties in such professional areas as medicine, engineering, architecture, dentistry, social work, theology, and library science, asking for separate recognition. It is certain that some of these professional faculties will seek separate recognition, particularly where they enjoy special privileges and higher salaries, for they will not wish to subject themselves to the salary-leveling influence of collective bargaining in a broad faculty unit. If faculty collective bargaining comes to such a private university as Havard, where the "each tub on its own bottom" tradition has long allowed the university's professional school faculties great freedom to run their own operations, separate units can hardly be avoided. Whether fragmented bargaining will serve the interests of a university, its separate schools, and its general and individual faculties, will have to be discovered in practice. As for the argument, advanced by the Fordham and other university trustees but rejected by the NLRB, that the management function is vested in the faculty, the Board may well one day be perplexed by evidence showing that, at an institution like Harvard, the graduate and professional schools do enjoy great autonomy within the university and are, indeed, "run by their faculties."

NLRB's approval of a separate unit for the law faculty at Fordham produced a surprising result. There is reason to believe that the law faculty did not feel a strong need to bargain collectively with the Fordham governing board and was, instead, content to depend on individual bargaining or informal collective bargaining to protect its salary advantages and other perquisites. As it turned out, the general faculty rejected collective bargaining and AAUP as a bargaining agent by a vote of 236 to 222, whereas the law faculty approved collective bargaining and its own agent, the Law School Bargaining Committee, by a vote of 16 to 10. The law faculty's bargaining agent is reported to have kept its negotiations with the university at a low-key level. But should it decide to bargain aggressively and win a contract that further strengthens the economic status of law professors, the rest of the Fordham faculty would probably change its mind at the first opportunity and itself vote to engage in collective bargaining.

The Medical Faculty at Wayne State University

The Wayne State University representation case was the first in which a state labor board has responded directly to a petition that a professional school faculty within a university be approved as a separate bargaining unit.[16] The ruling of the Michigan Employment Relations Commission on this point is in direct conflict with that of the NLRB with respect to the law faculty at Fordham University. At Wayne the medical faculty did not want to be included in a broad university faculty unit. Some of its members organized a Wayne Medical Faculty Association, which collected enough signatures to enable it to petition for recognition as the bargaining agent for a separate medical faculty unit. The university governing board and AFT opposed a separate unit for the medical faculty. AAUP, as in the

16. In the CUNY and SUNY cases, faculty members teaching graduate or professional courses were included in the units, inasmuch as none of the parties to the PERB proceeding argued otherwise.

Fordham case, supported the separate unit, a position seemingly in conflict with its general position that professional faculties are part of a single academic profession and of the faculties of their universities.[17] AAUP does not authorize separate chapters for such faculties, but does seek their membership in AAUP, and fosters their participation in the activities of its universitywide chapters.

The trial examiner recommended to MERC that it follow the rule that a faculty unit, such as the one at Wayne, should be "the largest . . . which, in the circumstances of the particular case, is most compatible with the effectuation of the purposes of the law and to include in a single unit all common interests." He then proceeded to a detailed examination of the specific ways in which the Wayne medical faculty appeared to be both a part of the university faculty and a separate entity. It is fair to say that there were at least as many facts and arguments in support of the medical faculty's contention that it had "little or no contact with the rest of the University" as had been present at Fordham in support of the law faculty's similar contention. The examiner nonetheless concluded that

> it would unduly fragmentize a *teaching faculty unit* if individual schools or colleges are permitted to have separate representation, especially where one of the parties is seeking the broader unit.

MERC accepted this recommendation. However, it excluded some employees from the unit that the examiner had recommended should be included, and thereby it weakened the force of his contention that "a teaching faculty unit" ought not to be fragmentized. Since the Medical Faculty Association was not seeking to be a bargaining agent candidate in an election in which the entire university faculty was the unit (or part of the unit), its petition was dismissed. In other words, medical faculty members at Wayne were made eligible to vote in the general election, along with other members of the university faculty, for one of the bargaining agent candidates or for the "no bargaining" option.

17. Although the trial examiner states that AAUP was in favor of "excluding the medical school faculty," he also notes that the "Federation [AFT], as well as the AAUP and the Intervenor [the WSU Faculty Association], did not take a strong position on either the inclusion or the exclusion of the medical school faculty, but in general appears to be willing to abide by whatever decision the Commission reaches in this regard."

THE DEPARTMENT CHAIRMAN ISSUE

What to do about department chairmen in determining faculty bargaining units has proved to be a deeply troublesome issue, particularly in the cases reaching the NLRB from private colleges and universities. The trouble begins with the uncertainty and vacillation that bargaining agent candidates and institution governing boards have shown on the issue. Faculties and candidates for bargaining agent are initially disposed to support the inclusion of chairmen in units on the ground that they are the agents of their faculty colleagues, both in managing the internal affairs of the departments and in handling departmental relations with deans, provosts, presidents, other departments, and the faculty as a whole. This position is probably strongest at institutions where chairmen are elected by departmental faculties for limited terms, take care of routine business, and preside at department meetings where all important decisions are made by vote of the department's members. Administrative officers and trustees, on the other hand, often begin by favoring the exclusion of chairmen from faculty units on the ground that they are management's "first-line supervisors," who carry out institutional policies within their departments concerning budgets, faculty appointments, and teaching and research assignments. Management also quickly discovers that when the contract stage of collective bargaining is reached, chairmen acquire new responsibilities in seeing that the agreement is so administered at the departmental level as to avoid or minimize the complaints and grievances of individual faculty members under the contract. In industrial labor-management relations language, chairmen would be viewed by their departmental colleagues as "stewards" and by the administration as "foremen."

Institutional practices with respect to department chairmen vary greatly. In some measure these local differences explain why governing boards and candidates for bargaining agent take other positions on the chairman issue than the above analysis suggests. Where chairmen are appointed by the administration for indefinite terms and wield unchecked authority in their departments, a bargaining agent candidate may conclude that they are indeed part of management and seek their exclusion from the faculty unit. The governing board, on the other hand, may believe that such chairmen would be a healthy influence in the councils of the labor organization and favor their inclusion in the unit. Both sides are also likely to be influenced by their estimates of how department chairmen will vote in the representation election if they are made part of the unit. Management may be tempted to want chairmen included in a faculty unit, guessing that, as senior faculty statesmen, they will have Old Guard leanings and vote either for the "no bargaining" option or for the most conservative candidate for bargaining agent. The bargaining agent candidates may oppose the inclusion of chairmen, fearing that their votes will reflect pro-administration leanings.

One further note: In an occasional case, the inclusion or exclusion of deans, associate deans, or assistant deans has been a disputed issue in determining the membership of a faculty bargaining unit. Up to now, deans have almost always been excluded on the ground that they exercise "supervisory" authority. Associate and assistant deans, on the other hand, have sometimes been included in a faculty unit (SUNY), sometimes excluded (CUNY). Where they are included, it may be presumed that governing boards and all candidates for bargaining agent agree on this point, or, if it is a disputed issue, that the labor board finds that these officers do not exercise supervisory authority.

DEPARTMENT CHAIRMEN AS "SUPERVISORS" UNDER FEDERAL LAW

The rulings of the NLRB on the chairman issue in two early cases at Long Island University (see below) and in later cases serve to underscore the contention that when a faculty exercises its statutory right to engage in collective bargaining with its "employer," both parties must accept the risk that bargaining patterns will be shaped to some extent by legalisms. The precise language of the National Labor Relations Act, as interpreted and applied by the NLRB, determines whether department chairmen are to be viewed as part of the faculty or part of the administration at private educational institutions, rather than judgment being made by a careful weighing of desirable organizational arrangements and practices as the academic community may see the issue. The federal statute provides that "the term 'employee' . . . shall not include any individual employed as a supervisor," which means that supervisors are denied the right to be part of an employee bargaining unit.[18] The statute then defines supervisor in these terms:

18. In addition, the provision in the statute means that employers are free from the *duty* to bargain collectively with supervisors. Supervisory employees may, however, organize, and the law does not prevent their employers from bargaining with such supervisory organizations on a voluntary basis. See Charles J. Morris, ed., *The Developing Labor Law*, pp. 204–5, 428, 772.

> The term "supervisor" means any individual having authority in the interest of the employer, to hire, transfer, suspend, lay off, recall, promote, discharge, assign, reward, or discipline other employees, or responsibility to direct them, or to adjust their grievances, or effectively to recommend such action, if in connection with the foregoing the exercise of such authority is not of a merely routine or clerical nature, but requires the use of independent judgment.[19]

Careful reading of this statutory provision indicates that a "supervisor" is anyone who (1) himself appoints, dismisses, or takes certain other direct action with respect to other employees, (2) responsibly directs them or adjusts their grievances, or (3) effectively recommends such action to some higher authority. NLRB rulings concerning department chairmen have largely depended on the third test: Does the evidence show that chairmen "effectively recommend such action"?

Long Island University

In the two Long Island University cases, the first faculty collective bargaining cases to reach the NLRB, the Board was immediately faced with the chairman issue. In the C. W. Post Center case, AFT, the only candidate for bargaining agent, asked that chairmen be excluded from the unit. In the Brooklyn Center case, however, where AAUP and AFT were rival candidates, both labor organizations wanted chairmen included.[20] Somewhat surprisingly, in both cases the university's governing board favored their inclusion. Thus, in the Brooklyn Center case all of the parties wanted chairmen included. The NLRB nonetheless ordered chairmen excluded from both units, explaining its ruling on the ground that, since department chairmen are "individuals" who "make effective recommendations affecting the status of faculty members and have authority to hire and discharge nonprofessional em-

19. NLRA §§ 2(3), (11). Supervisors were not excluded from employee bargaining units under the Wagner Act of 1935. This provision was added to federal labor law in 1947 by the Taft-Hartley Act. The federal statute also defines the term "employer" to include "any person acting as an agent of an employer, directly or indirectly," but this provision has not yet proved significant in faculty bargaining unit cases. The NLRB has apparently not yet squarely faced the contention that the role of an educational institution's faculty members is such that they act as agents of their employer, "indirectly" if not "directly."

20. 189 NLRB No. 109, 77 LRRM 1001 (1971); 189 NLRB No. 110, 77 LRRM 1006 (1971). AFT and AAUP as the petitioning and intervening labor organizations had attempted to organize these two campuses as independent units. No party to either case argued that collective bargaining at Long Island University should take place on an institutionwide basis. The employer in both cases, however, was the governing board of Long Island University.

ployees," they are "supervisors" and "the statute requires their exclusion" from the units.[21] The Board did examine with some care the evidence on the exact status of chairmen at both campuses, noting, for example, that at the Brooklyn Center department chairmen were elected by their departmental colleagues, whereas at the C. W. Post Center they were usually selected by the dean in consultation with the respective departmental faculties.

Fordham University

In the Fordham case, AAUP, the sole candidate for bargaining agent, adhered to the position it had taken in the Brooklyn Center case and favored the inclusion of chairmen. The Fordham governing board, taking the opposite stand from that of management in the LIU cases, wanted them excluded. The NLRB also changed its position and now, by a two-to-one vote, ordered department chairmen included in the unit. The Board majority attempted to distinguish its ruling from that in the LIU cases by finding that at Fordham a chairman did not exercise individual authority in faculty personnel decisions, but shared his authority with the members of his department "acting as a group." It also asserted that:

> To the extent that the chairman's recommendations concerning these matters are given more weight than those of other faculty members, the fact appears to reflect the chairman's superior knowledge and experience, and does not indicate possession of the type of authority contemplated in the statutory definition of a supervisor.

The majority also found that the recommendations of the chairmen concerning the salaries of their colleagues were not always accepted at higher levels and could not be said to be "effective."[22]

The dissenting NLRB member, having reviewed the status and duties of department chairmen at Long Island University and Fordham with particular respect to their authority in the making of faculty personnel decisions, concluded that "the department chairmen's situation at Fordham is substantially akin to that at C. W. Post.... Accordingly, as the Board did in C. W. Post, [he] would find the department chairmen at Fordham to be supervisors within the meaning of the Act."

21. 189 NLRB No. 110, 77 LRRM 1006 (1971).
22. 193 NLRB No. 23, 78 LRRM 1177 (1971).

At this point in the continuing effort of the NLRB to adapt and apply the National Labor Relations Act to the employment relationship between an educational institution and its faculty, the question could properly have been raised whether Board members were bringing to their work an adequate understanding of a university as a special kind of corporate enterprise. At the end of their ruling in the Fordham case on the department chairman issue, the two board members in the majority wrote:

> In addition, it is significant that the department chairmen consider themselves, and are considered by faculty members, to be representatives of the faculty rather than of the administration. There is some indication that the University views them similarly. Thus, the catalogues of the various schools refer to chairmen as members of the faculty rather than as part of the administration. The letter of appointment used by the University indicates that a faculty member is responsible to the president or dean, rather than to his department chairman.

These observations are highly pertinent as part of an attempt to understand the role of department chairmen at an educational institution and to arrive at a satisfactory disposition of this particular issue in a disputed faculty bargaining unit case. But the trouble with these remarks is that, with one exception, no labor board, federal or state, has yet been willing to let a dispute concerning department chairmen's inclusion in, or exclusion from, a faculty unit depend on how department chairmen, their colleagues, and the institution view their role. Labor boards may take notice of such information or evidence, but in the end they fall back to the known territory of statutory language and of the experience they have had in applying that language to the labor-management relationship in industry.

The University of Detroit

The NLRB was by no means free from the department chairman issue at this point. A month after its Fordham ruling, the NLRB once more, in the University of Detroit case, ordered chairmen included in the bargaining unit. This time the university governing board had asked that chairmen be included, and AAUP, the petitioning labor organization, that they be excluded. The NLRB now focused its attention even more sharply on the question whether chairmen, in playing their role in faculty personnel decisions, made recommendations concerning the appointment, promotion, tenure grants, and discharge of faculty members that in the end proved "effective." The Board concluded that the evidence showed that they did not, since their recommendations were among several, including those of their department colleagues, that were considered by the university officials who possessed the authority to make binding decisions.[23]

Adelphi University

In March 1972, in its ruling in the Adelphi University case, the NLRB swung back to its position in the Long Island University cases and ordered department chairmen excluded from the faculty unit.[24] This time the governing board wanted them excluded, and AAUP, as the petitioner, and AFT, as an intervenor, wanted them included. The record showed that the role of chairmen at Adelphi was not substantially different from that at Fordham and the University of Detroit, with two exceptions: at Adelphi, chairmen appeared "effectively to recommend the hiring and reappointment (or nonreappointment) of part-time (but not full-time) faculty members, and to allocate merit increases, without the approval of the department's faculty." In the view of the NLRB, this made them supervisors.

The NLRB did take notice that at Adelphi the president could remove a chairman before his term expired only with the concurrence of a majority of the members of the department in question. This rather unusual arrangement might have seemed to render department chairmen at Adelphi less subject to administrative control than they are at many other institutions and thus to constitute an argument for placing them in the faculty unit. But by now the crucial, almost the exclusive, test in the eyes of NLRB members was whether chairmen "effectually recommended" any faculty personnel actions.

Seattle University and Florida Southern College

Application of the "effectually recommended" test by the NLRB produced two further rulings in 1972 in representation proceedings involving Seattle University and Florida Southern College. In the former case, department chairmen were ordered excluded from the unit and in the latter, included. AAUP was the sole petitioner at Seattle and NEA at Florida Southern. AAUP sought to represent "an

23. 193 NLRB No. 95, 78 LRRM 1273 (1971).
24. 195 NLRB No. 107, 79 LRRM 1545 (1972).

all professional employees unit," NEA, an "all professional, fulltime faculty members" unit—department chairmen to be included in both units. At Seattle the employer asked that chairmen be excluded; the record in the Florida Southern case does not clearly indicate the employer's stand on the issue.

Four members of the NLRB participated in the Florida Southern case and found that the chairmen were not supervisors since they made no effective recommendations in personnel matters and in general acted only as coordinators of their departments and provided a liaison between the dean's office and their departments.

The final ruling in the Seattle case was made by an NLRB regional director. The record showed that department chairmen at Seattle unquestionably exercised more authority than they did at Florida Southern. But the evidence was such as to lead the regional director to be somewhat guarded in his written opinion. He found that the chairmen's recommendations in personnel matters were "nearly always respected" and, again, that they were "given great weight by their superiors." He also found that the chairmen were involved in the formulation and effectuation of university policy "to some extent." It was thus not quite possible to say that their recommendations were "effective." The regional director nonetheless found that the chairmen were "at least managerial employees, and, in some instances, supervisors." On that finding, he ordered them excluded.[25] This was one of the first cases in higher education in which the NLRB, following its policy in unit determination cases in industry, allowed a regional director to make the final ruling.[26] The regional director's use of the "managerial employee" concept must strike the nonlawyer unfamiliar with NLRB practice in industrial representation proceedings as curious, for it had not been used by the full Board in any of its prior rulings in faculty unit cases. Moreover, the federal statute, while carefully

25. Florida Southern College, 196 NLRB No. 133, 80 LRRM 1160 (1972); Seattle University, Case No. 19-RC-6163.

26. Prior to 1961, the NLRB itself made the rulings in all unit determination cases, based on the record of a regional-level hearing. Thereafter, the Board delegated authority to the regional directors to make final rulings. A director may, however, transfer cases involving novel issues of law to the Board for decision. Any party to a representation proceeding may also ask the Board to review a director's ruling, but only where substantial questions of law or policy are raised, or where it is asserted that there has been a clear error on a substantial factual issue, the conduct of the hearing was prejudicial, or compelling reasons exist for reconsideration of an important Board rule or policy. See Morris, *The Developing Labor Law*, pp. 828–29.

defining a "supervisor" and providing for his exclusion from an employee unit, is much more vague about the status of managerial employees. Indeed, the statute does not use that term at all. It does include within the definition of "the term 'employer' ... any person acting as an agent of an employer." But the statute does not spell out the distinguishing characteristics of such an employer agent, as it does for a supervisor. Moreover, if the ground is to be shifted from the "supervisor" to a "management employee" or "management agent" test in NLRB unit rulings with respect to department chairmen, the question is properly raised whether the NLRB ought not to reconsider its earlier rulings in the Fordham and Adelphi cases, in which it rejected the argument made by the governing boards that faculty members should not be allowed to invoke the right to collective bargaining under federal law because they were part of management. It was one thing for the NLRB to conclude that faculty members (except for department chairmen in some cases) did not fall within the statute's precise definition of supervisor; it would appear to be quite a different issue whether they may not be "agents of the employer," or "managerial employees," under the statute. If this more ambiguous concept (in the statute's terms) is to be used to exclude department chairmen from bargaining units, why should it not be used to exclude faculty members from the right to bargain under federal law? At the very least, the ruling in the Seattle case suggests that as future rulings in faculty unit cases become the responsibility of regional directors, NLRB's record for consistency in these cases may become even less noteworthy than it already is.

These latest federal rulings suggest that, in faculty collective bargaining, the fate of department chairmen at private colleges and universities remains uncertain in any case where the parties to a representation proceeding are in disagreement. Unless the record shows that the authority of chairmen at an institution is either nominal or definitive, it appears that the NLRB and its regional directors will exercise considerable freedom in deciding to include or exclude chairmen from faculty units.

THE CHAIRMAN ISSUE AT STATE INSTITUTIONS

In the early faculty unit determination cases at public institutions, the chairman issue was not troublesome. Through 1971, chairmen were included in virtually all units, including those at Boston State College,

Southeastern Massachusetts University, the University of Rhode Island, CUNY, SUNY, Rutgers, Central Michigan University, and Oakland University. At most of these institutions the parties seem to have been in agreement that chairmen should be included.[27]

There have been second thoughts at some of these institutions since contracts were negotiated. The president at Southeastern Massachusetts University, who has since resigned, thinks it was a mistake from management's point of view to permit chairmen to be members of the faculty bargaining unit. At Central Michigan University, many of the chairmen are reported to be unhappy about their presence in the faculty unit and to find themselves in something of a no man's land. They feel that their own interests have been poorly represented by the bargaining agent and that they have lost their status as part of the administration. At Oakland, the administration did apparently seek to have chairmen excluded from the unit but, with the approval of the state labor commission, agreed to let them make their own decision. The chairmen then voted eleven to seven to be included in the unit.

Eastern Michigan and Wayne State Universities

The Eastern Michigan and Wayne State University cases were the first in which a state labor board found the parties in disagreement over the chairman issue and ruled that they be excluded. In the East-

27. State public employee bargaining laws do not always follow the National Labor Relations Act in expressly excluding supervisors from employee units, but the same result usually prevails through either other statutory language or the exercise of administrative discretion by state labor boards. The Massachusetts statute excludes from the definition of "employee," and thus from employee bargaining units, "persons whose participation or activity in the management of employee organizations would be incompatible with law or with his official duty as an employee." The New York statute excludes from the term "public employee" any person who has been "reasonably designated from time to time as managerial or confidential upon application to the appropriate board.... Employees may be designated as managerial only if they are persons (a) who formulate policy or (b) may reasonably be required on behalf of the public employer to assist in the preparation for conduct of collective negotiations, administer collectively negotiated agreements, or have a major role in personnel administration." It is reported that this language was altered by the New York legislature in 1972 "to provide a fuller definition of 'managerial' and 'confidential' employees" (Terrence N. Tice, "New State Labor Laws, 1972," in *Collective Bargaining on Campus II.*)

The Michigan Employment Relations Commission excludes supervisory employees from general employee bargaining units, but permits them to organize their own supervisors units. This has been done in the community college sector. There is such a unit, for example, at Macomb County Community College. But no department chairmen at a four-year institution have yet gained recognition as a bargaining unit.

ern Michigan case the governing board and all of the labor organizations except AAUP wanted department chairmen excluded from the unit on the ground that they were supervisors. In the Wayne case the governing board wanted chairmen in five of the eleven major colleges of the institution excluded. The labor organizations wanted all chairmen included on the ground that they "are merely the spokesmen for their fellow department members under the collegial system of self-government prevalent among university faculties."

At Eastern Michigan the trial examiner found the evidence to show that the 26 department heads presided over faculty groups varying in size from a low of 14 to a high of 125, that they had to be full professors, and that they held office for indefinite terms. His findings further showed that when a vacancy existed, a screening committee composed of members of the department, but chaired by the dean, set up criteria for the position, secured candidates, and "assist[ed] in the process of making a selection of a candidate for the position." Department heads were paid "a differential of from $1,000 to about $3,000 more than other faculty members." A detailed examination of the powers and duties of the chairmen showed that they were "responsible for recruiting and recommending the employment of faculty, and recommending promotions, salaries, and tenure status of faculty within their department." They also "recommend[ed] a budget and handle[d] the expenditure" of department funds. They determined teaching work loads and prepared class schedules. These findings led the examiner to conclude that "the chairman exercises more than mere group responsibility for the affairs of his department." As a consideration that might have supported the opposite conclusion, the examiner noted that "department heads seek and utilize the advice and consent of other members of the department," although "they are not always required to do so." The examiner made no attempt to determine or weigh the extent to which the recommendations of chairmen were "effective" with deans, the president, and trustees, although he did conclude that they exercised "responsible supervisory authority." The use of "responsible" rather than "effective" action as the test was, of course, quite permissable since the Michigan statute contains no definition of supervisory authority, let alone the detailed one of the federal statute. In any event, the examiner recommended that chairmen be excluded from the faculty unit, and the labor commission accepted his recommendation.

The full labor commission also accepted the examiner's recommendation concerning department chairmen in the Wayne case. The examiner confined his attention to the status of the department chairmen in the five colleges concerning which the parties to the proceeding were in disagreement. He began his analysis by observing that "a decision . . . must rest on a close analysis of [the chairmen's] authority and how effectively it is exercised." His analysis is indeed "close" but may lack the understanding that labor board officials need in evaluating the place of department chairmen in an academic community. The examiner observes that

> a great deal of testimony was taken as to the duties and authority of department chairmen . . . , which . . . is somewhat difficult to reconcile due to the large measure of autonomy given to individual departments within a college and due to the varying methods of operation and individual characteristics of the particular department chairmen.

On the one hand, his finding is that

> promotions, raises, and refusal to renew contracts of non-tenure teaching faculty must . . . bear the recommendation and endorsement of the department chairman, and the record substantiates that these recommendations are almost always accepted and approved by the dean's office.

On the other hand, the examiner is troubled by "the fact" that the

> decisions and recommendations [of the department chairmen], and even the choice of a chairman himself, are reached frequently through the collegial decision-making process peculiar to higher education,

involving consultation by the chairmen with their colleagues. In spite of this "fact," the examiner persisted in his conclusion that:

> the department chairmen have and exercise the authority to make effective recommendations as to the hiring and change of status of faculty members and other employees of the university.

Admittedly, the role of chairmen did vary from one department to another in the Wayne colleges under examination (which is not in itself necessarily bad academic practice), but the evidence noted by the examiner did seem to show that the "collegial decision-making process" was operating satisfactorily in at least some of the departments in question. Thus, his recommendation that all of these chairmen be excluded from the faculty bargaining unit is both perplexing and disturbing.

The University of Delaware

Early in 1972, the Governor's Council on Labor in Delaware ordered a representation election at the University of Delaware. As the petitioning labor organization, AAUP asked that department chairmen be included in the unit. The university's governing board asked that they be excluded. The Council on Labor ordered an election in a unit from which chairmen were excluded. In its brief opinion the Council stated that it was excluding chairmen "because of their management responsibilities" as set forth in the university's *Faculty Handbook*.

AAUP's Vacillation on the Chairman Issue

AAUP, AFT, and NEA have all vacillated from case to case in their stands on the chairman issue. As the leading national professional association of college and university professors, AAUP might have been expected to adhere more faithfully to what it deems to be correct practice in the matter. And it does have a position. It holds that a chairman should serve "as the chief representative of his department within an institution."[28] It also asserts that chairmen should be selected for stated terms either by department election or, if by administrative officers, following consultation with members of the department. Although on occasion AAUP might choose to argue for the exclusion of chairmen from a bargaining unit where these conditions are not met, in so doing, it concedes the point that chairmen are part of management at such institutions. A stand more consistent with AAUP's broad principles

28. "Statement on Government of Colleges and Universities," *AAUP Policy Documents and Reports*, 1971 ed., pp. 33, 36. The statement was jointly formulated by AAUP, the American Council on Education, and the Association of Governing Boards of Universities and Colleges. It was approved by the AAUP Council in 1966 and the AAUP Annual Meeting in 1967. The full paragraph on the department chairman is as follows:

"The chairman or head of a department, who serves as the chief representative of his department within an institution, should be selected either by departmental election or by appointment following consultation with members of the department and of related departments; appointments should normally be in conformity with department members' judgment. The chairman or department head should not have tenure in his office; his tenure as a faculty member is a matter of separate right. He should serve for a stated term but without prejudice to re-election or to reappointment by procedures which involve appropriate faculty consultation. Board, administration, and faculty should all bear in mind that the department chairman has a special obligation to build a department strong in scholarship and teaching capacity."

would seem to require it to favor inclusion of chairmen within the faculty bargaining unit under all circumstances, with pressure then being exerted where necessary on institutions to correct faculty practices with respect to the appointment, terms, and duties of chairmen, either through revision of institutional bylaws or specific language in the collective bargaining contract.

The vacillation of AAUP on the chairman issue from case to case is explained in part by the inability of the national organization to dictate to its chapters on this and similar unit membership issues. It is the local AAUP chapter, just as it is the AFT local or the NEA local affiliate, that offers itself as candidate for bargaining agent and that makes the decisions at the campus level concerning the posture and tactics to be employed in the certification campaign and in the bargaining process that follows. The local affiliates of all these organizations can and do depart in significant ways from the goals and standards set at the national level. AAUP, as well as AFT and NEA, can exercise important supervisory powers from its national headquarters. Each of the national organizations can take the extreme step of withdrawing its recognition of an unusually obstreperous or recalcitrant local unit. But unless there is an open break between the national organization and one of the local units, officers and members of the local unit are free within wide limits to fix the aims and policies of that unit.

The Faculty Committee Issue

Whether faculty members should be excluded from a bargaining unit because of their service on certain faculty committees was considered for the first time by the NLRB in the Adelphi University case, decided by the Board in March 1972.[29] Once more the outcome depended on the application of the statutory provision defining a supervisor. The status of the members of two faculty committees was in question: the Personnel Committee, composed of eleven faculty members elected by their colleagues for three-year terms on a staggered basis, and the Grievance Committee, composed of three tenured faculty members elected for two-year staggered terms. The function of the first committee was to consider and make recommendations on such personnel matters as faculty appointments and promotions at the associate professor and professor levels, awards of tenure, sabbatical leaves, and suspensions or dismissals of faculty members during the

29. 195 NLRB No. 107, 79 LRRM 1545 (1972).

term of their contracts. The Grievance Committee's function was to hear and recommend the adjustment of all faculty grievances except in dismissal proceedings. AAUP as the petitoner and AFT as an intervenor argued that the members of the two committees should be included in the bargaining unit; the employer was reported as taking no position on the substantive issue, but asking the NLRB to determine the status of the faculty members serving on the two committees "in light of the uncontroverted facts."

Neither committee exercised final authority in its recommendations. The Personnel Committee's recommendations were sent directly to the board of trustees. The Grievance Committee's recommendations were transmitted, at its discretion, to the grievant and to appropriate administrators or other faculty bodies, with a possible final appeal by the grievant to the board of trustees. Evidence was submitted at the NLRB hearings indicating that over a two- to three-year period all of the committees' recommendations had been accepted and implemented. Two issues of statutory interpretation were present: (1) Were the committees' recommendations "effective," as used in the definition of "supervisor"? and (2) Were the recommendations made by "individuals"? The NLRB could hardly fail to be impressed by the evidence showing that the recommendations of the two committees were effective; yet two of the three panel members concluded that the supervisory action here was taken by a group and not by individuals. The committee members were held not to be supervisors and could thus be members of the employee bargaining unit. The third member of the NLRB panel dissented, indicating that he would exclude the committee members from the unit under the supervisor language of the statute. With reference to the Personnel Committee he wrote:

> The members of the committee would clearly be supervisors under the Act if they exercised their authority as individuals. In my view, it makes no difference that they exercise this authority on a collective basis through committee decision rather than as individuals. If the committee, when considered as a whole, would satisfy the definition of a "supervisor" under the Act, then a conclusion that each member of such a committee is imbued with some supervisory authority is logically sound, and I would so find.

Under this NLRB ruling, then, as long as faculty members exercise their authority through committees, they can continue to perform certain "supervisory" functions within the academic community without endangering their membership in the faculty bargaining unit. But this result depends on a two-to-one vote of the NLRB, with the majority avoiding an embarrassing ruling by resorting to a technicality— "supervisors" exercise their authority as "individuals." Of course, a faculty can avoid the threatened disruption of its ranks for bargaining purposes by asking the administration and the board of trustees to take over faculty personnel decisions and the settlement of grievances. Or it can encourage the president and the trustees to reject enough recommendations coming from faculty committees handling these matters to prevent the record from showing that these recommendations are always "effective." For a faculty to take either of these steps will require it to turn its back on the principle that faculty judgment should be controlling in many matters of internal management of an educational institution. Another way out of the dilemma would be for everyone to agree that when faculty members accept assignments as department chairmen or membership on certain committees, they in effect leave the faculty and become part of management. If this were done on a short-term basis, with faculty members rotating in and out of these assignments, the effects on faculty cohesion for purposes of collective bargaining could be seriously disruptive. If it were done on a long-term basis, the involvement of faculty members in certain essential roles or tasks in a manner consistent with faculty democracy would become impossible.

The consequences of labor board rulings on the disputed exclusion-inclusion issues examined in this chapter are already being felt at some institutions, and are potentially very serious as they may affect many more institutions in the years ahead. Advocates of faculty collective bargaining generally assert that the academic profession must try to develop special bargaining models that will meet the needs of higher education. Such models *are* desirable. Colleges and universities should not be locked into the industrial bargaining model. The question is: Do collective bargaining statutes and labor board rulings permit experimentation and innovation in the bargaining process in higher education? To the extent that so-called faculty bargaining units are compelled by law to accept large numbers of employees who have not traditionally been regarded as members of the academic profession, or are denied the membership of persons who help give a faculty its character and strength, the emergence of new bargaining models for higher education is jeopardized.

CHAPTER FIVE

The Role of Labor Organizations in Faculty Representation Elections

Workers seldom turn to collective bargaining on a wholly spontaneous basis. They may be ripe for organization and for collective bargaining because of their dissatisfactions and expectations, but without some prodding—without someone to give them direction, to show them what to do—they may well remain quiescent. Collective bargaining statutes typically establish the right of workers "to organize" and "to bargain collectively through representatives of their own choosing." They also provide that the workers' representative may be an "individual or labor organization." The latter is usually defined broadly as "any organization of any kind . . . in which employees participate" whose "purpose, in whole or in part" is to deal with an employer concerning "grievances, labor disputes, wages, rates of pay, hours of employment, or conditions of work."[1]

This statutory language allows a faculty to take the initiative by asking one of its own members to act as its "representative" and to set in motion the steps that must be taken if the faculty is to engage in collective bargaining under law. The use of an "individual" as a representative in collective bargaining is certainly not common in industry. No faculty has yet tried this approach, although it may offer a means of developing a bargaining model suitable to the special needs of a faculty and the higher education setting. An existing faculty organization is occasionally designated as the bargaining agent, but almost never where it is a part of the formal institutional governance system. Instead, faculties, like workers in industry, seem to be dependent on a positive effort *to organize* them by an outside agency or by a campus agency that is external to the governance structure. Certain faculty leaders

---

1. The quotations come from the National Labor Relations Act. State statutes are similarly worded. The use of "or" rather than "and" as the conjunctive in the definition of a labor organization permits an organization to qualify under the law if it serves any one of the enumerated purposes.

115

may participate in organizational efforts, but almost always as officers or representatives of a labor organization that seeks to become the faculty's bargaining agent. Often these faculty leaders are assisted, or even prodded into action, by agents of the organization who come to the campus from local, state, or national headquarters.

Faculty collective bargaining has not lacked for labor organizations to provide the prodding. A total of five candidates (or types of candidate) for bargaining agent have figured in the representation elections held thus far. In each election the ballot has included one or more of these candidates, together with a "no agent" or "no bargaining" option which, under the law, provides an employee group with an opportunity to reject the proposal that it engage in collective bargaining.

The Three National Labor Organizations in Faculty Bargaining

Three of the five possible candidates for bargaining agent are well-known national organizations, each of which has been trying to carve out for itself a significant share of the business in this new field. They are the American Federation of Teachers, the American Association of University Professors, and the National Education Association. The first is a traditional labor union and is affiliated with the AFL-CIO. The latter two, before becoming involved in the business of collective bargaining, long identified themselves as professional associations seeking to advance the interests of the teaching profession in a variety of ways, NEA almost exclusively in primary and secondary public education, AAUP in higher education, public and private. An occasional employer has tried to avoid bargaining with AAUP by arguing that it does not qualify as a "labor organization," but AAUP has had little difficulty in persuading the NLRB and state labor boards that it meets the statutory definition.

These three national organizations have come close to dominating the representation function in faculty collective bargaining at four-year institutions.[2] Although each had certain handicaps to overcome in entering this new area of labor-management relations, they were available and active from the start as candidates for faculty bargaining

2. Independent faculty organizations have won representation elections in a few instances, but in the most notable cases, at City University of New York and State University of New York, these agencies then affiliated with NEA. AAUP is the joint bargaining agent with a local faculty association at St. John's University.

agents. They have provided the aggressive organizing effort without which it is unlikely that many faculties would have reached the stage of full involvement in collective bargaining with their governing boards.[3]

It is always a state- or local-level affiliate of one of these national organizations that offers itself as a candidate for faculty bargaining agent at a college or university. Thus, at Oakland University the bargaining agent is the local chapter of AAUP; at Southeastern Massachusetts University it is Local No. 1895 of AFT, which takes the name of Faculty Federation; and at Central Michigan University it is the Faculty Association, a campus unit of the Michigan Association of Higher Education, which is a state affiliate of NEA. To simplify discussion here, the local labor organizations will usually be referred to by the names of the national organizations, where such affiliations exist. It must be borne in mind, however, that the local organization often claims and exercises considerable autonomy, and that, legally, the local organization *is* the bargaining agent.

National Education Association

NEA is the oldest of the three organizations. It traces its origins back to the National Teachers Association, which was founded in 1857 when ten state teachers associations joined forces in establishing a national organization which they hoped would "elevate the character and advance the interests of the profession of teaching, and . . . promote the cause of popular education in the United States."[4] In 1870, this association and an organization of public school superintendents merged and took the name National Education Association. Throughout most of its history, NEA's purpose has been to serve the professional interests of public school personnel—administrators as well as

3. The availability of NEA and AFT as rival bargaining agent candidates in the public school sector has been identified as a positive force leading to "this movement toward collective teacher action." Writing in 1966, Robert E. Doherty and Walter E. Oberer declared: "The rivalry between the National Education Association and the American Federation of Teachers . . . is almost as important a cause of the present efforts to formalize the employer-employee relationship in public education as is dissatisfaction with conditions of work." And again they make the point in even stronger terms: "the growing competition between the two major teacher organizations . . . might be as important a cause of organizational activity as all the other reasons combined" (*Teachers, School Boards, and Collective Bargaining: A Changing of the Guard,* pp. 21, 32).

4. Ibid., pp. 22–23. The historical account of NEA and AFT draws on the Doherty and Oberer volume as a principal source.

teachers. A traditional criticism of NEA until recent years was that administrators exercised too much influence over its policies and programs. In any event, its early growth was slow. Its membership did not reach 10,000 until 1918, when reportedly it enrolled only 5 percent of the nation's public school teachers. Thereafter, it grew more rapidly, particularly in recent decades. The *NEA Handbook 1971–72* put NEA membership at 1,103,485 and memberships in its state affiliates at 1,726,751; affiliated local associations numbered 8,950.

Following World War II, NEA became increasingly active as a political force at the local, state, and federal levels. It campaigned aggressively for the "cause of popular education," but always as its leaders viewed that cause, and supported specific and often controversial means for its implementation, such as teacher certification laws that placed emphasis on courses in "education" in the curricula of teacher-training institutions. The association also began to lobby effectively on behalf of its members' "conditions of employment," although it usually refrained from identifying this activity in trade union terms, preferring instead to suggest that what was good for its members was also good for public education.

Along the way, NEA developed a minor interest in higher education, principally because of a necessary recognition that the development and control of teacher-training programs was a function of higher education. This interest developed through a series of organizational arrangements, leading ultimately to the formation of the American Association for Higher Education (AAHE). This affiliate, like the parent organization, accepted college administrators as well as professors. Its members were from the start heavily concentrated in teachers colleges and in departments and schools of education at broad-purpose colleges and universities. During the 1960s, the relationship between AAHE and NEA became increasingly troubled. NEA had grown more and more teacher-oriented, while AAHE retained its joint administrator-teacher character. And AAHE vigorously opposed collective bargaining in higher education, whereas NEA was deciding to challenge AFT as the means through which public school teachers could utilize collective bargaining in a more aggressive attempt to improve their conditions of employment.

In 1968, AAHE voted to drop its departmental status within NEA and to become an "associated organization." For all practical purposes, AAHE thereby became an independent agency. Its membership is still heavily limited to professors and administrators identified with the discipline of education. It has played no role in faculty collective bargaining. NEA has attempted to fill the gap created by AAHE's departure through a series of internal organizational rearrangements, which need not be examined here. NEA has won some notable victories in faculty bargaining agent elections, but the resulting increased membership in higher education still accounts for a very small segment of its total membership.[5]

During the early 1960s, NEA and its affiliates, with much larger memberships of public school teachers than the AFT had, resisted the idea of collective bargaining, arguing that it was inconsistent with the professional status and goals of teachers. NEA's leaders also feared that established and satisfying relationships between teachers and school boards and administrators would be impaired by collective bargaining, asserting that a consultative and cooperative approach to shared responsibilities and activities would be replaced by an adversary one. Strikes or the threats of strikes, an essential characteristic of collective bargaining, were said to be unprofessional and, in the public sector, illegal.

By the middle of the decade, the trend toward a more militant representation of the interests of public school teachers had become unmistakable, and NEA's younger and more aggressive leaders argued that the organization could continue to oppose collective bargaining only at the price of turning the public school teacher movement over to AFT. Their contentions found favor with large numbers of NEA members, and the organization decided to support "collective negotiations," its term for collective bargaining. For a while, the NEA continued to oppose teacher strikes, but when some of its local affiliates nonetheless went on strike, the national organization was compelled by circumstances to support them. From July 1960 through June 1971, there were 631 "strikes, work stoppages, and interruptions of services" by public school teachers. Of these, 439 were called by NEA or its affiliates, 156 by AFT locals, and 36 by an independent organization or were jointly sponsored or had no organizational backing.[6] A sig-

---

5. NEA and AFT reports of membership totals do not disclose how many members either organization has gained through collective bargaining activities among college faculties.

6. Data are from "National Education Association Memorandum on Teacher Strikes, Work Stoppages, and Interruptions of Service, 1970–71," 71 *Government Employee Relations Report*, 1051–60.

nificant number of NEA strikes occurred before 1968, when the NEA's Representative Assembly went on record in support of strikes by its affiliates. NEA had found that it could not hold its public school members unless it supported its affiliates, although its action was inconsistent with its long-standing national policy.

American Federation of Teachers

AFT was founded in 1916, when several local teachers unions in the Chicago area were granted a charter by the American Federation of Labor. Unlike the NEA of those days, its principal purpose was to bring public school teachers into the American labor movement and to win better wages and working conditions for them. From the beginning, it stressed the existence of an adversary relationship between school teachers on the one side and school boards and administrators on the other. It thus argued that teachers should join an organization independent of their employer and then at the first favorable moment attempt to use collective bargaining as the best way of improving their compensation and work conditions. However, as public employees, teachers did not win the statutory right to engage in collective bargaining until the 1960s and were everywhere denied the legal right to engage in strikes; hence AFT's efforts during its first four and a half decades were largely directed to the limited end of "organizing" teachers.

AFT did not positively endorse teacher strikes until 1960. In scattered instances during the late fifties and early sixties it did persuade school boards to recognize it as a bargaining agent for teachers on a voluntary basis. In 1962, the United Federation of Teachers, AFT Local No. 2, led a successful strike and won recognition as the bargaining agent for the teachers of New York City. After this victory, AFT became aggressive in urging collective bargaining on public school teachers throughout the country.

As early as the 1930s, AFT established a few locals for professors at urban institutions, but here, too, the purpose was to identify professors with the American labor movement for the long-run benefits that might accrue to both sides, rather than the immediate one of engaging in collective bargaining.[7] It gained its foothold in higher education as a labor organization before either NEA or AAUP. Thus, by 1969 it

7. This characterization is based in part on an article by Israel Kugler, "The Union Speaks for Itself," 49 *Educational Record* (Fall 1968), 414–18.

had been selected as bargaining agent, virtually without challenge, at Boston State College, Southeastern Massachusetts University, Bryant College of Business Administration, and the United States Merchant Marine Academy. These were neither well-known nor typical four-year institutions, and AFT's early foothold has not given it any continuing advantage in soliciting faculty support at other institutions. In 1971, AFT reported its membership at 246,747, mostly public school teachers. Its membership among college teachers is not reported. There were 931 AFT locals.

American Association of University Professors

AAUP, founded in 1915 by a group of distinguished faculty members at several of the nation's leading universities, has for more than half a century been the only national professional association that represents professors exclusively, without regard to academic disciplines or types of institutions with which they are identified. In 1972, it had 91,316 members. This figure was well below the membership total of NEA or AFT, but probably represents about one-third to one-half of the full-time members of the American academic profession and certainly a far larger and more varied part of the professoriate than was identified with either of the other organizations.

AAUP's leading concern has always been the protection of academic freedom, but it has also long been interested in defining and protecting such "conditions of employment" in higher education as compensation, tenure, and the processing of grievances.[8] On the other hand, AAUP has always disclaimed the label "faculty union." Until recently it also rejected such terms as "employer," "employee," and "adversary relationship" as properly descriptive of the internal organization of a college or university, insisting instead that faculty members are "officers" and, as such, part of a "shared authority," or "joint custodians," scheme of governance.

AAUP reacted slowly and cautiously to the appearance of faculty collective bargaining in American higher education. In 1966, it reasserted its belief that a faculty ought not to settle for anything less than a direct role in institutional governance and, in particular, that a

8. The term "grievance procedure" has only recently come into widespread usage in academic life. But "academic due process," which AAUP has long sought to define and defend, is a forerunner of the current concern about the proper means of settling grievances.

faculty should claim the right to be a principal participant in the policy-making process with respect to educational, faculty personnel, and budgetary matters. It was clearly fearful that it could not simultaneously support the professional interests and well-being of college professors through traditional means and use the direct means of a labor organization, including the strike, to improve the "wages, hours, and working conditions" of its members. Certainly AAUP had no inclination to abandon its status and activities as a professional association in favor of an exclusive role as a labor organization. In spite of these fears, the AAUP Council voted in May 1966, "as a temporary policy to furnish *interim* guidance," to authorize AAUP chapters to seek recognition as bargaining agents at institutions where "effective faculty voice and adequate protection and promotion of faculty economic interests" did not exist. Three limitations were established: a chapter must first obtain the approval of the AAUP general secretary; no strikes or work stoppages were to be called; no agency shop (compulsory union membership or dues payment) arrangements were to be established.[9]

In 1968, AAUP went a step further to emphasize that conditions at particular institutions might be so unsatisfactory to the faculty that collective bargaining could well seem to be the best way of improving its status. Bertram H. Davis, the general secretary of AAUP, wrote in the *AAUP Bulletin*:

> It may be well to remember that there are more depressing alternatives than faculty unionization. Indeed, given a choice solely between administrative tyranny—that kind of administration which . . . keeps the faculty not on its toes but on its knees—and collective bargaining. . . . a faculty member not totally insensitive to his environment would probably have little hesitation in going the union way.[10]

The national AAUP, however, still recommended as the preferred approach that faculties seek to strengthen the role of the faculty senate

9. "Representation of Economic Interests," 52 *AAUP Bulletin* (June 1966), 229–34.

10. Davis, "Unions and Higher Education: Another View," 54 *AAUP Bulletin* (September 1968), 317–20. See also "Policy on Representation of Economic and Professional Interests," *AAUP Policy Documents and Reports,* 1971 ed., pp. 39–41. The original formulation of this new policy statement was approved by the AAUP Council in April 1968, and the statement was then "concurred in" by the next AAUP annual meeting. It was further revised and approved by the Council in October 1969.

within the governance systems of their institutions, looking toward a "shared authority" or cooperative control of policy making.[11]

In some ways, AAUP found itself in the same position in higher education that NEA had occupied a few years earlier as public school teachers began turning to collective bargaining. If it resisted collective bargaining and discouraged its local chapters from offering themselves as candidates for bargaining agent, it ran the risk that, where other organizations were selected as the faculty bargaining agent, some of its chapters might not survive. The failure of AAUP to play a significant role in the efforts to organize the CUNY faculty for collective bargaining, after the enactment of the Taylor Law in 1967, undoubtedly caused a good deal of soul-searching in the organization's Washington office. AAUP had long enjoyed much faculty support at the oldest and strongest of the CUNY institutions, such as the City College. Moreover, in December 1964, the principal national officers, committee chairmen, and staff members of AAUP had met with the president-elect of the AAUP chapter at the City College and the chairman of the Legislative Conference at CUNY for a two-day discussion of the possible roles of AAUP, the Legislative Conference, and the CUNY AFT local in whatever faculty collective bargaining might take shape at CUNY.[12] The Legislative Conference chairman later told us that the meeting revealed that AAUP was unlikely to show much interest in helping the CUNY faculty get ready for collective bargaining. Up to then there had been a willingness within LC to entertain the possibility that it and AAUP might work together in support of a movement toward collective bargaining at CUNY. Three or four years later "the loss of CUNY" must have seemed to some AAUP leaders a heavy price to have paid for the association's failure to have become more actively involved in collective bargaining between 1965 and November 1967, when the Legislative Conference petitioned the Public Employment Relations Board (PERB) in New York for recognition as the bargaining agent at CUNY.

---

11. "Faculty senate" has become a generalized term intended to describe any of several arrangements by which a faculty plays a formal and significant role in university governance. Some actual senates are small representative councils elected by the faculty at large; others are the entire faculty itself or all tenured members of the faculty. The term is here used to mean any formal arrangement by which a faculty is given an effective role in institutional governance, particularly with respect to educational policy and faculty personnel policy.

12. This meeting was reported in Ralph S. Brown, Jr., "Representation of Economic Interests: Report of a Conference," 51 *AAUP Bulletin* (September 1965), 374–77.

In October 1971, the AAUP Council took a major step toward a complete and enthusiastic commitment to faculty collective bargaining. The Council announced that henceforth the association would "pursue" collective bargaining "as a major additional way" of achieving AAUP's goals; that it would encourage "interested and well-qualified Association chapters themselves to seek certification as the exclusive representatives of the faculty" in order to avoid the election of other bargaining agents that "have not demonstrated any sustained sense of obligation to press beyond the letter of the contract in order to secure academic justice"; and that such association "resources and staff" would be made available "as are necessary for a vigorous selective development" of collective bargaining beyond "present levels." In defense of this step, the Council repeated the argument that AAUP, alone among national organizations, understood and represented the academic profession's basic purposes and principles and that for AAUP to ignore the trend toward faculty collective bargaining would leave the field open "to organizations without the established dedication to principles developed by the Association and widely accepted by the academic community." Those principles would soon be in "serious jeopardy." And it emphasized the "pressing need to develop a specialized model of collective bargaining for higher education, rather than simply to follow the patterns set by unions in industry."[13]

This new stand by the AAUP Council presumably took effect immediately as an association policy, but it was decided to ask the association's 1972 annual meeting to concur in the Council's action. In an attempt to inform AAUP members fully about the new policy and to enable local chapters to instruct their delegates how to cast their votes, a detailed and candid statement of the pros and cons of the situation was published in the March 1972 issue of the *AAUP Bulletin*, just prior to the annual meeting.[14] The record of the association's reaction to the collective bargaining problem, beginning with the 1964 meeting with CUNY faculty members, was reviewed. No attempt was made to conceal the fact that the Council had carefully considered two alternatives to the one approved: (*a*) that the association withdraw from collective bargaining, although continuing to offer "assistance . . . to chapters wishing to engage in collective bargaining through

13. See "Council Position on Collective Bargaining," 57 *AAUP Bulletin* (December 1971), 511–12.
14. "Council Position on Collective Bargaining," 58 *AAUP Bulletin* (March 1972), 46–61.

other entities"; and (*b*) that the association adhere to the existing policy (which meant that "national Association resources [invested in] these efforts [would] not substantially [exceed] the present level"). In the preliminary Council vote, thirteen members preferred alternative *a*, two preferred alternative *b*, and nineteen the position adopted. In a final vote the new policy carried twenty-two to eleven.

The president of the association, the chairman of Committee A on Academic Freedom and Tenure, and the first vice-president joined forces in submitting a dissenting statement, published as part of the report in the *Bulletin*, to which they gave the title "The Manifest Unwisdom of AAUP as a Collective Bargaining Agency." Among other things, this dissenting statement revealed that Committee A had submitted a recommendation to the Council, "with just one dissent," favoring withdrawal of AAUP "from involvement as a rival, competitive labor organization seeking representational status." It is clear that some of AAUP's top leaders believed that AAUP's traditional role—as a professional association committed, in cooperation with other national education organizations representing university presidents and trustees, to the development and enforcement of sound principles of academic freedom and tenure—was in irreconcilable conflict with its new role as a labor organization seeking to improve the economic status of college professors through the adversary confrontation with college trustees and administrators inherent in collective bargaining. The plain speaking in this dissenting statement is suggested by the following excerpts:

> Once the AAUP becomes substantially and unambiguously involved in competitive collective bargaining, the risk is great that we may see the end to our capacity to make inquiry or investigation into academic freedom and tenure complaints on any campus with a collective bargaining representative other than our own.
>
> . . . [the] customary manifestations of competitive collective bargaining cannot possibly come free of cost to the Association. In all likelihood, the principal cost would become evident in the loss of our identity and the consequent impairment of our influence in higher education generally, in exchange for limited success as one among several labor agencies.
>
> . . . When it is borne in mind that nonacademic professionals, who would probably be included in most appropriate bargaining units, amount to one fourth to one third of the total staff of some institutions, the impact on our membership and identity becomes quite clear.
>
> In brief, the consequence of adopting the Council's proposal may

well be to convert the AAUP into the AUUP, the American Union of University Professionals, with a substantial change in the character of its membership, its identity, and its image, sharp impairment of its ability to carry out its historic role and an indeterminately severe curtailment of the effectiveness of the Association's staff and of Committee A and other committees in resolving complaints and furthering basic Association principles and standards.

... From a unique national academic association with membership and influence in virtually all institutions of higher education, [AAUP] would become one of several unions with influence largely confined to those campuses it represents.

Perhaps the most remarkable passage in the statement is one that confirms the observation increasingly heard among old-line academicians that it may become necessary "to reinvent the AAUP" if the association persists in its collective bargaining role:

... Indeed, we would predict that, if the AAUP engages directly in collective bargaining, and if in so doing it suffers the distortion of its basic purposes (as we believe it inevitably will), some new organization can be expected to appear to defend central academic values with an objectivity the AAUP will have denied itself.

The 1972 AAUP annual meeting, after a lengthy discussion, approved the new policy statement on collective bargaining by a very large majority. Though no analysis of the vote is available, it is apparent that the opposition came largely from senior faculty members representing AAUP chapters at strong public and private universities and colleges, and that much of the support was provided by young faculty members, some still without tenure, representing a much larger group of public and private institutions where all of the educational, governmental, and financial problems of a troubled period in higher education were in one degree or another present.[15]

15. This dichotomy in membership has been present in AAUP almost from its beginning. Although the association was founded in 1915 by professors who were identified with outstanding institutions and were themselves distinguished teacher-scholars, its membership appeal was soon necessarily extended to a much broader spectrum of the professoriate, in terms both of institutional affiliation and scholarly standing. The dichotomy within the association's governance structure can be discerned in the contrasting personnel of its top elective offices and the chairmen of its most prestigious committees on the one hand, and of the members of its Council on the other. Its presidents and Committee A and Z chairmen have, virtually without exception through the years, been distinguished members of the academic profession. Its Council members, elected on a regional basis from ten districts, have, by design, been more broadly representative of every segment of the academic profession and every type of educational institution.

In all of this public manifestation of divided counsel, AAUP was perhaps providing its rivals in collective bargaining with ammunition to use against it at the campus level in future contests for bargaining agent designations. But it was also revealing itself as the only national association representing the nation's professoriate that was prepared to debate the pros and cons of faculty collective bargaining and to take a stand based on an effort at reasoned discussion. In contrast, AFT had never claimed to be anything other than a labor union in the classic mold, fully committed to the use of traditional methods of winning "more" for its members. And NEA had committed itself to collective bargaining by teachers at every level of the nation's educational system before the issue had really been identified as one deserving careful consideration by the professoriate.

Strengths and Weaknesses of the Three Organizations

Neither AFT nor NEA has welcomed AAUP's entrance into the competition for the right to represent faculties in collective bargaining. Both have attacked this new rival as inexperienced in labor negotiations, lacking adequate resources in dollars and manpower, and still indifferent or ambivalent in attitude.[16] Both AFT and NEA were aware that they shared handicaps in competing with AAUP for bargaining agent designations by college faculties: neither had ever given its undivided attention to higher education or the academic profession; neither had ever enjoyed a significant membership among teachers across the full spectrum of academic disciplines and at all types of colleges and universities.

AAUP, on the other hand, faced its own set of difficulties. As an agency attempting to double as a professional association, similar to the American Bar Association or the American Medical Association, and as a labor organization, similar to AFT and NEA, it found itself handicapped in its appeals to certain segments of bargaining units. Until 1972, it restricted eligibility for "active membership" to persons

16. Israel Kugler, long the leading figure in the AFT higher education organization in New York City, has been particularly vitriolic in his attacks on AAUP, although he has also on occasion advocated a merger between AAUP and AFT. Myron Lieberman, director of program development in the Office of Teacher Education at CUNY, while an enthusiastic supporter of faculty collective bargaining and at times friendly to both NEA and AFT, has been a persistent and bitter critic of AAUP; see his "Professors, Unite!" *Harper's,* October 1971, pp. 61–70.

holding "at least a one-year appointment to a position of at least half-time teaching and/or research, with the rank of instructor or its equivalent or higher or other acceptable evidence of faculty status, in an approved institution."[17] Thus, some professional and instructional employees who had been included in faculty bargaining units by labor boards were excluded from the association's active membership ranks. Collective bargaining statutes do not require that employees in a bargaining unit have access to membership in any labor organization that offers itself as a candidate for bargaining agent or wins that designation in an election.[18] Wholly apart from what the law might require, AAUP discovered that it was not politically feasible to persuade certain employees who had been placed in a bargaining unit to vote for AAUP as the bargaining agent, at the same time that it told them that they were not eligible to become active members of AAUP. This dilemma was encountered in the SUNY election when PERB placed several thousand noninstructional professional employees in the faculty bargaining unit. AAUP itself has estimated that 30 percent of the members of the SUNY bargaining unit were ineligible for AAUP membership. Although it risked losing its identification as a "professional association" that served the interests of those persons who had met exacting requirements for membership in the academic profession, AAUP in 1972 amended its constitution so as to admit to active membership, in addition to persons holding positions "of teaching and research," "any professional appointee included in a collective representation unit with the faculty of an approved institution."

AAUP may have an advantage over NEA and AFT in being able to argue that it has always been exclusively concerned with the interests of teachers in higher education; but the other two organizations have

17. "Association Membership," 57 *AAUP Bulletin* (September 1971), 324.

18. § 7 of the federal statute provides that "employees shall have the right to self-organization, to form, join, or assist labor organizations, etc. . . ." § 8, in listing "unfair labor practices" in which labor organizations are forbidden to engage, refers to restraining or coercing employees in the exercise of their rights under § 7, but it also provides "that this paragraph shall not impair the right of a labor organization to prescribe its own rules with respect to the acquisition or retention of membership therein." A labor organization designated as a bargaining agent has the duty to fairly represent all employees in the approved unit, but to date this duty has not been held to prevent it, if it wishes, from setting membership rules that prevent some workers in the unit from joining the organization. It should be noted that federal and state civil rights and equal employment opportunity statutes place varying restraints on labor unions with respect to membership rules that discriminate on the basis of race, national origin, sex, age, etc.

the advantage of being able to draw on stronger bureaucracies and greater financial resources in attempting to organize college faculties for collective bargaining. This advantage may well be more seeming than real. AFL-CIO has recently been making vigorous efforts to organize white-collar workers and, to a lesser degree, professional employees, but whether it is prepared to make a heavy investment in an intensive campaign to draw college professors into the labor movement is uncertain. AFT's membership consists largely of public school teachers in urban areas in such states as New York, Michigan, Illinois, Pennsylvania, and California. As AFL-CIO unions go, AFT, some forty years after its founding, remains one of the lesser lights of the trade union movement.

NEA would clearly like to build a strong base in higher education. Moreover, in representing the interests of public school teachers, it has an obvious reason for wanting to win the allegiance and support of those members of the professoriate who offer teacher-training courses at the colleges and universities with strong programs in this field. This explains the vigorous and successful efforts NEA has made to win the bargaining agent designation at the so-called state colleges, particularly where control of an entire state system is at stake, as in New Jersey, Pennsylvania, and Nebraska.

NEA, like AFT, may, however, be unwilling to invest any significant part of its substantial reserves and operating income in a broad effort to organize college faculties. Once the merger between the Legislative Conference at CUNY and the New York State NEA affiliate had been effected, it was at once clear that NEA expected the dues income from the CUNY faculty not only to put that operation on a self-sustaining basis but also to constitute a source of income for the state and national NEA organizations. Similarly, at Central Michigan University the faculty members who are members of the NEA bargaining agency appear to be restless because dues income is flowing outward from the campus. The national organizations and state affiliates of NEA and AFT have undoubtedly been willing to invest limited portions of their funds in attempts to organize faculties and win representation elections, but they also expect the resulting operations to be placed on a self-supporting basis promptly and then to provide increased dues income to state and national headquarters.

AFT argues that if a faculty intends to bargain collectively, it should choose a true union as its agent and join the national labor movement.[19] AAUP counters with the argument that unions are essentially blue-collar organizations and that the college teacher's professional problems and concerns require that he turn for his bargaining agent to the one national organization that understands this side of his work as well as his economic needs. Both NEA and AFT argue that they will prove more effective bargaining agents than AAUP because of their prior experience with collective bargaining in the public schools. Or the same argument is modified to suggest that college teachers should join public school teachers in presenting a united teacher front against "the establishment" that controls education's purse strings. But here NEA and AFT have to contend with the college professor's traditional unwillingness to regard the public school teacher as his professional counterpart and ally.

In appealing to faculties at state institutions, where a substantial majority of the academic profession is now employed, both AFT and NEA can claim more experience and success than can AAUP in lobbying at state capitals on behalf of their members. So far, these efforts have been made on behalf of public school teachers, who are considerably more numerous and politically consequential than are college teachers. Neither organization is finding it entirely easy to convince college teachers that it can and will lobby with equal effectiveness for them. AAUP lacks strong organization at the state level. It has been setting up state "conferences," but in most instances they still lack strength and experience.

AAUP—however it resolves its other problems in pursuing a more aggressive course as a labor organization—is likely for some time to be handicapped by the limited financial resources it can devote to its

19. In rare instances a labor union other than AFT has made a tentative effort to organize a faculty or part of a faculty, as in the case of the Teamsters Union at Wisconsin State University—Whitewater. The Teamsters Union is not affiliated with AFL-CIO. AFT appears to be AFL-CIO's preferred instrument for the effort to organize college professors. It may face a competitor within the AFL-CIO structure in the much stronger American Federation of State, County, and Municipal Employees (AFSCME), which is already engaged in an aggressive effort to organize noninstructional employees of public colleges and universities. There is an outside chance that the industrial union approach of the early CIO days might gain favor in higher education as a means by which both management and labor could avoid the disruptive and troublesome need to bargain with each other on a fragmented basis. Under such circumstances some other AFL-CIO union than AFT might appeal successfully to faculty members. However, to the extent that labor relations laws protect professional workers against inclusion in the same bargaining units with nonprofessionals, faculty members cannot be forced into "industrial" units with other employees of their institutions.

efforts to organize college faculties for collective bargaining purposes. Although it has more than 90,000 members, its dues have always been modest by labor union standards and it has not accumulated sizable reserves.

The Financing of Faculty Bargaining

The processes of collective bargaining can prove costly, both while the work force is being organized and the contract negotiated and over the longer pull as the contract is being administered, particularly if frequent arbitration of grievances is necessary. In industry bargaining, either the so-called union shop or an agency shop has commonly been written into the contract, in part to provide the union with sufficient guaranteed income to meet its operating costs. Under the union shop, all workers at a plant or in an industry are required to join and pay dues to the recognized union. Under the agency shop, the worker can avoid union membership but must pay dues at least sufficient to meet his share of the union's cost of serving as his representative in collective bargaining. In some states the law prohibits the agency shop for public employees—the Taylor Law in New York is an example—and in some, "right to work" laws ban agency shop agreements in private enterprises.

Thus far, no contract at a university or four-year college includes a union or an agency shop provision, although some community college contracts do contain agency shop clauses. Even where the agency shop is not illegal—as in Michigan and in collective bargaining under federal law at private educational institutions—faculty bargaining agents at the senior institutions have not yet found it feasible to ask management to agree to a contract provision calling for compulsory payment of dues by all members of the bargaining unit. The difficulty is less getting management to agree than it is apprehension about the reaction within the faculty. An administrator at one Michigan university told us that management would not resist an agency shop clause, for "this would have a quieting effect on the union; it would not have to keep on trying to impress the faculty all the time by making new gains." (He could, of course, be wrong in this judgment. An agency shop agreement compelling *all* faculty members to pay dues to the union might put the union under increased pressure to show everyone that it could produce continuous gains justifying the dues payments.) Bargaining agent officers at the same university told us that they were doubtful that an agency shop agreement would command majority support within the faculty. That being the case, they were fearful that, if a contract containing an agency shop provision were submitted to the entire faculty, it would be rejected and their organization might also be voted out as bargaining agent as soon as a new election could be petitioned for under the state law.

Faculty membership in bargaining agent organizations, as well as payment of dues, remains, then, on a voluntary basis at all four-year institutions. Bargaining agents have had to take their chances on acquiring dues-paying members, and the record is almost everywhere discouraging. For one thing, college faculties are simply not accustomed to paying to any organization the sizable dues of $100 or more a year that bargaining agents have often set as necessary to meet the actual costs of collective bargaining. As a result, the proportion of the eligible members of faculty bargaining units who are paying dues to bargaining agents is surprisingly small. It is difficult to obtain precise information on this point. Bargaining agents seldom publicly report their dues-paying memberships on any dependable basis. Estimates given to us in interviews at a number of institutions varied sharply, depending on who was answering the question. Administrators usually said that the estimates given to us by bargaining agent officers were on the high side. One faculty officer candidly gave us his answer in terms of "paid-up members" and "members in arrears." But no faculty spokesman at any other institution used such a distinction in his answer.

At CUNY the Legislative Conference claimed a membership of 60 percent of the eligible faculty soon after the first contract was negotiated. After recent additions to the faculty made necessary by the university's open admissions program and the sharp increase in dues following the LC-NEA merger, the membership was set for us (in a 1972 interview with a bargaining agent officer) at "about 3,800 out of a potential 8,000." At Southeastern Massachusetts University, officers of the AFT local claimed a membership of 100 out of a potential 220. At Central Michigan University an administrator said there were 170 dues-paying members out of a total of 590; local NEA officers did not set the figure appreciably higher. At Boston State College, an administrator estimated the AFT membership at 150 out of 250. At Oakland University, where there are 193 members of the bargaining unit, the AAUP chapter claimed 155 members. At Rutgers the AAUP chapter set its membership at a much lower proportion of the potential total. At SUNY the Senate Professional Association–NEA agent claimed no more than 30 percent of the potential and this was probably an inflated estimate. Three factors may explain this low figure at SUNY: the dispersion of the 16,000 members of the unit throughout the state on some twenty-six separate campuses; the diverse professional roles and interests of these 16,000 individuals; and the after-effects of a campaign in which four different candidates for bargaining agent fragmented the loyalties and support of the group.

One discerning observer of faculty collective bargaining has written that "the relatively low level of [bargaining agent] membership does not necessarily indicate a lack of support for organization *per se*. It reflects a combination of apathy, distaste, professorial parsimony, and the existence of conflicting faculty allegiances among the competing organizations."[20] This situation is sufficiently serious at the institutions where faculty collective bargaining is taking place to suggest that all bargaining agents will begin developing a case for including an agency shop provision in contracts as soon as this becomes legally possible and politically feasible.

CIVIL SERVICE ASSOCIATIONS AS CANDIDATES

A fourth candidate for bargaining agent that has occasionally been available to faculty members at public institutions is a statewide association of civil service employees. The Civil Service Employees Association in New York State qualified as a candidate for bargaining agent in the SUNY election, as did a similar association in the Southeastern Massachusetts University election. Neither candidate fared well. In Hawaii the Government Employees Association was the first organization to file petitions, late in 1970, with the Public Employment Relations Board, claiming the support of 30 percent of the employees in the two bargaining units fixed by statute for the state university–community college system, and asking that representation elections be held. AFT, NEA, and AAUP affiliates also subsequently qualified as candidates for bargaining agent for the faculty unit. The Government

---

20. Joseph W. Garbarino, "Creeping Unionism and the Faculty Labor Market," (draft prepared for *Higher Education and the Labor Market*, forthcoming publication of the Carnegie Commission on Higher Education). Mr. Garbarino is professor of business administration and director, Institute for Business and Economic Research, University of California, Berkeley.

Employees Association (GEA) may be presumed to have fallen within the civil service association classification, but at some point it affiliated with the American Federation of State, County and Municipal Employees (AFSCME) and became Local No. 152 of that AFL-CIO union. The faculty election in Hawaii was thus the first in which two AFL-CIO unions competed for the bargaining agent designation.

It is significant to note that even though the Hawaii statute designated the faculty of the University of Hawaii–Community College system as the proper bargaining unit, there was considerable disagreement among the bargaining agent candidates and the university about which employees should be regarded as falling within the classification of "faculty." This made it necessary for the state PERB to hold hearings and determine the membership of the bargaining unit.

The representation election was not held until October 1972. GEA-AFSCME ran a poor fourth in the race, behind AAUP, AFT, NEA, and the "no bargaining" option, which finished in that order. (AAUP's candidacy was joint with the local Faculty Association, which had earlier been established at the instigation of the faculty senate of the university to participate in a representation election, should one be held.) [21]

Faculty members in state institutions have joined civil service associations, sometimes in significant numbers, presumably in order to gain one more organizational means of self-protection in the political setting in which they work. But the academic profession has not ordinarily thought of itself as part of the civil service. No such orga-

---

21. In the runoff election between AAUP and AFT, the latter emerged victor with 995 votes to AAUP's 805. The results were announced by the separate campuses making up the single bargaining unit. AAUP ran ahead of AFT at the main (Manoa) campus of the university, 672 to 549, but well behind AFT on the other campuses (a small branch campus of the university at Hilo and the community colleges of the state which had been made part of the unit by the state legislature) with 114 votes for AAUP and 435 for AFT. The great majority of these latter votes were cast at the community colleges.

There was a total of 761 nonvoters, 595 of whom were at the main campus. This suggests that AAUP's campaign on the main campus, where its strength was obviously concentrated, had not managed to overcome the disinclination of a large segment of the faculty there to take part in a faculty collective bargaining election.

These election results at the University of Hawaii are not necessarily at odds with the judgment expressed later in this chapter that AAUP is likely to do well at universities at the top of state systems of higher education.

It may also be noted here that, in an election at Temple University in Pennsylvania in December 1972, AAUP defeated AFT by a vote of 621 to 436. AAUP also defeated NEA at Regis College (Denver) in a runoff election in January 1973.

nization has yet been chosen by the faculty of a four-year college or university as its bargaining agent.

LOCAL ORGANIZATIONS AS CANDIDATES

As a fifth option, a faculty can choose to bargain through an independent organization at the local campus level. This kind of agent can have a strong "do-it-yourself" appeal to a faculty. The faculty of Macomb County Community College in Michigan has been bargaining for many years with management through a local Faculty Federation, which it chose in preference to an AFT local. AFT's attempt to organize this faculty failed, we were told by faculty members, because its agents "came on too strong" in their approach. At CUNY and SUNY the faculty originally voted for local faculty organizations as their bargaining agents, but in both instances these independent agencies encountered problems that led them to affiliate with NEA.

A local bargaining agent can be a specialized organization, such as the Legislative Conference at CUNY, that has had prior experience in serving a faculty's economic or professional interests outside the area of educational policy. Or it might be a faculty senate or council that has a recognized place in an institution's governance system and has traditionally been concerned with such matters as educational policy rather than employment conditions. There has been considerable debate about the legality and desirability of a faculty senate doubling as an instrument of university governance and a collective bargaining agent. The strongest argument in favor of such an arrangement is that a faculty might thereby have the best of two worlds: selecting the faculty senate as the bargaining agent would preserve the "shared authority" system of running a university long favored by AAUP and AAHE, and at the same time enable the faculty senate to use collective bargaining as a means of settling disputed issues of wages, hours, and conditions of employment on an adversary basis.

There is a legal question whether a faculty senate, in which administrators at the management level (president, provost, dean, and the like) are voting members, or which is supported financially by the institution, can qualify as a bargaining agent. Would a senate thereby fall within the prohibition against "company unions" under the unfair labor practices provisions of labor laws? The federal statute, in § 8(a)(2), declares it to be an unfair labor practice for an employer "to dominate or interfere with the formation or administration of any labor organization or contribute financial or other support to it." This difficulty might be overcome by changing the governance system of an institution so as to remove administrators from senate membership and by requiring the senate to provide its own income. But could a faculty senate bring pressure on its members to pay dues? Could it remain part of a shared authority system of institutional governance at the same time that it was negotiating with the governing board and with administrators as the governing board's agents? Probably, in making such adjustments a faculty senate would find that it was giving up its role within the shared authority governance structure and becoming a local labor union similar to the Legislative Conference at CUNY or the Faculty Federation at Macomb County Community College. These issues remain hypothetical, for no faculty senate at a four-year institution has yet been chosen as a faculty bargaining agent.[22] If a faculty desires to bargain through a wholly local agent, it will almost certainly turn to an organization that has no regular role in institutional governance. In any event, such independent or local bargaining agents are still far from common. One example beyond those already mentioned is the Law School Bargaining Committee at Fordham University. Its existence suggests that, in the context of faculty bargaining at a broad-purpose university, the faculty members of certain graduate or professional schools will seek separate recognition as bargaining units and then elect bargaining agents of their own devising.

An independent faculty association may prove a more popular and effective bargaining agent at private colleges and universities than it yet has at public institutions. Among other things, a faculty that has been accustomed to handling its own affairs is likely to become quite dissatisfied if its members find that a significant part of the dues they are paying to the local affiliate of a national organization is going off campus to support a state or national bureaucracy. We found more than a little faculty sentiment of this kind at such public institutions as Central Michigan University, Henry Ford Community College at Dearborn, and Southeastern Massachusetts University. At Central Michigan each faculty member who belonged to the NEA bargaining unit in 1971 was paying dues of $117 a year, of which, we were told,

22. The Senate Professional Association, which won the faculty bargaining agent designation in the election at SUNY, was created by the University Senate to play this one special role. It never functioned as a faculty senate itself, and, in any event, its decision to affiliate with NEA removed any possibility of its being regarded as part of the governance system of the university.

$107 went off campus to the state and national NEA organizations. This kind of feeling will be encouraged if the bargaining relationship at an institution becomes stabilized to the point where a faculty is persuaded that it can bring the necessary manpower and expertise to the bargaining process without assistance from the state or national headquarters of such organizations as NEA, AFT, and AAUP. There is, however, evidence of an opposite trend: the discovery that effective collective bargaining, even in higher education, is not for amateurs.

THE BOX SCORE OF BARGAINING AGENT DESIGNATIONS

As of the end of the 1971–72 academic year, bargaining agents had been selected by the faculties of thirty-three four-year colleges and universities and in six multicampus situations (the City University of New York, the State University of New York, Rutgers University, and the state college systems of Nebraska, New Jersey, and Pennsylvania). See Table 5, page 54. NEA, AFT, and AAUP all had important designations to their credit and were serious contenders to represent faculties at other institutions in all parts of the country, if collective bargaining continued to gain ground in higher education. Each had won several of its designations on an essentially unchallenged basis. No one of the three organizations had yet demonstrated an ability to win contested elections on a regular basis; no one of the three had a lead in this respect.

Among the four-year institutions where elections had occurred, NEA had a lead over its two rivals, for in addition to its single campus victories it had been designated agent for five statewide or citywide multicampus systems. At CUNY and SUNY, however, NEA did not appear on the ballot—the Senate Professional Association at SUNY and the Legislative Conference at CUNY won these elections and then affiliated with NEA. NEA lost contested elections to AAUP at the University of Rhode Island and the University of Delaware, but defeated AAUP at Youngstown State University. Many of NEA's designations have been won at institutions with teachers college backgrounds, where it may be expected to have a continuing advantage over AAUP and AFT. NEA's standing with faculties at multipurpose universities and liberal arts colleges remains relatively untested. NEA was also a clear leader over AFT at two-year community colleges, with some ninety designations, and may be expected to dominate bargaining in this sector. AFT was the agent at some thirty-five community colleges, and AAUP at one. AAUP has a weak membership base at community colleges and is unlikely to win more than an occasional designation at these institutions.

In addition to the four-year institutions at which AFT won the designation as bargaining agent, it was an aggressive candidate at CUNY and SUNY, but lost both elections to independent faculty associations which, as has been indicated, later decided to affiliate with NEA. It also lost contested elections to AAUP at Adelphi University and Wayne State University.

AAUP appears to be the only agent that is beginning to make headway in the private sector. AAUP's victories over NEA at the University of Rhode Island and the University of Delaware also augur well for its prospects in faculty elections that may be held at other universities at the top of state systems of public education. Indeed, for all of its lack of experience in collective bargaining and its vacillation in committing itself to a full-scale attempt to win representation elections, AAUP appears likely to dominate whatever faculty collective bargaining takes shape at strong broad-purpose universities, public and private, and at private liberal arts colleges.

NEA will continue to dominate bargaining at community colleges and at those state colleges and universities that have strong teacher-training programs, with AFT winning occasional elections at these institutions, particularly at those located in or near large industrial cities. If the NEA-AFT mergers in early 1972 at CUNY, and in the New York state teachers organizations, foreshadow similar mergers in other states and cities, an NEA-AFT joint candidacy may pose a stronger challenge to AAUP at many institutions. On the other hand, NEA and AFT may discover that they have merely merged their respective shortcomings as seen by many academicians, to the advantage of an AAUP candidacy in a straight race between NEA-AFT and AAUP.

THE LEGAL PROCESS FOR SELECTING A BARGAINING AGENT

The law provides for the recognition of a labor organization as the bargaining agent of a group of employees in a number of ways. Federal practice only will be examined; state practices may vary but are usually similar to the federal model. The National Labor Relations Act permits an employer and a labor organization to reach an agreement themselves without any intervention by the NLRB: to agree that the proposed employee unit is an appropriate one, that the labor organization has demonstrated (usually by means of a "card check") that it is supported by a majority of the employees in the unit, and that no other labor organization is petitioning for recognition. This is known as "recognition without an election." Under these circumstances, there is no formal certification of the bargaining agent by the NLRB. The AAUP chapter was so recognized as the faculty bargaining agent at Bard College. However, as the federal statute is currently interpreted and applied, an employer normally is not required to recognize a union on the basis of a card check. The United States Supreme Court has declared:

> When confronted by a recognition demand based on possession of cards allegedly signed by a majority of his employees, an employer need not grant recognition immediately, but may, unless he has knowledge independently of the cards that the union has a majority, decline the union's request and insist on an election, either by requesting the union to file an election petition or by filing such a petition himself.[23]

Federal law also provides for NLRB certification of a bargaining agent, following a "consent election" held on an expedited basis, where there is no disagreement between the employer and the candidate for bargaining agent about the appropriateness of the unit or the adequacy of the petition, and both parties agree that an election is desirable to show that the petitioning organization does have the support of a majority of the employees in the unit. Finally, if there is more than one candidate for bargaining agent and the parties are in disagreement concerning the nature of the unit, a representation proceeding is held by a hearing officer designated by an NLRB regional director. A ruling on the disputed issues is made by either the regional director or the NLRB itself, and a "directed-election" is conducted by a Board agent.[24]

23. NLRB v. Gissel Packing Co., 395 U.S. 575, 591 (1969).
24. For a detailed account of the complex procedures in the designation of bargaining agents under federal law, see Charles J. Morris et al., eds., *The Developing Labor Law*, pp. 246–67, 825–32. For an excellent treatment of the NLRB's changing attitude through the years on certification of an agent without an election—for example, on the issue of whether under certain circumstances an employer has the right to insist that an election be held—see Howard Lesnick, "Establishment of Bargaining Rights without an NLRB Election," 65 *Michigan Law Review* (March 1967), 851–68.

In the collective bargaining elections held thus far, it is difficult to identify and weigh all the factors that have influenced faculty members. The actual campaigns have not been well recorded. Typically, rallies and debates are held, campaign flyers are circulated by the different factions, and a good deal of informal discussion takes place. The printed evidences of such campaigning are fugitive. Voting is by secret ballot. Usually, only the total votes are announced, with no breakdowns in the voting by schools, departments, disciplines, faculty ranks or age groupings, campuses in multicampus elections, or by any of the other categories that might prove useful in analyzing voting behavior in a collective bargaining election. One can only guess at the voting patterns that have helped shape the result. With these limitations in mind, it is nonetheless useful to examine the conditions and steps that led to faculty bargaining elections at several institutions.

Southeastern Massachusetts University:
Faculty Bargaining through AFT

The faculty at Southeastern Massachusetts University voted to engage in collective bargaining, with AFT as its agent, in April 1969. Ninety-four faculty members voted for AFT, fifty-five for the "no bargaining" option, and eight for the Massachusetts State Employees Association.[25] The institution is of recent origin and has grown substantially in less than a decade of operation. It was established by act of the Massachusetts legislature in 1960, by merging two small state institutions—the Bradford Durfee College of Technology in Fall River and the New Bedford Institute of Technology. It has its own board of trustees. First called the Southeastern Massachusetts Technological Institute, it gained a president in 1962 and opened its doors in 1964, having been provided with a handsome and costly new campus on a splendid rural site between Fall River and New Bedford. The institution occupies an anomalous position in the state system of higher education. Under a master plan, the University of Massachusetts, with

---

25. We had the benefit of extensive interviews at Southeastern Massachusetts University with numerous administrators and faculty members and with the trustee who was board chairman at the time of the representation election. We have also had access to documentary materials bearing on the faculty's decision to engage in collective bargaining.

its main campus in Amherst, a medical school in Worcester, an undergraduate college of arts and sciences in Boston, and other branches under consideration, is presumably responsible for graduate and professional education leading to the doctorate or equivalent degrees. The University of Massachusetts also offers undergraduate studies in many fields; in this it is supplemented by eleven state colleges, which are controlled by a single board of trustees.

The designation by the legislature, in 1969, of the new institution as Southeastern Massachusetts University was thus surprising, for it had been assumed that the University of Massachusetts alone would enjoy university status. The term is, of course, also used by Michigan and other states to designate regional institutions below the level of an all-purpose state university. But in Massachusetts, Southeastern is the only regional university, and any other institutions that gain university status are likely to do so as branches of the University of Massachusetts.

The short history of Southeastern Massachusetts University has been played out against a background of political influences from without, as well as considerable internal controversy. Politics undoubtedly helped bring the institution into existence, provided it with a costly physical plant, gained it its name as a university, and exacerbated its difficult internal problems of growth. Everyone with whom we talked at Southeastern Massachusetts agreed that the faculty decision to turn to collective bargaining grew out of a serious conflict between the faculty and the president, and also a sharp split between Old Guard and Young Turk elements within the faculty, with the Old Guard providing a substantial number of the votes to engage in collective bargaining. Typically, the older faculty members were carry-overs from the two technological schools. Because of the limited educational purposes of the earlier schools, these teachers did not have Ph.D. degrees and their interests and work were not centered in the arts and sciences. Making up the Young Turk faction were the faculty members who had been recruited in large numbers over a period of three or four years to staff the new institution's greatly expanded programs and to meet the much increased student load. Ph.D. degrees were emphasized as important to the new institution's being accredited as one whose central program was to be in the arts and sciences.

The new institution's president was a powerful force in its early development. He attempted to provide strong and aggressive leadership and was intensely devoted to the new institution and ambitious for it. He quickly put his faith in the young faculty members and in the administrative staff that he had shaped. In so doing, he ran a calculated risk. The older faculty members were numerous, they could not all be got rid of, and in their own way they, too, were loyal to the institution and anxious for its success. One of the leaders of the Old Guard group spoke to us of "the painful process of growing" that characterized the years from 1964 to 1969. He believes, however, that "much of the pain could have been avoided." In his judgment "new faculty members were hired in too much of a hurry. Some of them should have been looked at more carefully, for they proved to be rebellious and anarchistic." He also expressed the judgment that older faculty members "were systematically disadvantaged" by the president and the deans. "They were denied salary increases and whenever possible they were encouraged to resign." As time went by, the Old Guard element in the faculty coalesced around an AFT local at the institution as their power center. To a less evident extent, the Young Turks found a power center in the AAUP chapter.

Out of this background of dissatisfaction and conflict, three developments influenced the faculty decision to engage in collective bargaining. One was the failure of the faculty senate under the existing system of university governance to achieve authority and prestige. One of the leaders in the AFT group, who was also a member of the senate, told us that he had held off the movement toward faculty unionization and collective bargaining for a year, hoping that the senate "could be made to work." In the end, he became convinced that the president was determined that it should be "nothing more than a debating society and a sounding board."

The second development was a controversy over the system by which faculty salary increases were determined. For several years the legislature had been granting the state's educational institutions 5 percent increases in their faculty salary appropriations to be used for "merit increases." Reversing a tradition of using this money for across-the-board increases, the president and the deans embarked on a program of granting "special merit" increases to part of the faculty in a highly selective fashion. Their wish to introduce a true merit system as a means of building a strong faculty may have been commendable, but it is widely believed at Southeastern Massachusetts that the new merit increases were granted in an authoritarian manner and were based on grossly unfair judgments.[26] Two of the younger faculty members who later became deans told us that they felt they had been granted salary increases that were out of line and that could not have been based on careful evaluation of their work as teachers.

Third, certain controversial faculty personnel actions became campus *causes célèbres* and increased tension significantly. One of these cases involved failure to reappoint a nontenured teacher who enjoyed considerable popularity with students. To the extent that these cases frightened some of the young faculty members and led them to vote for collective bargaining, the Old Guard–Young Turk division was somewhat blurred.

When the representation election was held in April 1969, the AFT local was the focal point for the proponents of collective bargaining. Two factors appear to have explained the failure of the AAUP chapter to challenge the AFT candidacy. First, in 1969 the national AAUP organization was still ambivalent about collective bargaining and was not encouraging its chapters to offer themselves as bargaining agent candidates. Second, some of the most militant younger members of the faculty were opposed to collective bargaining and thus, insofar as they were attempting to make the AAUP chapter their power center, they did not urge it to enter the contest.

Central Michigan University: Faculty Bargaining through NEA

The faculty at Central Michigan University voted in September 1969 to engage in collective bargaining. NEA was the only candidate for bargaining agent; it received 239 votes, and the "no bargaining" option, 221 votes. Several considerations seem to have influenced those who

---

26. Some of the anger within the faculty aroused by the special merit increases is perhaps explained by a belief at Southeastern Massachusetts, which all parties appear to have held, that the faculty had few outstanding members, old or young. No one took the position, however, that the faculty was poor or that the quality of teaching was below the average at similar institutions. Faculty leaders told us that perhaps fifteen to twenty teachers deserved special recognition for the quality of their teaching and research. When we asked several deans how they managed to hold faculty members in the face of a limited ability (under the collective bargaining contract) to meet salary offers elsewhere, they replied, "Our faculty members do not get outside offers. They are well paid here in the light of academic salaries generally and they are mostly quite happy to stay where they are."

voted in the majority.[27] One senior faculty member has written that
there was "a heritage of general discontent" on the campus.[28] A new
president had taken office in 1968. He replaced a much older man who
had come to be viewed by many faculty members as both authoritarian
and conservative. But, as often in these situations, the faculty at Central Michigan was ambivalent about presidents, old and new. The old
president was a known quantity and many faculty members had
learned to live with him. The new president was young, able, and full
of plans for the institution's further development. Some older members of the faculty, who had known the institution as a teachers college
and were already troubled by its increase in size and development
into a regional multipurpose university, distrusted the new president
and thought he was likely to throw his support to the younger faculty
members in the liberal arts disciplines. Many of the 132 instructors
and assistant professors who had joined the faculty at the beginning of
the new academic years in 1968 and 1969 also felt a sense of insecurity.
They were dissatisfied with their pay and apprehensive about acquiring tenure. The president himself has recognized that there was faculty
unrest at both ends of the spectrum. In his words, "The old faculty
was alarmed by growth and change; the new faculty was concerned
about getting tenure." There was also some distrust of the president
among faculty members, old and young, growing out of his strong interest in students. One faculty member is reported to have said, "Mr.
B. gives students anything they want. We get what's left."[29] Although
the president later became a friend of faculty collective bargaining, he
made a speech shortly before the election in which he seemed to be
counseling the faculty to vote against collective bargaining. This
action did not sit well with some faculty members.

There was also a heritage of faculty distrust of the university's
governing board. This feeling was accentuated shortly before the election by what appeared to be an arbitrary, unilateral action of the
board with respect to the faculty salary schedule. In line with the prac-

27. We had the benefit of interviews with many faculty members and with the
president and other administrative officers at Central Michigan. We have also
drawn on the speeches and articles of President William Boyd and of Neil
Bucklew, vice-provost for academic affairs. John C. Helper, professor of English,
has written a useful analysis of the coming of collective bargaining to Central
Michigan in "Timetable for a Take-over," 42 *Journal of Higher Education*
(February 1971), 103–15.
28. Ibid., p. 104.
29. Ibid., p. 105.

tice at many teachers colleges, the institution had long been granting salary increases on a straight across-the-board basis. The trustees (and the president) favored the introduction of a merit component into the system. A committee of the faculty senate had been studying the problem and, we were told, was about to recommend a revised salary schedule that would have provided for merit increases. The trustees apparently became impatient, suspended the old schedule for the next year, and gave the faculty the impression that it intended to develop its own merit system without consulting with the faculty senate. One faculty member put it to us this way:

> If the president had said nothing, the deans had said nothing, the Board of Trustees had said nothing, collective bargaining at Central Michigan would have lost. In the old days, the simple act of joining AAUP at Central Michigan was a sufficient protest. This is a wholly different struggle from the idealistic battles we fought in the 60's. Now it is power and gut-level strategy.

There were many similar elements in the situations at Central Michigan and Southeastern Massachusetts Universities. One difference was that conflict at Central Michigan was not exacerbated by political interference by state officials. There was some tension, however, between the president and the board of trustees at the time of the faculty decision to engage in collective bargaining. This appears to have been alleviated thereafter, rather than heightened as at Southeastern Massachusetts.

The faculty was clearly ambivalent about the existing governance system. Some faculty members regarded the senate as both ineffectual and controlled by an Old Guard element. Departments were strong, but many were viewed as being run on an authoritarian basis by their chairmen. AAUP had a chapter at Central Michigan, but we were told that some of the younger, more aggressive faculty members had given up on AAUP because of its ambivalence toward collective bargaining, both nationally and locally, and had transferred their loyalties and energies to the local NEA organization. One or two faculty members belonged to AFT, but there was no AFT local on the campus. In the end, NEA was the only candidate for bargaining agent on the ballot.

If the election had not been held so quickly after the beginning of a new academic year, the result might have been different. Opponents of collective bargaining, including some old-line AAUP leaders, were regarded as making good headway in their campaign against the proposal, and there are those at Central Michigan who believe that, had another week or two been available, the opposition would have won enough additional support to have changed the outcome. In spite of the several causes of faculty discontent, bargaining and NEA as the agent won by just 18 votes in an election in which 460 faculty members participated.

Events at Central Michigan since 1969 suggest that a faculty decision to engage in collective bargaining, even where made by a bare majority vote, is not likely to be reversed soon, particularly if the process seems to be producing satisfactory results for the faculty. Six months of negotiations at the bargaining table following the election produced a one-year contract in which the faculty appeared to have gained a rather handsome economic package of salary and fringe benefit improvements. This contract was submitted to the entire faculty and was approved, 369 to 82, to take effect in July 1970. The negotiation of the second contract, a year later, proved somewhat more difficult, particularly since the trustees demanded a three-year agreement. The first version of the second contract was rejected by the faculty, but a few adjustments were quickly made, including a reopener clause with respect to a salary increase in the third year, and the contract was then approved by a substantial majority in May 1971.

Northern Michigan University:
Faculty Bargaining and NEA Rejected

The faculty at Northern Michigan University, in the Michigan Upper Peninsula, rejected collective bargaining by the substantial margin of 168 to 97, in April 1971. As at Central Michigan, a local NEA unit was the only candidate for bargaining agent, so the choice was a straightforward one between NEA as the bargaining agent and no bargaining. Since NEA had not petitioned for an election until a majority of the faculty had signed its authorization cards, the election showed that faculty members do not necessarily vote for collective bargaining because they have signed a potential agent's cards asking for an election.

The president of Northern Michigan, as had his counterpart at Central Michigan, made his opposition to collective bargaining known to the faculty. Having sought the counsel of a Detroit law firm, he demonstrated that the unfair labor practices provisions of collective bargaining statutes by no means prevent an employer or his agent from stating the case against collective bargaining as he sees it, during the campaign preceding a representation election. The fixing of an exact line between permissible and prohibited conduct by the employer has required numerous labor board rulings and court decisions in both federal and state practice. In general the employer must refrain from "election interference": he is forbidden either to promise certain positive benefits if collective bargaining is rejected or to threaten the loss of existing ones if it is adopted.[30] At any rate it is clear that if a president or trustees remain silent during the campaign preceding a faculty collective bargaining election, they do so, not because the law compels a hands-off policy, but for other reasons, such as a belief that faculty members should be permitted to conduct their own debate and make their own decision, or a fear that any statements on their part opposing collective bargaining will have a boomerang effect.

At Northern Michigan the president did not remain silent, nor did he expect other administrators to do so. He sent a series of memoranda to faculty members in which he expressed his belief that there were other "mutually acceptable and effective procedures" than collective bargaining by which the administration, the trustees, and the faculty could come to grips with "the issues of adequate salary, due process, objective evaluation procedures, and the like." He also wrote,

30. A federal court has declared that "interference is no less interference because it is accomplished through allurement rather than coercion" (NLRB v. Crown Can Co., 138 F.2d 263 [1943]). And the U.S. Supreme Court has warned against "the danger inherent in well-timed increases and benefits" which suggest "a fist inside a velvet glove" (NLRB v. Exchange Parts Co., 375 U.S. 405, 409 [1964]). The Supreme Court has attempted to indicate the proper limits of employer campaign propaganda in the following general terms: "[A]n employer is free to communicate to his employees any of his general view about unionism or any of his specific views about a particular union, so long as his communications do not contain a 'threat of reprisal or force or promise of benefit.' He may even make a prediction as to the precise effects he believes unionization will have on his company. In such a case, however, the prediction must be carefully phrased on the basis of objective fact to convey an employer's belief as to demonstrably probable consequences beyond his control. . . . [A]n employer is free only to tell 'what he reasonably believes will be the likely economic consequences of unionization that are outside his control,' and not 'threats of economic reprisal to be taken solely on his own volition' " (NLRB v. Gissel Packing Co., 395 U.S. 575 [1969]).

For an excellent summary of federal law governing employer activity, see "Interference with Protected Rights and Restrictions on Preelection Activity," in Morris, *The Developing Labor Law*, pp. 63–110.

State labor laws in general also prohibit certain unfair labor practices by employers. Thus, the Michigan statute provides that: "It shall be unlawful for a public employer or an officer or agent of a public employer (a) to interfere with, restrain, or coerce public employees in the exercise of their rights [to organize or to bargain collectively]; (b) to initiate, create, dominate, contribute to or interfere with the formation of or administration of any labor organization."

"I am convinced that the industrial-union model is simply inappropriate to the functioning of the University and to the setting required for effective learning and instruction for which we are responsible." And again, "In my opinion, the union model tends to separate the 'production worker' from 'management' in a manner inconsistent with the goals and purposes of higher education." He also reviewed the gains in faculty compensation during the three years of his presidency and asserted that faculty compensation had increased by 36.4 percent. He reviewed the faculty's role in the university governance system, which included participation in an Academic Senate, a universitywide Advisory Council, a Faculty Advisory Committee on Budget, a Curriculum Committee, and a Hearings Committee on Nonreappointment of Nontenured Faculty.[31]

As at Central Michigan, AAUP did not appear on the ballot at Northern Michigan as a candidate for bargaining agent, but in this instance it engaged in campaigning that almost certainly influenced the outcome. The officers of the local AAUP chapter, who were apparently friendly to the NEA effort to organize the faculty, reported to the faculty early in the campaign that the chapter had voted not to offer itself as a rival candidate for bargaining agent. A group of faculty members then organized an Ad Hoc Committee for AAUP Principles and, with the help of the executive committee of the Michigan State Conference of the AAUP, conducted a campaign at Northern Michigan in support of the "no bargaining" option in the forthcoming election. A two-page letter, sent to all members of the Northern Michigan faculty by the president and immediate past president of the AAUP state conference (both of whom were members of the faculty of the University of Michigan) urging rejection of NEA as bargaining agent, appears to have had a substantial impact on the outcome of the voting.

The University of Rhode Island: An AAUP Victory

One of the most interesting and perhaps significant of the faculty decisions thus far on whether or not to engage in collective bargaining occurred at the University of Rhode Island in December 1971. Three well-organized faculty groups took part in the campaign that preceded

31. Memoranda from the president to the faculty members, dated March 12 and 26 and April 2, 1971. We had access to written materials circulated at Northern Michigan by all interested persons and organizations during the weeks preceding the election. We did not visit the campus.

the making of the decision.[32] There were two candidates for bargaining agent, NEA and AAUP, and a faculty group that favored the "no bargaining" option. The local NEA organization filed a petition with the Rhode Island State Labor Relations Board in April 1971, asking to be certified as the bargaining agent of the faculty. Hoping perhaps to race quickly home with the prize, it told the faculty that it expected "an election within a few weeks if competing organizations and/or the Board of Regents do not challenge the election." The local AAUP chapter did soon file an intervenor's petition, and the regents did challenge the NEA's proposed bargaining unit. The Rhode Island labor board held hearings during the summer and made its ruling in October. The principal disputed issue concerned department chairmen. The board ordered them included in the unit and set the election for December 1.

During the preelection period, the three groups circulated considerable campaign literature, which on the whole was well reasoned, readable, and hard-hitting. In the main, NEA and AAUP ignored the no-bargaining group and its arguments. Each labor organization made its own positive case and attacked that of the other. NEA stressed its experience and success in bargaining for public school teachers. It attacked AAUP as an organization that had turned to collective bargaining belatedly and reluctantly. AAUP claimed that it was the one national organization that had always been exclusively concerned with the professional interests of college teachers. It suggested that NEA would not hesitate to trade off faculty interests at the University of Rhode Island for school teacher gains throughout the state.

The no-bargaining group had obviously done a good deal of careful research. Its literature provided data concerning collective bargaining at such public institutions as Southeastern Massachusetts University, SUNY, and the New Jersey state colleges, purporting to show that the contracts there, far from bringing significant salary increases to the faculties, had in one way or another harmed faculty interests by establishing more rigid academic calendars or heavier teaching-load requirements. It argued that "coercion" was "the major tool" of NEA and accused AAUP of being "a reluctant contender." It asserted that the faculty at the University of Rhode Island already occupied a

32. Copies of all materials circulated to the faculty during the preelection campaign were made available to us. We also talked and corresponded with members of the university community, but did not visit the campus.

strong position under the existing system of institutional governance, particularly with respect to the determination of educational policies and the making of faculty personnel decisions. It contended that the best way to gain additional authority for the faculty in budget matters would be to work toward an extension of the shared authority system to cover financial policy making. It reminded faculty members that only dues-paying members of the labor organization designated as the exclusive bargaining agent would have the legal right to vote "in determining the demands to be made and in accepting the contract"; that the faculty as a whole would have no control over the bargaining unit; and that the existing faculty senate would be destroyed because "there is no limit to the subjects that can be covered by collective bargaining." Thus, the contract could cover any and all of the subjects at that time regarded as the senate's prerogatives.

From April until the December election, the university administration conducted itself with care and discretion. The president announced in April that the university would make meeting rooms, bulletin boards, and mailing facilities available to all groups. He stressed "the neutral postion of the University as institutional employer" but reserved "his own rights as a member of the faculty to express his personal opinions on the subject of collective bargaining." He then remained silent until mid-November when he sent a letter to all faculty members, accompanied by a speech he was to make two weeks later before the Conference of Southern Academic Deans in Florida. In the letter he deplored, as having "no place in an academic community," the propaganda used by industry management in "emphasizing all the bad points of unionization." He stated further that he had been advised by counsel that it was legally permissible for him, "both as a member of the faculty and as President of the University" to reply to requests from the university community that he express his views on collective bargaining. In the speech he reviewed the development of collective bargaining in industry generally and in higher education. He stressed the contrast between the minimal role played by labor in the operation of a private business and the substantial role of most faculties in university governance. He offered his judgment that faculties had more to gain through attempting to strengthen the shared authority model than they did by turning to the adversary model of collective bargaining.

The two bargaining elections in December at the University of

Rhode Island provided a series of surprises. With 566 of 669 eligible persons voting in the first election on December 1, the "no bargaining" option, with 281 votes, came within one vote of gaining an outright majority. AAUP received 161 votes and NEA 121 votes, for a total of 282 votes between the two organizations. There were three challenged votes. The board of regents, on recommendation of the president, promptly announced that it was requesting the Rhode Island labor board to forgo any effort to decide what to do with the challenged ballots and instead to proceed directly to a runoff election on December 15, the date that had been agreed upon by all parties should the first election be indecisive.

During the two-week interval between the two elections, NEA leaders at the university renewed their support of collective bargaining and strongly urged their supporters to vote for AAUP in the second election. AAUP leaders, surprised and pleased by their victory over NEA in the election, renewed their campaign with increased vigor and distributed literature stressing AAUP's determination, if it became the bargaining agent for the faculty, to protect and strengthen the position of the faculty senate in university governance, to bargain aggressively for more faculty power in the selection of department chairmen, the awarding of tenure, the protection of the interests of probationary teachers, and for larger across-the-board salary increases, as well as a merit increase system that would "genuinely and fairly" reward faculty members above general increases. There was a promise of something-for-everybody in this approach.

In a victory against long odds, AAUP did close the gap on December 15. AAUP increased its support over the first election by 132 votes, to emerge the victor with a total vote of 293. The "no bargaining" option picked up eight additional votes, but with 289 votes was once more denied victory by a narrow margin.

It would appear that the AAUP and no-bargaining groups held their lines between the two elections, and that the NEA people were able to deliver their votes to AAUP without significant losses. Why did the NEA people throw their support to AAUP? This move on their part was not inevitable, for, as we have seen in the Northern Michigan case, one labor organization may well be tempted to urge its followers to vote for the "no bargaining" option rather than support another labor organization for bargaining agent. By so doing, it holds open the possibility that it may yet be chosen as the bargaining agent in a later election, held as soon as the law permits a second try. The NEA leaders at the university may have genuinely preferred collective bargaining at the earliest possible moment, even at the price of conceding control of the bargaining to AAUP. Another explanation, offered by persons close to the scene, was that the NEA leaders expected to wield substantial influence within the AAUP chapter and thereby to play a part in the bargaining with the employer.

The latter explanation is a persuasive one, for it is based on a characteristic of organizational affiliations of faculty members at many institutions that is easily overlooked. In industry trade union practice, where two or more labor unions are attempting to organize a work force preliminary to bidding for recognition as the bargaining agent, workers necessarily choose sides and join one union or another. A worker seldom becomes a member of two competing unions. In higher education, on the other hand, faculty members can and do readily join AAUP, NEA, and an independent faculty organization, simultaneously, either because they see these organizations as offering separate and distinct advantages or because they are splitting their bets and making certain that they will back the winner. To put the point differently, at the campus level, AAUP, NEA, and even AFT, are open membership organizations. All faculty members are welcome; all are wanted as dues-paying members. Moreover, the local leadership within each organization is often fluid; it is "up for grabs," at least until one organization is chosen as the bargaining agent and collective bargaining begins in a serious way.

In our interviews at a number of institutions, faculty members were quite candid in telling us such things as, "I am an officer in AFT, which is the bargaining agent here. I am also an elected member of the faculty senate. And I belong to AAUP. I want to be sure that I am active in whichever organization accomplishes the most for the faculty as time goes by."

Other Decisions Against Faculty Bargaining, the Fordham Example

It is said that, in the public school sector, the "no bargaining" option might just as well not be available to teachers in representation elections, for it never wins.[33] This has not been true in higher education, for collective bargaining has been rejected by faculties in formal repre-

33. Doherty and Oberer, *Teachers, School Boards, and Collective Bargaining,* p. 84.

sentation elections at a number of institutions: at Northern Michigan, Manhattan College, Fordham University, Lawrence Institute of Technology, the University of Detroit, Pace College, Seattle University, and Rhode Island College.[34] This result may be temporary, for the law usually allows labor organizations to petition for subsequent elections at intervals of one year. Thus, at Rhode Island College, after having twice voted against collective bargaining, the faculty selected AFT as its bargaining agent early in 1972.

Fordham University provides a final example of a faculty's action on a proposal to engage in collective bargaining. It will be recalled that the university's governing board had unsuccessfully attempted to persuade the NLRB that it should reject petitions to hold a representation election at Fordham, arguing that the authority exercised by the faculty, its committees, and certain of its individual members was such as to make the faculty part of management and thus ineligible for bargaining rights as labor. During the two months that led up to the NLRB supervised election in November 1971, the university's administration conducted a vigorous campaign in an effort, this time successful, to persuade the faculty to reject collective bargaining. During this period, letters were sent to the faculty by the vice-president for academic affairs, the executive vice-president, and several deans. Toward the end of the campaign, the case they attempted to make against collective bargaining was supplemented by two long letters from faculty members, one of which was signed by twenty-eight faculty

34. Four of the institutions are identified with the Catholic church. It may be guessed that many of the votes against bargaining at these institutions were cast by faculty members in religious orders. This guess could be wide of the mark, for possibly many of the lay teachers at such church-related institutions have conservative leanings that would lead them to vote against unionization and collective bargaining. The margin of defeat was narrow in every instance. With AAUP as the bargaining agent candidate in each case, bargaining was rejected by the following votes: Fordham, 236 to 222; Manhattan, 130 to 121; Detroit, 206 to 168; Seattle, 64 to 46.

Collective bargaining may also have been rejected by the faculties at the C. W. Post Center of Long Island University and at Eastern Michigan University, where representation elections produced close results between a bargaining agent candidate and the "no bargaining" option. There were sufficient challenged ballots in both instances to affect the outcome, and, as of January 1973, these challenges were still under consideration by labor boards.

Since June 1972, faculties have rejected collective bargaining at Baldwin-Wallace College (Ohio), Jacksonville University (Florida), Michigan State University, Philadelphia College of Art, Tusculum College (Tennessee), and Villa Maria College (Buffalo).

members calling themselves the "Committee to Examine Alternatives to Unionization."

Because the opponents of collective bargaining carried the day at Fordham, and because administrative officers did play an active role of opposition without subjecting themselves to unfair labor practices charges under the National Labor Relations Act, it is appropriate to examine here the case they attempted to develop against the AAUP candidacy for bargaining agent:

1. Faculty compensation, it was asserted, had improved at Fordham during the two preceding years at well above the national rate revealed in the annual AAUP reports on the economic status of the profession. The rate at Fordham for 1970–71 was said to have been just under 7 percent, and for 1971–72, 11.5 percent. This favorable position, it was argued, demonstrated that the governing board and administration were making vigorous efforts to improve the faculty's economic status. (The AAUP chapter countered by showing that faculty compensation at Fordham was significantly below that at New York University, an institution with which Fordham might expect to be competitive.)

2. The "University Statutes," as approved in 1970, provided for extensive faculty participation in the internal governance system at Fordham and deserved to be tested out in practice. A joint letter from three deans put it this way:

> If you have not read the *Statutes*, or even a part of them, we would ask you to do so before you vote. Then we would invite your reflection: do these pages articulate a strong position for the faculty in the governance of the University, stronger than we have seen in the past? are the rights of the individual faculty members and faculty groups protected against arbitrary decision? is the door open to change? development? progress? what more could a union add?
>
> The *Statutes* are a beginning. They are a formula for growth. They should be given a chance.

In support of the contention that the faculty was already playing a powerful role in university governance, statistics were supplied concerning faculty personnel actions during the two-year period 1969–71. These purported to show that the administration was accepting the great majority of faculty recommendations: in 207 cases of faculty members up for reappointment, no final decision to reappoint was made "against the recommendation of the Department or School," and only 3 refusals to reappoint were made where reappointment had been recommended; faculty recommendations for promotions were followed in all but 15 of 104 cases; "a majority faculty recommendation" concerning a tenure grant was followed in 67 of 70 cases.

3. It was repeatedly asserted that AAUP was a reluctant and vacillating participant in collective bargaining. For example, it was observed that a minority report of the national association's 1966 Special Committee on the Representation of Economic Interests had urged "that under no circumstances should our local chapters transform themselves into union locals and stand for election as exclusive bargaining agents." It was also repeatedly argued that the AAUP chapter's claim that it would not become a "labor union" by engaging in collective bargaining was specious.

4. If the faculty voted for collective bargaining, all aspects of the university's educational program and campus governance system would be subject to negotiation in the bargaining process. Faculty groups interested in educational innovations would find that they "must deal with their union representatives and ultimately across the bargaining table with University representatives." One dean wrote:

> I have spoken with faculty at both the City University and at St. John's. Everyone with whom I have spoken predicted that much of our freedom to innovate and experiment would be lost in a collective bargaining situation. They doubted that our Council and its committees, our flexible calendar and teaching schedules, and our generally informal spirit of cooperation among faculty and students, could survive intact after unionization.

5. The administration claimed not to be opposing collective bargaining because of any fear that its power and influence might suffer; quite the contrary,

> under formal, legalistic collective bargaining, the Administration would exercise far more power than it does at present under the system of shared governance. Although it would not wish to do so, the Administration could, under formal collective bargaining, exercise all the prerogatives of management in determining policies, developing plans, and in making personnel appointments. . . .
>
> The University, no less than the union, will insist upon "working by the book."

It is impossible, of course, to say how faculty members reacted to these arguments or to the strong case on behalf of collective bargaining made by the AAUP chapter during the campaign. It may be that faculty lines in this and similar collective bargaining elections are drawn on the basis of allegiances, commitments, and attitudes that transcend the particular arguments made during the preelection campaign. At Fordham the 458 yes and no votes were cast by faculty members of varying age and appointment status, on two different campuses, organized into separate schools, graduate and undergraduate, and some two score academic departments. People at Fordham have their guesses about the patterns that took shape in the final voting. But the formal result certified by NLRB showed only that 236 faculty members voted for the "no bargaining" option and that 222 voted for AAUP as bargaining agent.[35]

THE REJECTION OF FACULTY BARGAINING: A SIGNIFICANT TREND?

Whether the faculties that have rejected collective bargaining have acted wisely in their individual situations is properly open to doubt and debate. Some of these faculties may change their minds and opt for bargaining at one of the continuous opportunities at regular periods that the law extends to them to reverse their decisions. But at this stage of the coming of collective bargaining to campuses, it is an encouraging result that at least an occasional faculty, for reasons that seem persuasive to it, should reject bargaining. Collective bargaining is not so clearly the ideal or best way of managing labor relations, or of structuring the governance system, at every college and university in the land that it deserves to be adopted and implemented everywhere at the earliest moment. We believe that it is a promising means of meeting the two purposes just mentioned and that it, along with other promising means, old and new, should be the subject of substantial experimentation at a wide range of institutions, differing from one another in function and location, as part of higher education's constant search for better ways of engaging in its work and serving its great purposes. But so also, for the present, is experimentation with other quite different arrangements much to be desired. Thus, it is fortunate that professors, unlike public school teachers, have thus far refrained from establishing a pattern of an invariable acceptance of collective bargaining as soon as the opportunity is available.

35. It should be recalled that the NLRB recognized the law school faculty at Fordham as a separate bargaining unit, and that faculty did vote to accept an independent law school bargaining committee as its agent.

CHAPTER SIX

The Bargaining Table: Process, Impasse, Agreement

THE BASIC PURPOSE OF COLLECTIVE BARGAINING IS THE REACHING OF A binding agreement between management and labor on certain disputed issues of "wages, hours, and conditions of employment," which will thereafter control the employer-employee relationship, usually for a fixed period called "contract time," at the end of which the agreement must be renegotiated. The process of collective bargaining divides, then, into two parts: negotiating an agreement and living under that agreement. The first will be examined in this chapter and the second in the next chapter.

Certain observations can be made about the negotiation of agreements between faculties and governing boards at four-year colleges and universities, although seldom is a full story available in any one instance. In the main, the procedures of industrial bargaining have been adopted in higher education. Management and the bargaining agent designate negotiating "teams" which then meet at the "table," usually in closed sessions, and "bargain" as long as is necessary to reach an agreement. These commonly used terms—"teams" and "table" and "bargain"—can be misleading if they are thought of as describing a uniform process or ritual. The law grants the parties to collective bargaining great freedom to select their own mutually agreeable and effective ways of proceeding. It does usually require that they meet at convenient times, negotiate in good faith, and reduce an agreement to writing at the request of either party. But the law is silent on such procedural details as the size and character of the negotiating teams, the place and circumstances of their meetings, and the extent to which the teams shall be instructed by the principals they represent, supported by resource persons or back-up personnel, or required to submit the agreements they reach to their principals for approval.

Labor and management can authorize their representatives at the bargaining table to sign an agreement for them. Or one or both parties can require their agents to refer an agreement back to them for consideration and ratification. There are obvious advantages both ways. If representatives at the table have final authority, they may be sustained through a difficult series of negotiations and come to work together effectively, precisely because each side knows that when the other has finally made a commitment, the agreement is binding. On the other hand, there are sometimes advantages for one or both sides in being able to say, "This seems all right to us, but we have to check it out with our people."

Practices in negotiating agreements thus vary greatly with respect to both form and dynamics. Outward form is not always identical with inner substance, for both sides in collective bargaining frequently share a wish or need to let form conceal substance, to protect the "trade secrets" of the negotiating process from public scrutiny and even from scrutiny by the people they represent. Or stated the other way around, the negotiators join forces in making statements for public scrutiny that present something less than a full or accurate record of how they have hammered out an agreement. The negotiating process is, more often than not, a delicate one. Even though their interests and goals differ sharply, successful negotiators find that they must establish a substantial esprit de corps; they must respect confidences; they must allow each other the privilege of taking credit for gains won in hard-fought bargaining; they must assist each other in concealing the extent to which demands were tempered or abandoned and concessions made in the interest of arriving at compromises and trade-offs without which no agreement would have been reached.

The negotiating process is an important example in contemporary society of collective decision making and of group dynamics. Moreover, important issues are at stake; the subject matter of the interaction is a series of complex problems to which there are seldom easy or simple answers. Both sides come to the table armed with "facts" that each is prepared to interpret and apply to its advantage in trying to reach agreement on specific points. But, since "the objective of bargaining is agreement . . . the end may be consummated in spite of the facts."[1] Both sides have emotional and political needs. Each must "win" some points, even where the facts and analysis may support the

1. William E. Simkin, "Fact-Finding—Its Values and Limitations," 61 *Government Employment Relations Reporter* (1970), 511. The author presented this paper before the National Academy of Arbitrators in 1970, when he was chairman of the Federal Labor Relations Panel; he was also formerly director of the Federal Mediation and Conciliation Service.

other side's contention. In a good bargaining relationship, each side must also be aware of the other side's strengths and weaknesses and of its interests. Good bargaining must be aggressive and hard fought, but it must in some degree be understanding and resilient. For either party to go beyond a certain point in its assurance about its facts, its adherence to its "principles," and its insistence on its demands, ensures the failure of the process of collective bargaining as a viable means of reaching agreement on difficult issues, about which, if men insist, they can continue to disagree indefinitely.

Bargaining: A Task for Professionals or Amateurs?

In industrial bargaining the negotiating teams are usually manned by persons who have considerable experience in labor-management relations. Depending on the corporation's size and bargaining history, team members may or may not hold regular jobs as part of management or labor. But they are seldom amateurs who once every two or three years step out of their roles as managers and workers to negotiate a complex labor agreement. If they are not themselves professionals in labor-management relations, they have learned to draw on the assistance—either as the team's "chief negotiator" or as back-up personnel—of lawyers, economists, personnel administrators, accountants, efficiency experts, and even theorists in social relations and psychology, who can bring information and know-how to bear in identifying options and exercising choices with respect to complex problems of wage and hour schedules, work loads and productivity standards, layoff and call-back practices, pensions, vacations, sick leaves, and the impact of all such matters on manufacturing practices, cost analysis, interpersonal relations, and the worker's adaptation to the work environment.

In higher education, particularly at independent institutions, there has been a strong inclination to draw at least some of the members of the two negotiating teams directly from an institution's governing board, administration, and faculty. Thus, at Central Michigan University, where two agreements have been negotiated, the labor teams consisted entirely of faculty members who were officers or members of the organization that had won the bargaining agent designation. At the first round of negotiations, management's team was made up of the president, the provost, the university's attorney, and the deans of the five component schools of the university. The deans were thereby to be exposed, we were told, to the reality of collective bargaining. The second time, only two deans served on the team, the other places being taken by officers from the business area of administration. No trustee served on either management team. In the negotiations at several of the Massachusetts state colleges, the management teams have usually consisted of two members of the professional staff of the state board of trustees, and the president, a dean, and a business administrator from the individual college. On the faculty side, the teams have consisted of faculty members associated with the bargaining agent organization and one professional or consultant from the AFT or NEA state organization. In such situations, where the teams are relatively large and varied, it is a reasonable assumption that the chief negotiator on each side will play a dominant role in the reaching of an agreement. But there is also evidence that in higher education up to now other members of the teams have been assertive and stubborn and that this helps explain the substantial delays in reaching agreement that have sometimes occurred.

At multicampus institutions, such as CUNY and SUNY, the negotiation of a contract is necessarily a centralized undertaking in which both sides make significant use of persons with professional experience or competence in collective bargaining. On the management side, the administrative staff of such a system is sufficiently large and specialized that one or more administrators can be assigned to the management team directly from the labor relations area. Thus, at CUNY a vice-chancellor for staff relations is responsible for the entire process of collective bargaining, including acting as management's chief negotiator at the bargaining table. At SUNY, "management" is not the board of trustees but "the Executive Branch of the State of New York"; thus in the negotiation of the first contract, management's role was played by a state official, the director of employee relations, who was responsible to the governor. At both CUNY and SUNY, faculty members from different campuses served on the labor negotiating teams, and were joined in each instance by salaried members of the professional staffs of the bargaining agent organizations.

The proper role of the president in the negotiation of a faculty contract has occasioned much debate. At some institutions the president has been a member of management's team, but his direct participation in negotiations is widely believed to be a mistake. According to one argument, the risk is great that he will thereby use up far too much of his limited credit with the faculty: he will be blamed for the concessions made to management but be denied any credit for the gains made by the faculty. But the need a president feels to stay close to the negotiations if he is to fulfill his responsibilities as the institution's chief executive is great, indeed often irresistible. Too much is at stake for him to let others control this aspect of the institution's decision making without any intervention on his part. One president of a state four-year institution who remained aloof from the first round of negotiations on his campus told us that when the final draft of the contract was placed on his desk, he discovered it was too late for him to react to the contract in any meaningful way. He indicated that he had learned a lesson and intended to stay in closer touch with what was going on when the time came to negotiate a second contract. At another public institution, it was clear that the president, although not a member of the negotiating team, watched over the negotiation of the first contract with considerable care and helped determine the management postition from the sidelines. At still another public institution where the president was a member of management's team, we were told that he was kept away from most of the sessions—particularly the difficult ones—but was always carefully briefed about the progress of the bargaining. He was, however, brought into the negotiations to receive some of the credit when management was prepared to concede a point or when it was thought important that he state the case in support of basic educational interests or the welfare of the institution.

Even under the best of circumstances, presidents, and provosts and academic deans as well, are discovering that the contract negotiation stage of collective bargaining poses a dilemma for them. If they participate, it can only be on the side of management. But they, like faculty members, are salaried employees of the institution. Administrators and faculty members view themselves as professional people; they work together on campus and cope with the same or related problems. At strong institutions, they are part of a true shared authority system of governance. Tension and conflicts do take shape between faculty members and administrators as they view the institution's problems from their separate vantage points. But many administrators, including presidents, often come to identify more closely with faculty members than they do with trustees. If they are direct participants in collective bargaining, they are likely to be viewed as the faculty's adversaries. If they withdraw to the sidelines while the faculty and the governing board fight it out at the bargaining table, they surrender their right and need to help shape policies in which they have vital interests.[2]

The direct involvement of administrators and faculty members in the negotiating process usually requires large expenditures of time and energy. Thus, as noted, when it came time to negotiate the second contract at Central Michigan, only two deans were placed on management's team. We were told that the second round of negotiations then proved to be at least as protracted and difficult as the first round, which suggests that faculty collective bargaining will not become easier at an institution as time goes by. At Henry Ford Community College the negotiation of a new contract in 1970 required a total of 187 hours at the table between January and September, even though bargaining had been going on there for some five years.

The second round of negotiations at CUNY, which got under way in the summer of 1972, proved exceedingly complex and contentious. The first-round contracts expired on August 31, 1972. As late as February 1973, the two adversaries still seemed far from agreement. The new bargaining agent, the Professional Staff Congress, representing the university's entire professional work force, was taking a particularly belligerent stance. The Board of Higher Education and the university administration also appeared determined to win significant changes in the original agreements. A "no contract, no work" referendum had been approved by the employees, but no strike had yet been called.

The membership of the employee bargaining team is determined by the labor organization rather than the faculty as such. Labor's bargaining team is usually drawn, at least in part, from the ranks of those faculty members who are loyal members of the organization, be it AFT, NEA, AAUP, or an independent faculty association. A representative or two from state or national headquarters of the labor organization may be drawn into the negotiations, either as a team member or in an advisory role. Or the local bargaining agent may engage the services of a nearby labor lawyer on a part-time basis. Protracted and arduous negotiations can present obvious difficulties for faculty members as well as for administrators. Apart from rotating the assignment, a faculty will usually find that one of the prices it must pay for collective bargaining is the expenditure of much time and energy by those

2. John Gianopulos, "Collective Bargaining: What Part Should College Presidents Play?" 49 *College and University Business* (September 1970), 71, provides an interesting analysis of the subject.

members who serve on the bargaining team. Thus, at Central Michigan University, where labor's teams in both rounds of negotiations were made up entirely of faculty members, four teachers repeated the assignment, serving on both teams.

There is something to be said for "bargaining by amateurs" in higher education, that is, for direct participation in the bargaining sessions by administrators and faculties. This practice might well prove, in time and with experience, to be simply a new manifestation of the shared authority principle of university governance. (After all, it takes time and trouble to operate any shared authority governance system at a college or university with results that are reasonably satisfactory to all parties.) Something like this appears to have happened at Rutgers University under the name of collective bargaining. There, the administration and the faculty, which selected the AAUP chapter as its bargaining agent, have used the framework of collective bargaining as a means of reaching a series of understandings on such matters as salary increases, establishment of a sabbatical leave program, and a way of avoiding a threatened faculty cut-back. The two contracts thus far negotiated have been short. Apart from covering salary increases, they were largely concerned with providing means for deciding substantive issues and policies on campus, sometimes through a memorandum of agreement between the bargaining agent and the administration, sometimes through action by the university senate or other regular agencies of university governance. Under these circumstances, decisions with respect to new issues and problems can be reflected in university bylaws, regulations, and policies, rather than in the detailed legal language of a series of ever-longer contracts arrived at through protracted negotiations at the bargaining table. This judgment of the Rutgers situation, reached on the basis of information gathered prior to June 1972, is strongly confirmed in an "Op-Ed" article in the February 2, 1973, issue of the *New York Times*, written by Edward J. Bloustein, who became president of Rutgers in September 1971, some time after the faculty's decision to engage in collective bargaining. President Bloustein writes:

> My generally optimistic view of the impact of faculty collective bargaining on universities is possibly colored by the special character of the Rutgers contract. Appointment and promotion of faculty and the development of most aspects of educational policy remain outside the purview of the A.A.U.P. Rutgers contract, except to the extent that the fairness and integrity of these processes is protected.

A somewhat different model of negotiations between a faculty and an administration took shape at the University of Scranton during the 1970–71 academic year. Scranton is a private institution with a Roman Catholic affiliation. Both labor and management were ready for some measure of collective negotiations in the economic area. But both parties were apparently reluctant to proceed to full-scale collective bargaining under either the federal law or a Pennsylvania "little Wagner" statute. The president, Father Dexter Hanley—a former professor of labor law at the Georgetown University Law Center in Washington, D.C.—was not happy with the thought of the *exclusive* bargaining rights that would be acquired by any faculty labor organization which gained recognition under a statute. The faculty, for its part, was not fully persuaded that the university senate was the proper body to negotiate with the university concerning a new salary scale. Thus, both sides agreed on the creation of a new faculty agency, the Professional Negotiating Team, to be composed of five members: the three officers of the local AAUP chapter and two other faculty members elected at large. A constitution was drawn up and approved by the full-time faculty. The trustees gave the arrangement unofficial approval. An administration team, consisting of the president, the comptroller, and "the chief academic officers of the university," was appointed, and after several months of negotiations, the two teams approved a "master agreement" in February 1971 to run for three years. The administration agreed to a new salary scale and apparently received in return some faculty concessions in the teaching load area. The agreement was approved by the faculty by a five to one majority.[3]

3. Dexter L. Hanley, S.J., "Issues and Models for Collective Bargaining in Higher Education," 57 *Liberal Education* (March 1971), 5–14. One of the authors of the present book heard Father Hanley discuss the Scranton experiment at a meeting on faculty collective bargaining, called by the Association of American Colleges. We have not visited the University of Scranton or talked with its faculty members about the experiment. An officer of one of the three national organizations active in faculty collective bargaining told us that "Father Hanley went to the University of Scranton intending to organize a company union, and he has succeeded."

The Scranton experiment has its ambiguities. As long as the "Professional Negotiating Team" is not recognized or certified as the bargaining agent by a public labor board, it presumably does not possess the exclusive bargaining right over all negotiable matters that labor laws, federal and state, allow. But it might at any time seek such recognition by circulating cards for employee signatures and petitioning for a representation election. Or another candidate for bargaining agent might make such a move, if the PNT appeared to be faltering to a point where its continued faculty support was in doubt. There are other legal subtleties in such a situation that stimulate the interest and concern of labor lawyers.

This experiment at Scranton suggests the possibility that an administration and faculty, with the informal approval of the governing board, can establish a mechanism, internal to the institution, that enables faculty and administrative teams to meet and negotiate an effective agreement concerning certain matters respecting "wages, hours, and conditions of employment." In the opinion of President Hanley, "mutual trust" has been "engendered" through this informal bargaining process: "No conflicts of interest developed and the bargaining was conducted in an atmosphere of collegial concern." An advantage of this kind of arrangement is that members of the academic community not only retain complete control of their traditional functions but also avoid unwanted or unnecessary interference with the existing governance system which might occur were the bargaining to take place under federal or state law. But the arrangement must command the continuing support of a majority of the faculty, for, if significant dissatisfaction takes shape, a labor organization can force a recognition election on the basis of the signatures of 30 percent of the faculty. At the ensuing election, a simple majority of the members of the unit, as determined by the labor board, can then force the entire group to accept formal collective bargaining under law, with a single bargaining agent possessing the exclusive right to represent the entire faculty. In other words, it is not wholly clear that faculty bargaining can ever be said to be taking place on a voluntary basis, outside the reach of law and government agencies. As long as management and labor negotiate freely, effectively, and without disagreement or conflict, the law and the labor board may be kept at arm's length. But once embarked on collective bargaining, a faculty and the institution's governing board must recognize that circumstances may arise that will entitle one or both sides to invoke the relevant law, federal or state, and request the intervention of public agencies.

Experience at other institutions than Rutgers and Scranton suggests that it will not be easy as time goes by to employ the formal, legal process of collective bargaining as an effective means of fostering a shared authority system of university governance or of protecting institutional autonomy. The parties to collective bargaining may begin by using a do-it-yourself approach to reach friendly agreements on a few basic issues, but end up concluding that the bargaining process is much too difficult and complex and the outcome much too crucial to be entrusted to amateurs or left to informal, friendly understandings. As issues grow more numerous, contentions more diverse, and solutions more elusive, the tendency will be strong on both sides to turn to the services of lawyers, economists, personnel administrators, and arbitrators for both the negotiation and administration of contracts.

Impasse at the Bargaining Table: What Then?

No labor relations statute, federal or state, compels either party to the negotiations to accept the other's final offer or to reach agreement. The legal obligation is to bargain collectively, in good faith and at convenient times, concerning wages, hours, and conditions of employment. Such bargaining, however, may well lead to disagreement, an impasse, at the table.[4] The law does not require that an impasse be broken at the table. Indeed, in the private sector the law recognizes the strike and the lockout as appropriate means for labor and management, respectively, to use in attempting to compel the other to accept its demands and offers. In the public sector, although the strike is generally illegal, government employees nonetheless do resort to it at the impasse stage in collective bargaining.

With only one exception above the two-year college level, neither the strike nor the lockout has yet been used as a way of trying to break impasses in faculty collective bargaining. There have, however, been numerous impasses in faculty bargaining in the sense that negotiations were protracted and agreement on difficult issues was reached

---

4. There is an enormous body of federal administrative and court law attempting to define "good faith bargaining" and "impasse":

"There exists in the law generally, and in the field of labor relations particularly, a tendency to rely on catch phrases and key words to describe recurring problems. The shorthand term most frequently used under the National Labor Relations Act refers to the reciprocal duty between the employer and the representative of the majority of its employees to bargain in 'good faith.' What constitutes 'good faith' . . . is not readily identifiable, although hundreds of cases and exhaustive commentaries have undertaken the task. . . .

". . . Where there are irreconcilable differences in the parties' positions after exhaustive good-faith negotiations, the law recognizes the existence of an impasse. Some difficulty exists in drawing a line between an impasse reached by hard and steadfast bargaining and one resulting from an unlawful refusal to bargain. . . .

"Where an impasse is reached, the duty to bargain is not terminated but only suspended" (Charles J. Morris et al., eds., *The Developing Labor Law*, pp. 271, 330).

only after the discussions were temporarily suspended or third-party assistance was resorted to in the search for a compromise or trade-off acceptable to the two principal parties.

Four decades of collective bargaining in industry and government have produced a variety of post-impasse procedures, in both law and practice, for reaching an agreement without a strike. Most of these involve third-party intervention through the processes of conciliation, mediation, fact-finding, and arbitration. The intervenor can be an individual or an impasse resolution committee. Such third parties have training and experience in helping the parties to the negotiations overcome their difficulties. They may be government officials, supplied by the Federal Mediation and Conciliation Service or a similar state agency, they may be identified with a private organization, such as the American Arbitration Association, or they may be free lances, usually lawyers or economists, who specialize in this kind of work. Resort to one or more of these procedures may take place before or after a strike. If before, the hope is that the impasse can be broken without a work stoppage; if after, the hope is to find an agreement by which the strike can be ended.

"Conciliation" and "mediation" originally referred to somewhat different processes but are now used interchangeably to describe the effort of a neutral agent, or third party, to help the opposing sides work their own way out of their impasse. A mediator usually meets with the parties to the dispute in private and leads a freewheeling discussion in which all options are examined in a search for a solution that is certain to require some give and take on both sides. "The mediator has unusual opportunities to explore a wide variety of solutions—to 'try them on for size.'"[5] But he has no authority to make findings or rulings; it is the parties who must make the decisions. In mediation the search is not for the correct or best or fairest solution, but for one that is acceptable to both sides.

"Fact-finding" describes a somewhat more regular or formal process; the fact-finder reviews the record, gathers new evidence through hearings, and then normally recommends a way out of the impasse, based on the facts as he finds them. Such recommendations are not binding, but if not promptly accepted by both parties they are usually made public

5. Simkin, "Fact-Finding," p. 513.

with the expectation that thereby both sides will be put under additional pressure to accept the proposals.[6]

In practice, the distinctions between mediation and fact-finding have been substantially blurred. Mediators and fact-finders use whatever means are available to them—often the same means—to accomplish the result that is expected of them: helping the parties end their disagreement.[7] The test of a good mediator or fact-finder lies not so much in his understanding of what is meant by "mediation" or "fact-finding" as it does on whether he can help both sides find a basis for agreement on disputed points.

Arbitration, as will be seen in the next chapter, is the last stage of the system by which the parties to a collective bargaining agreement attempt to settle disagreements on "grievances" during contract time. But it can also be used as the final step in the series of attempts to break an impasse at the bargaining table where the expiring contract specifies resort to arbitration under these circumstances; the parties agree on an ad hoc basis to let their dispute be settled by arbitration;

6. Professor Carl M. Stevens of Reed College has paraphrased the provision in the Oregon public employees bargaining law dealing with fact-finding as follows: "if a public employer and a labor organization find that after a reasonable period of negotiation they are deadlocked, then either or both may petition the Public Employee Relations Board to initiate discretionary fact-finding. If the board elects to initiate fact-finding, it appoints a three-man fact-finding committee to investigate the dispute and to make written findings of fact and recommendations for resolution of the dispute. The Board is required to make the findings and recommendations of the fact-finding committee public five days after the report is received unless the parties have reached an agreement before that time.... The Oregon law provides: 'Nothing in this section prohibits a fact-finding committee from attempting to mediate a dispute at any time prior to the submission of its findings and recommendations.' This kind of language is an invitation to the committee to roll up its sleeves and get into the dispute-management business" ("The Management of Labor Disputes in the Public Sector," 51 *Oregon Law Review* [Fall 1971], 191, 199).

7. Simkin writes:
"...labels are quite secondary....
"Fact-finders do or do not mediate. Some fact-finders who mediate find no facts. Persons appointed as mediators frequently do not mediate in any meaningful way but may announce some real or alleged facts and conclusions....
"When non-economic but highly emotional issues are also involved, when there is an imbalance of economic power or when serious personality conflicts exist at the bargaining table—who can say honestly that recommendations are or can be based solely and solidly on facts?...
"Where fact-finding has been successful, I would suggest—but cannot prove—that the fact-finder has mediated—deliberately, instructively or surreptitiously" ("Fact-Finding," pp. 511, 512, 513).

or the law requires this final step. Arbitration, either as a way of settling grievances under a contract or of breaking an impasse in the negotiation of a contract, involves a search for the right or correct way of resolving a disputed issue by one or more impartial experts who hold hearings, gather evidence, and render rulings which are usually binding on both parties. Advisory arbitration is possible in theory, but today "arbitration" almost always describes a form of third-party intervention in labor disputes that, by preagreement, is binding on the parties.

What everyone involved in the business of higher education must recognize is that collective bargaining does not guarantee that agreement can or will be reached at the bargaining table. Indeed, if the adversary aspect dominates the cooperative aspect in faculty collective bargaining, both sides must expect from time to time to find themselves in impasse situations where the solution will be provided by outsiders, by third parties, rather than worked out within the academic community. Such a solution may or may not conflict with the community's academic principles or educational programs. But it will entail a lessening of the autonomy hitherto enjoyed by both educational institutions and the academic profession.

THE STRIKE AND THE ACADEMIC PROFESSION

The strike has never been much used by college teachers as a means of bringing pressure on governing boards, administrators, legislatures, alumni, or society. Faculty strikes at four-year colleges and universities have been so rare that they can be numbered on the fingers of one hand. A few years ago work stoppages at St. John's University in New York, Catholic University in Washington, D.C., and San Francisco State College attracted much attention. None of these took shape out of a collective bargaining impasse or was strictly or even primarily concerned with economic issues. In recent years, there have been several economic strikes at two-year community colleges, but, thus far, the brief strike at Oakland University at the beginning of the academic year in September 1971, has been the only one at a senior institution. As faculties increasingly turn to unionization and collective bargaining, faculty strikes for economic reasons may well become more frequent if the theory of the strike as the sanction that makes collective bargaining work is borne out in practice. (See Tables 3 and 4, pages 44–49, for faculty attitudes toward the strike.)

Are Faculty Strikes Permitted by Law?

For faculty members at private colleges and universities, the strike is lawful. For faculty members at most public institutions, it is not. Federal and state laws recognize the strike and the lockout as valid ultimate weapons for use by labor and management in the private sector of the economy. The law encourages management and labor to turn to collective bargaining as a way of reaching agreement by peaceful, rational means, but at the same time views the availability of the strike and the lockout as essential to the successful use of collective bargaining. In particular, it is the strike—both as a threat and an actuality—that is said to enable labor to face management in the private sector at the bargaining table on equal terms.[8]

After forty years of collective bargaining, strikes are still a more serious cause of interruption of business in the United States than in any other principal democratic nation.[9] Strikes are now caused primarily by breakdowns at the negotiation stage of the collective bargaining process. Grievance procedures and provisions for binding arbitration in contract administration have proved effective means of reducing, although by no means eliminating, work stoppages during the life of collective bargaining agreements.[10] In the typical contract, both parties expressly agree to refrain from work stoppages as means of resolving disagreements while the contract is in effect.

Strikes by public employees are forbidden in most states, even in those that have laws authorizing collective bargaining by their employees. Two assumptions have undoubtedly played a part in the en-

8. Derek C. Bok and John T. Dunlop write that "the strike and the lockout are means of stimulating bargaining and inducing the parties to reach agreement." And again, "strikes and lockouts are tools in the agreement-making process" (*Labor and the American Community*, p. 229).

9. A study for the decade, 1955–64 shows that, measured by days lost per 1,000 persons employed in mining, manufacturing, construction, and transport, work stoppages in the United States substantially exceeded those in seven nations of Western Europe and in Australia, Canada, and Japan; only in Italy did the rate begin to approach that of the United States (ibid., p. 234). The record since 1964 may not show the United States at such a disadvantage, particularly when compared with England and Italy.

10. Bok and Dunlop state that 58 percent of all work stoppages and 87 percent of idle man-days are caused by breakdowns in the negotiation or renegotiation of contracts (ibid., p. 253).

actment of laws forbidding such strikes. One is that the public has a greater interest in the continuity of the services supplied by public employees than in those provided by workers in private business. This belief is asserted most strongly with respect to services upon which the public safety and public health are said to depend, but all public services tend to be viewed as essential, for they are usually provided by government on a monopolistic basis. The other assumption is that, in public employment, labor is not pitted against a management that seeks to increase profits at the expense of wages. Both of these assumptions have come to be questioned as time has gone by. Both have also had to hold their own against the counterargument that public workers should enjoy the same opportunity as private workers have to better their conditions of employment through collective bargaining and the strike. This contention has gained weight as the scope of governmental services and the number of public employees have sharply increased in recent years.

The distinction between faculties at public and private institutions with respect to the *legal* right to strike may prove to be more seeming than real. Indeed, up to now, the only faculty strikes that have occurred at the impasse stage of collective bargaining have taken place at public colleges. These strikes have been part of a much broader phenomenon—resort to strikes by all kinds of public employees in spite of laws forbidding such action. The no-strike laws have proved difficult to enforce, even though some of them carry heavy penalties. The Taylor Law in New York is a good example, for its penalty clause provides jail sentences and heavy fines for persons or organizations convicted of violating its terms. Another common penalty in state laws forbidding strikes by public employees is loss of jobs by strikers. The difficulty with these tough penalties is that they are likely to be ignored or waived, as part of an effort by both sides to find an acceptable basis for ending the work stoppage and, after a strike, as part of an amnesty by which normal operations are resumed. On occasion, strike leaders or even a larger group of striking teachers or other public employees have gone to jail, but their brief jail terms have usually been endured in the belief that a principle is being upheld, a labor organization strengthened and solidified, or the public shown that the school teachers or other public employees have justice on their side and must be paid more. Fines against the organization that called an illegal strike have in the end either not been collected or have not proved sufficiently onerous to damage the organization's financial position. Where large numbers of essential public employees with special training and experience, such as policemen, firemen, transport workers, and teachers, have been dismissed during an unlawful strike, it has seldom proved feasible to let such dismissals stand after the strike is settled.

Some state laws that forbid strikes by public employees carry no express penalties for violations. Laws of this type define unlawful behavior, but leave it to persons or organizations whose interests are adversely affected by the illegal action to seek some sort of redress or remedial help in the courts. The most obvious step is to ask a court to issue an injunction forbidding continuation of the unlawful action. If a court of proper jurisidiction finds, after a proceeding in which both sides are entitled to be heard, that the evidence does reveal the existence of an unlawful strike, and if the petitioner can show that he is suffering irreparable harm, the court has authority to issue a restraining order forbidding continuation of the strike. Failure to observe this order places the strikers and, in particular, their leaders, in contempt of court, for which offense they can be fined or jailed at the discretion of the court.

The Michigan statute forbidding public employee strikes is one that carries no penalties. Thus, public agencies in that state have turned to the injunction as the most promising sanction for the enforcement of the law. But experience shows that judges are reluctant to become deeply involved in efforts to settle controversial strikes in the public sector. Such strikes are likely to have political repercussions from which judges wish to stay free, particularly where they are elected, and where labor is as strong a political force as it is in Michigan. Michigan judges have been slow to issue restraining orders or to find strikers in contempt of court and have instead tried to bring pressure on management and labor to end a strike through continued direct negotiations or through third-party intervention. They have insisted on a showing that the employer has bargained in good faith before the impasse occurred. Sometimes a judge, possessed of authority to issue restraining orders and to hold persons in contempt of court, has exerted just enough influence after all other efforts have failed and an unlawful strike is taking place to persuade management and labor to reach agreement.[11] At Oakland, no attempt was made to obtain an injunction against the unlawful faculty strike. Had it lasted longer, management might have elected to go this route.

A few states, such as Hawaii and Pennsylvania, have moved toward the legalization of public employee strikes, undoubtedly influenced by the difficulty other states have encountered in the enforcement of no-strike laws, and also by the contention that public employees ought to enjoy the same rights and opportunities in their relations with their employers that workers in private industry do. The Pennsylvania statute, enacted in 1971, establishes an outright ban against strikes by prison and mental hospital guards and by certain court employees. For all other public employees, the strike can be used only at the end of a complex sequence of required efforts to end an impasse by other means. The operation of the law has been described as follows:

> if the parties are unable to reach a complete agreement within twenty-one days after negotiations commence, or if there are fewer than 150 days before a proposed budget must be submitted for final legislative action, the parties are obligated to request in writing the services of the Pennsylvania Bureau of Mediation. If mediation is not successful within twenty days, the Bureau of Mediation notifies the Board, and the Board may in its discretion, appoint a fact-finding panel. The panel is authorized to hold hearings and subpoena witnesses. It has forty days in which to make its finding of facts and recommendations, and thereafter the parties have ten days to notify the Board whether or not they each accept those recommendations. If either party does not accept, the findings and recommendations are then publicized. After publication the parties have another ten days in which to accept the findings. Then, assuming the parties do not agree to voluntary binding arbitration, the public employees involved in the dispute have a limited right to strike. The limitation is that if the strike "creates a

11. Following a three-day strike in 1971 by certain of the service employees at the University of Michigan, the university sought injunctive relief in a state court. The judge delayed granting such relief and brought pressure on the two sides to use a state fact-finder. Both parties were apparently apprehensive about what the fact-finder might recommend and, with the judge's encouragement, returned to the table and negotiated a settlement themselves. As one university official put it, "The shadow of the fact-finder made it necessary for the Union to become more realistic in its demands." He conceded, however, that the university also gave some ground when the negotiations were resumed. Under such circumstances, a statutory prohibition against a strike by public employees becomes not so much a basis for the trial and punishment of lawbreakers as a further sanction that operates to persuade the parties to a dispute to make one last and, it is hoped, successful effort to reach agreement.

clear and present danger or threat to the health, safety, or welfare of the public" the public employer can seek an injunction in a court of general jurisdiction.[12]

The Hawaii statute, enacted in 1970, places public employees under similar obligation to try to settle impasses at the bargaining table through resort to various kinds of third-party intervention before they reach the point where they can legally resort to the strike. Neither state has yet had much experience with the actuality of legal public employee strikes, and it remains to be discovered how such a system will work in practice over a period of time. One thing is certain: the many qualifications and the complex procedures set forth in both statutes will pose difficulties for the courts and for administrative agencies during the break-in period. It is reported that "the Pennsylvania Labor Relations Board has literally been swamped with cases under the Act" and that it "has yet to issue definitive opinions on many unclear areas of the legislation, and [that] it will be some time before Board decisions are tested through the courts."[13] State legislatures will also have continuing roles to play in the implementation of right-to-strike statutes. Thus, the Hawaii statute provides that where both parties to a labor dispute in the public sector agree to binding arbitration as a means of avoiding a strike by public employees, "all items requiring any monies for implementation" in an arbitrator's ruling "shall be subject to appropriations by the appropriate legislative bodies...."

Professors H. H. Wellington and R. K. Winter, Jr., of the Yale Law School, suggest that states should "accept the strike" by public employees but work to "reduce its effects." In addition to immediate danger to public health and safety, the authors assert, attention should be given to the impact such a strike may have on "the inelasticity of demand for most governmental services" and on "the vulnerability of the typical large city political structure to the strike weapon." They call attention to a number of ways for reducing the impact of a strike by public employees. These include: contingency planning to minimize the social effects of a strike, efforts at partial operations during a strike, publishing the wages of striking workers by name, specifying in tax bills the allocation of tax revenues among the different functions of

---

12. This paraphrase of the statute is from John C. Wright, Jr., "The Pennsylvania Public Employee Relations Act," 51 *Oregon Law Review* (Fall 1971), 183, 187.
13. Ibid., p. 188.

government or the amounts attributable to collective agreements, and requiring a public referendum on agreements reached after a strike.[14]

Professor Carl M. Stevens develops a strong argument against the legalization of strikes in the public sector:

> In a sense, the public budget represents a political agreement, the parties to it being the various categories of public employees, the beneficiaries of public services, and, of course, the taxpayers. Each of the parties to the political agreement may want more, but if any one party gets more, the others will necessarily get less. The question then is, what strategies should the parties represented in the budgetary equation be allowed to use in attempting to effect a more favorable agreement? Political power is appropriate since the agreement itself is political. But the strike represents an attempt to achieve political results by using the wrong kind of power, *i.e.*, economic market power. Since the parties to the agreement wield markedly different amounts of market power, it might be inequitable to allow strikers to dominate the budgetary equation. Additionally, if all of the parties to the political agreement represented by the budget did resort to whatever market power they could muster, the results vis-à-vis the political decision-making process would be arbitrary, capricious, and illogical.[15]

To take the place of the strike in the sequence of steps in collective bargaining for public employees, Professor Stevens proposes a form of binding arbitration for the settlement of impasses at the negotiating table which he calls "one-or-the-other" arbitration. The arbitrator would be limited to a ruling accepting without change the last offer of one party or the other. This kind of arbitration would be strikelike in character in that the threat of such arbitration, like the threat of the strike, might stimulate the "processes of concession and compromise characteristic of normal collective bargaining."

> Each party would genuinely negotiate with his opposite number in an effort to reach agreement rather than risk the possibility of total defeat should the arbitrator select his opposite number's final offer. The parties would generate reasonable final offers since the arbitrator would be inclined to choose the most reasonable alternative.

14. Wellington and Winter, "Structuring Collective Bargaining in Public Employment," 79 *Yale Law Journal* (April 1970), 805, 842, 849–50. Regarding publication of wages of striking workers, the authors suggest that "where these salaries seem higher than those received for comparable work in the private sector, public sympathy for the strikers will not be very great."

15. Stevens, "Management of Labor Disputes," pp. 191, 193–94, 195, 196.

Are Faculty Strikes Consistent with Professional Values?

There are undoubtedly many reasons for the infrequency of faculty strikes, including, labor organizers would say, the professor's inertia about advancing his own interests in practical ways. But academicians have also been influenced by their belief in goals, principles, and obligations that they cannot reconcile with the strike, lawful or not, as a means of compelling others to make concessions to them. How can professors strike and still claim to be professional people committed to such an ideal as service to society through a continuous search for and purveyance of truth and to systems of individual and social decision making which depend on the use of accurate data and fair and non-coercive arguments to arrive at reasoned solutions to complex problems?

The president of Central Michigan University, in a generally sympathetic article on faculty collective bargaining, expresses his particular concern in these words about faculty strikes that violate the law:

> Illegal strikes represent a special danger to university communities because of what they will teach our students about contempt for law, about coercion as a means of influencing relationships, and about a resort to hypocrisy which is particularly repugnant in a university. When Governor Wallace defied the law by standing in a schoolhouse door, all of us liberals knew how to react. When the schoolmarm defies the law by leaving her classroom in an illegal [or legal?] strike, we are confused. There are grave consequences in this dilemma which all of us may have to face in the future.[16]

A searching attempt to weigh the propriety and morality of the faculty strike was made several years ago by Professor Sanford H. Kadish, professor of law at the University of California, Berkeley, at the time he was chairman of AAUP's national Committee A on Academic Freedom and Tenure (he later served as national president of AAUP). His analysis[17] is clearly his own but is also revealing of the agonizing reappraisal of the issue in which AAUP, as the academician's principal professional association, was then engaging.

Professor Kadish recognizes that the economic interest (collective

16. William B. Boyd, "Collective Bargaining in Academe: Causes and Consequences," 57 *Liberal Education* (October 1971), 316.
17. Kadish, "The Strike and the Professoriate," 54 *AAUP Bulletin* (June 1968), 160–68; article based on a lecture at the University of Illinois College of Law, April 1968.

bargaining) strike "imperils" many professional values to which the academician claims he is committed. One of these is the "service ideal"; yet in using the strike, "The professor brings education ... to a halt in order to win concessions from administrators, boards, or legislators." The irony is that the economic strike operates through professors cutting off a service for which both they and the governing boards are responsible on the premise that the boards will be the first to yield to the pressures to continue that service. The troubling suggestion here is that if trustees yield to a faculty strike so that the university may resume operations, they give the service motivation in higher education a higher regard than do the professors. Professor Kadish is also troubled by the impact of an economic interest strike on the large measure of autonomy the academic profession has traditionally claimed in its work, and asks whether it will not endanger autonomy because it shifts "the basis of professorial claims from common commitment and moral entitlement to the play of power in the competitive context."

Professor Kadish speculates about the kind of circumstances that would justify an economic interest strike by professors. He suggests that some educational institutions may not deserve to be regarded as colleges or universities in that they lack any semblance of collegiality in their organization and operation. They are business enterprises, even if nonprofit ones. Conditions at such institutions may justify teachers, who are in fact "employees" rather than professionals, in striking to better their economic lot.

A reluctance to condemn the faculty strike under all circumstances is understandable. Uncertainty about the propriety of the faculty strike is but one more manifestation of the difficulty the troubled professor encounters today as he tries to relate his professional ideals and aspirations to the confusions and limitations of both the educational environment and the social setting in which he works. This uncertainty of mind undoubtedly helps explain the vacillation that AAUP has shown in the last half-dozen years in its attitude toward faculty strikes. As recently as January 1966, the association was asserting that it "has never looked upon the strike as an appropriate mechanism for resolving academic controversies or violations of academic principles and standards" and that it "does not now endorse a strike against an academic institution." A few months later, in adopting an "interim policy" authorizing AAUP chapters to offer themselves as collective bargaining agents at their institutions, the association's national Council stated flatly that "no strike or work stoppage will be called or supported by the chapter or its officers."[18]

In April 1968, the AAUP Council approved for publication the report of the Special Joint Committee on Representation, Bargaining, and Sanctions recommending that the association no longer adhere to its no-strike position of January 1966.[19] Instead, the special committee "put forward in generalized and severely limited terms the suggestion that sometimes a faculty strike may be appropriate—almost because it becomes unavoidable." The committee accompanied its formal statement with a long explanation and elaboration. The strong arguments against faculty strikes were all carefully restated:

> ... Resort to the strike as regular mechanism for the resolution of conflicts with administrations or governing boards imperils the faculty's just claim to partnership in the government of the institution, by implying acceptance of the status of mere employees.... Employees strike against employers; co-ordinate and interdependent members of a community do not usually strike against each other.
> ... a strike is a witness of failure.... It carries the risk of further hardening of opposed positions, and of creating deeper rifts.... [I]t constitutes a reliance on concerted power by those who are preeminently charged with advancement and instruction in the uses of reason.

But, on the other hand,

> ... in the end, one must contemplate situations where self-respect demands an end to temporizing. No more than anyone else can pro-

18. *AAUP Policy Documents and Reports,* 1969 ed. (Washington: The Association), pp. 35–39. The quotations are from a statement which the association's executive committee authorized the general secretary to release. The statement carried qualifications to the effect that refusal by individual faculty members to cross picket lines maintained by their colleagues "should not be considered a violation of professional ethics" and, similarly, that refusal of a faculty member "to teach the classes of a colleague who has been dismissed in violation of accepted principles of academic freedom or tenure" is not a violation of professional responsibility.

19. "Faculty Participation in Strikes," 54 *AAUP Bulletin* (June 1968), 155–59; the report carried a notice that "comment by members, chapters, and conferences is earnestly solicited." It was later republished in the association's *Policy Documents and Reports,* 1969 ed., with a terser announcement that "comments on the statement" should be sent to the Washington office. At the annual meeting of the association in spring 1969, announcement was made that the statement was not being submitted to the meeting for endorsement "because further changes may be made in it." No reference was made to the statement at either the 1970 or 1971 annual meetings. It seemingly remains approved "for publication" only (55 *AAUP Bulletin* [June 1969], 151–52). In the 1971 edition of *AAUP Policy Documents and Reports,* the "comments invited" clause was dropped (pp. 42–46).

fessors be expected to go about their daily duties in an atmosphere poisoned by injustice and destructiveness.

... A strike is supposed to have a shock effect, and some shocks are salutary.... The faculty may find that it has valuable allies if with deliberate spontaneity it takes a bold stand.

... governors and legislators ... may become the common enemy.... [A] legislature ... may sometimes be moved only if the faculty confronts it with a dramatic defiance.

The committee suggested that economic strikes may be necessary in countering "gross disparities," "a severe cut in salary appropriations," or "scandalous teaching loads." Nonetheless, "the industrial pattern which holds the strike in routine reserve for use whenever economic negotiations reach an impasse" is "emphatically reject[ed]."

The committee stated its opposition to laws that deny faculty members, as public employees, the right to strike and reminded institutions that they must invoke sanctions against striking faculty members only in accordance with due process. There is a final warning to everyone that "a strike is not a carefree holiday; it is a hostile act leading to possible reprisals. As in war, even victory may be attended by casualties." On this note rests the academic profession's own effort to decide whether the faculty strike can ever be justifiable.

ARE FACULTY STRIKES EFFECTIVE?

It is not yet possible to measure the effectiveness of faculty strikes on an empirical basis. The few faculty strikes that have thus far occurred at four-year colleges and universities have had uncertain results. Indeed, in every instance they can be viewed as quasi-strikes only and are thus not entirely useful examples. Only one—at Oakland University—was a collective bargaining strike; the other strikes of this type have been confined to two-year colleges. Several community college faculties have struck at the impasse stage in negotiations in an attempt to win higher salaries or other improvements in working conditions. They do not appear thereby to have won significant gains beyond those that would have been won in any event. An administrator at Henry Ford Community College, in Michigan, told us that if the faculty there had gone on strike at the opening of the college year in September 1970—as it threatened to do in attempting to win further concessions at the bargaining table—"the board was prepared to close the college and sit that one out." And he added that even though

Dearborn was a strong labor community, sympathy for professors was at low ebb.[20]

In addition to the Oakland strike, there have been three work stoppages at institutions above the two-year college level in the last decade. Although none was a collective bargaining strike, they may be examined for whatever light they throw on the effectiveness of faculty strikes.

The St. John's University Strike

The first of the three strikes in a senior institution occurred at St. John's University in New York in January 1966. It was called by a group of faculty members affiliated with the American Federation of Teachers. Its primary purpose was to bring about the reinstatement of twenty-one faculty members who had been summarily dismissed as the culminating event in a troubled period at St. John's, during which the faculty's relations with the administration and governing board had gravely deteriorated. The strike failed of its objectives, for the university was able to continue in operation, and the dismissed faculty members were not reinstated.

AAUP refused to endorse the strike that AFT had called, but sent an investigating committee to the campus. Its study led to a published report and censure of the university administration in April 1966. In voting censure, the AAUP annual meeting took the unusual step of accompanying the censure with a statement that "although we do not recommend imposing an absolute obligation upon our members to decline appointments, we do feel that ... it would be inappropriate for our members to accept appointments at St. John's University."[21] There was much bitterness then and thereafter between AFT and AAUP over their separate roles in the St. John's situation.

Between 1966 and 1971, the university's administration altered many of its institutional regulations and practices and made an offer of redress to a number of the dismissed faculty members, looking toward removal of the AAUP censure. During this period, the AAUP chapter at St. John's and a local faculty association joined forces in persuading the faculty to vote to engage in collective bargaining negotiations with the university, with the two organizations as the joint bargaining agent. A contract was agreed to late in 1971. The AAUP censure of

20. We visited Henry Ford Community College in 1971 and had interviews with several administrators and faculty members.
21. 52 *AAUP Bulletin* (June 1966), 100, 124.

St. John's was removed shortly thereafter when the association had satisfied itself that all of the dismissed faculty members had had an adequate opportunity to accept the university's redress offer if they cared to do so.

In retrospect, although it took several years, it appears that more was achieved in this situation through the use by the academic profession of the censure sanction than through the faculty strike.[22] On the other hand, AFT's militant support of the faculty strike at St. John's may well have been a significant influence in the recent softening of AAUP's opposition to faculty strikes. AAUP has shown obvious sensitivity to the efforts that AFT and NEA have made in the last half-dozen years to persuade the academic profession that they can represent and defend the interests of professors more aggressively and effectively than AAUP can.

The Catholic University Strike

In April 1967, "a total and almost spontaneous refusal" by both faculty and students to hold classes at Catholic University qualified as the second faculty "strike" to take place at a senior institution. Prolonged dissension between the governing board and the faculty about many matters had culminated in a refusal by the board to retain a faculty member who had been recommended for promotion. This work stoppage was called a boycott by its participants, but its purpose was to win specified concessions from management with respect to conditions of employment. However labeled, it was immediately and decisively successful, for, after just four days, the bishops who composed the governing board of the university rescinded the dismissal decision. Thereafter, significant changes were made in the structure and personnel of the university's governing system, with a considerable strengthening of the role and influence of the faculty.

The San Francisco State College Strike

The third faculty strike at a four-year institution took place at San Francisco State College at the beginning of 1969 when from one-fifth to one-fourth of the faculty refused to meet their classes for a period of two months. The strike, occurring shortly after S. I. Hayakawa was named president of that deeply troubled institution, was called by

22. For the AAUP involvement, see 54 *AAUP Bulletin* (March 1968), 9; 54 *AAUP Bulletin* (June 1968), 155; 54 *AAUP Bulletin* (September 1968), 325; and 57 *AAUP Bulletin* (June 1971), 201.

faculty members identified with an AFT local, in support of a student strike which had begun two months earlier and which continued after the faculty strike was broken off. Some 204 members of a faculty of more than 1,000 members were hard-core strikers in the sense that they were found to have absented themselves from their classes without leave for five consecutive days and thus to be subject to the loss of salary payments under state law. The striking faculty members made a number of specific demands in the economic and institutional governance areas. The student and faculty strikes both had strong political overtones and were generally viewed as radical in character and purpose. Both were failures inasmuch as control over the college was successfully asserted and maintained by President Hayakawa, the Trustees of the California State Colleges, and a majority of the faculty. The college was not closed down during the strike, and at the end the strikers won few of their demands. Although most of the faculty did not participate in the strike, the aggressive use of picket lines and the threat of violence apparently greatly reduced class attendance during part of the strike. At the end of the two-month period, the faculty strikers, by a close vote, terminated their work stoppage. As seen by the chairman of the political science department, "by whatever criterion or standards one measures success, the strike by the AFT local was a failure."[23] In the judgment of three other members of the faculty, "the union lost on nearly every aggressive thrust . . . and the trustees gave away virtually nothing that had not been previously settled . . . the union failed in most of its economic demands and in its commitment not to return to work until there was a resolution of the student grievance."[24]

23. John H. Bunzel, "The Faculty Strike at San Francisco State College," 57 *AAUP Bulletin* (September 1971), 341, 344. Professor Bunzel was a principal faculty target of leaders of the student strike. In publishing his article, which appears to be a sober, carefully documented account of the strike, the editors of the *AAUP Bulletin* appended this somewhat unusual note: "The views expressed herein are the author's own, and the article is not to be confused with an Association case report. The editors invite the expression of differing views which would contribute to a debate on the appropriateness of a strike as a mechanism for resolving faculty-administration conflicts."

Subsequent issues of the *AAUP Bulletin* carried no communications from readers that seriously challenged the accuracy of the Bunzel analysis of the San Francisco State College strike.

24. Robert Smith, Richard Axen, and DeVere Pentony, *By Any Means Necessary*, p. 299. Smith preceded Hayakawa as president of San Francisco State, serving from June to December 1968. In 1970, he was a professor of education, Axen was professor and chairman of the department of higher education, and Pentony was dean of the School of Behavioral and Social Science and a professor of international relations.

The Collective Bargaining Strike at Oakland University

In view of the reluctance of AAUP at the national level to approve the use of the strike by a faculty for economic gain, it is ironical that the first senior institution in the country to experience a faculty strike at the impasse stage of collective bargaining was Oakland University in Michigan, where the local AAUP chapter was the bargaining agent. The strike was called by a vote of 112 to 64 at an AAUP meeting at the opening of the academic year in September 1971, and lasted two weeks. Negotiations at the bargaining table got under way in February 1971. After several months of aggressive, but intermittent bargaining, agreement had been reached at the end of the summer on most of the noneconomic issues. But the two parties were unable to reach agreement on the economic package and on two or three related issues, such as faculty research grants and the student-faculty ratio to be maintained by the university. The faculty's negotiators were demanding a 22 percent increase in total compensation, whereas the university's best offer was a 10 percent increase.[25] The state legislature had granted Oakland, in common with all of the other four-year colleges and universities in the state system of higher education in Michigan, increased funds for the 1971–72 fiscal year sufficient to permit an overall or average improvement in faculty compensation of 6.5 percent measured against the compensation base of the preceding year, or 8.1 percent measured against the salary base. AAUP's demand for much larger increases was presumably based on the assumption that the Oakland administration and governing board possessed the necessary legal authority and fiscal flexibility to transfer funds into the faculty compensation category from such other university budget categories as student aid. Management's negotiators rejected such a "reordering" of the university budgetary "priorities" as improper, and an impasse at the bargaining table resulted. It seems clear that the two negotiating teams at Oakland had not managed to develop a good working rapport during the extended bargaining sessions and that, at the end, the faculty bargaining team was making compensation demands that could not possibly have been met by the university.

AAUP proposed that the impasse be resolved by a binding agree-

25. Other reports place these figures at slightly different levels. Our account of the strike draws on interviews with Oakland faculty members and administrators and on Professor Jesse R. Pitts, of the Oakland faculty, "Strike at Oakland University," *Change*, February 1972, pp. 16–19.

ment by both parties to accept the ruling of a state fact-finder on the disputed issues, but the governing board took the position that it could not commit itself to a finding that it might not be able to fund. Members of the bargaining unit then voted not to meet their classes during the first week of the semester. The administration promptly directed students to leave the campus, closed university buildings to the faculty, and suspended all faculty salary and fringe benefit payments.

Negotiators for the two parties met regularly during the strike. Both parties also agreed to accept the help on a nonbinding basis of a fact-finder supplied by the Michigan Employment Relations Commission. Press stories reported the president of the university as stating that the fall semester would have to be cancelled if the strike continued beyond the opening weeks of the school year. He denied such reports, but it became apparent to both sides that, unless the strike was settled quickly, many of the university's commuting students would enroll in nearby public universities and community colleges.

There was no significant public support for the strike. Press coverage was surprisingly modest even in the nearby Detroit area and was virtually nonexistent outside the state.[26] The administration and the governing board appeared to be solidly united in resisting the faculty demands and were seemingly free from any pressure from state legislators or the governor to end the strike by making substantial additional concessions to the strikers. Nonetheless, the administration clearly wanted to end the strike and was prepared to make limited concessions. The state's agent appears to have played a useful role during the period of the strike. Functioning more as a mediator than a fact-finder, he persuaded both sides to give a little ground. Agreement was reached on a compensation formula, apparently suggested by the fact-finder, by which the faculty would not suffer financial loss for the two weeks of inactivity, and, even though no additional money was provided by the administration, would receive a 12 percent salary increase for the seven and a half month period from November 15 to the end of the academic year. Some adjustments were also made in the disputed student-faculty ratio policy.

Members of the bargaining unit voted to accept this settlement and

26. This first collective bargaining faculty strike at an American university passed without notice in the *New York Times*. In Michigan, the Oakland strike story was apparently overlooked in the furore over the Pontiac school bussing controversy.

to terminate the strike at the end of the second week. There were no claims from faculty members that they had won a notable victory by striking. One member of the Oakland faculty has written: "The strike had a relatively disappointing ending. Doubtless it had proved that professors can wage a soft strike. (A strike can last up to three weeks and result in no loss of salary simply by reshuffling the academic calendar.)" He also suggests certain losses by the administration: "there is a very serious question whether aggressive collective bargaining will not wear out and delegitimate any administrative team. More than two months after the strike, the adversary stance was still present."[27]

Faculty members had voted to end the strike on the basis of word that compromises on the salary increase formula and on one or two other disputed issues had been agreed to by the negotiating teams. However, several weeks of subsequent effort were necessary to produce a formal contract.

The experience at Oakland suggests that if a strike is called for the opening of an academic year, administrators may more easily close buildings and keep students off campus than if it were called during the academic year. The effective date of collective bargaining contracts in higher education will typically coincide with either a fiscal year beginning July 1 or an academic year beginning in September. Thus in some degree the timing of impasse strikes will be controlled by the rigidities of the collective bargaining calendar. A faculty might try to gain leverage by agreeing to begin the academic year without a contract and then selecting a more auspicious moment to call a strike if further negotiations did not lead to an agreement.

The Oakland strike also suggests that a faculty's bargaining power to improve compensation is sharply limited where the state legislature provides funds for all public institutions on a uniform formula or systemwide basis. Under a lump-sum appropriation system, bargaining is generally limited to the discretionary authority at the campus level to shift funds from one budget line or category to another. In Michigan, the thirteen state four-year colleges and universities possess considerable local autonomy in deciding how to use the funds available to them from various sources, including money appropriated by the legislature. But they have limited ability to increase income. Although Michigan is a strong labor state, the legislature has been remarkably

27. Pitts, "Strike at Oakland University," p. 16.

resistant to pressures from an individual institution to provide a larger appropriation because it is paying higher salaries than its competitors. The governing boards of the separate institutions can presumably obtain additional income by increasing student tuition and fees; at the same time, they must keep these charges at competitive levels, and, in voting substantial increases, they run the risk of encountering political repercussions and perhaps legal challenges to their authority. The only other source of institutional income is gifts, and governing boards seem unlikely to view this source as a promising means of funding compensation increases won through collective bargaining or strikes.

There is some evidence that certain Michigan state institutions have accumulated budget surpluses or reserves and used them to provide their faculties with larger increases than have been possible at other institutions. Administrators at Oakland claimed that they were contending with accumulated deficits and showed some bitterness about the rumor of reserves being used at other institutions to make more generous compensation concessions to faculties. Such advantages, if they have indeed existed, will probably quickly disappear, with the result that all the state institutions engaging in collective bargaining with their faculties will find themselves working within income limitations that are largely controlled by the state government at Lansing.

The Outlook for Faculty Strikes

For a faculty to win a strike, it must pinpoint an adversary and it must hurt that adversary in some significant degree. The strike may be said to be against the college or the university. But the decision that the institution is being hurt and that concessions can and should be made must come from persons on the other side of the bargaining table. In this setting, usually the president can be ruled out as the primary target of a faculty strike, for his control over resources is limited. A president can certainly be hurt by a strike, and indeed he, more than almost any other person involved, may desperately wish an end to a faculty strike and do everything in his power to effect a solution. His role, at best, will be as a counselor and a mediator. A strong president may bring effective pressure on a governing board to end a strike by persuading it to offer additional concessions. However, if a faculty, thinking that its president can manage such a result, goes out on strike, it may well succeed only in undermining his standing with the governing board and thereby hasten the day of his departure.

In the private sector, the top management and board of directors of the business are the principal adversary. So, too, in the public sector, except when a strike settlement requires increased institutional income (not just a reordering of priorities for the use of funds already available or in sight) and legislative bodies, mayors, governors, and ultimately taxpayers and voters become the adversaries. In industry, the consumer and the stockholder may ultimately pay for a generous strike settlement, but they are seldom identified by labor or themselves as adversaries. Faculty strikers will usually find in the final analysis that they are dealing with trustees. Trustees cannot be hurt in the sense that corporate profits will be lost during a strike. They cannot be hurt in the sense that their own income or property is endangered. They can be hurt in the sense that their pride and satisfaction in effective fulfillment of the trust imposed in them is injured. More specifically, they may be troubled by mounting evidence that real and perhaps lasting damage is being done to their institution through the loss of students to other institutions, through the hardening of lines beween the faculty and the president and other administrators which will impede effective cooperation after the strike is over, or through a bad press and loss of public approval and support of the institution.

Professor C. Dallas Sands, professor of law at the University of Alabama and a member of the national AAUP Council, argues that "management" in higher education will be subject to strong pressures to settle or avoid faculty strikes by making concessions:

> it has not been demonstrated that the compulsion to maintain the continuity of an institution's operations is sufficiently less where it is not committed by nature to the end of earning profits. The officers of a college or university are surely no less sensitive to the disruption of its normal operations than is the management of a private enterprise.
>
> ... Next to student riots, a faculty strike would probably be the most visible external sign possible that in some respect things were not right at the institution. Administrators are generally anxious enough to avoid the display of such signs that the threat of a strike could well have greater influence than the strike itself.[28]

It will be dangerous to assume that university managements will react to strikes in this manner. Much will depend on the state of affairs at an institution, as well as on the exact circumstances surround-

28. Sands, "The Role of Collective Bargaining in Higher Education," 1971 *Wisconsin Law Review* (no. 1), 150, 163–64.

ing a strike. If an institution has serious budgetary or educational problems, its governing board may welcome the opportunity offered by a faculty strike to close the institution for a semester or a year as a means of dropping costly educational programs and courses with small enrollments, reducing the size of the faculty, or changing the tenure system. On the other hand, the board at a troubled institution might move to end a strike quickly in the belief that a prolonged strike would force it to close the institution's doors permanently. But it will necessarily hesitate to end a faculty strike by bettering its last salary offer, if that move will bring the institution closer to bankruptcy.

Finally, faculties must recognize that their standing with governing boards is, more often than not, something less than good. Trustees can reveal such human qualities as stubbornness, irritability, and aggression just as readily as a combative faculty can. Under such circumstances a faculty must be prepared to discover that, by waging an economic strike, it has locked itself into a situation where neither side is prepared to manifest much sweet reasonableness or spirit of compromise, at least during the two- or three-week period that a faculty strike can last without costing anyone anything, that is, the period for which classes can be made up during the remainder of the academic year, without tuition being rebated to students or their parents, and with faculty recovering salary payments withheld during the strike.

Public opinion has strongly affected the outcome of many strikes by workers in private industry and by such public employees as school teachers, policemen, and transportation workers. If strikers receive friendly treatment in the press and on television and the public comes to believe in the legitimacy of their demands, management is likely to be willing to settle promptly, concluding, among other things, that the cost of the settlement can successfully be passed on to the consumer either in the form of higher prices or higher taxes. There is no evidence thus far that striking college professors will enjoy a good press or find public opinion rallying to their support. In the case of a private college or university, the general public in the vicinity of the institution may well prove disinterested. The institution's own public, in the sense of its alumni and the parents of its students, will usually be remote from the event and its underlying issues. Unless a faculty strike is prolonged, such a public will prove difficult to propagandize to shape an opinion, one way or the other.

At public colleges and universities, an immediate public is available and will probably be interested in what is happening. That striking professors at a public institution can generally count on a friendly and supportive local public opinion is doubtful. A member of the central administration at CUNY told us that if the faculty did go out on strike in the event of an impasse at the bargaining table in the fall of 1972, he doubted public opinion in New York City would respond favorably to the strikers. If the issue were higher salaries, "the Board of Higher Education," he said, "can point out that the top salary for a professor at one of the community colleges is already $31,275. The people of New York aren't going to be impressed by any argument that CUNY professors are underpaid!" (He might have added, "Neither will the public be impressed by the faculty union's effort to win lifetime tenure for all term-appointment instructors through the grievance-arbitration system, or tenure for all fiscal officers, registrars, doctors and dentists, lecturers, and teaching assistants in the bargaining unit, as a matter of right.") This administrator may have underestimated the possibility that open admissions at CUNY has established a new, more acute public interest in the university which could be marshaled in support of the striking faculty. Working against such a result would be the belief, said to be widely held by minority groups in New York and by CUNY students, that teachers have been using collective bargaining to promote their own economic interests, with the cost of teachers' high salaries being met at the expense of student interests and welfare.

The effectiveness of a strike by professors, particularly at a public institution, might also depend in considerable measure on the degree of support provided by other unionized employees at the same institution or in the same community. Refusal by other employees to cross a professors' picket line might make it difficult for a college or university to remain open. Whole-hearted support of an AFT-backed strike at CUNY by the powerful New York City Central Labor Council would undoubtedly strengthen the position of the striking teachers. But such support is not automatically given to every group of striking workers. The CUNY work force might well discover that other AFL-CIO unions in the city were not prepared to offer such backing at any significant cost to their own interests. Moreover, at CUNY and other colleges and universities, a willingness by the governing board to close the institution down during a strike would to some extent undercut the value to the strikers of an effective picket line or of other forms of interunion support.

The specific variables, then, that affect the outcome of a particular faculty strike at a particular moment are likely to be both numerous and confused. The faculty may or may not be solidly united in support of a strike. At a multipurpose university, professional school faculties, such as those in law, medicine, or engineering, may refuse to support a strike by their militant colleagues in the arts and sciences. Even the faculty of arts and sciences, where the inclination to strike may be strongest, is likely to include some mavericks who oppose the strike. In the event picket lines are established, the mavericks (or the large number of faculty members who do not belong to the bargaining organization) may be quite willing to cross the lines. What about students? The initial inclination of student leaders to support a faculty strike against administrators, trustees, and legislators, whom they view as the enemy, may not be sustained when the student body at large realizes that a closed university is not serving their interests at all, or that a generous strike settlement will be reflected in increased student charges. Further, students are at the center of one serious difficulty: a student body once dispersed will not easily be brought back together on short notice, and many students will enroll at other institutions and thereby make a new commitment for a semester or even a full academic year.

It may well be that a strike must be quickly settled, as it was at Oakland, if the weapon is to have any value to a faculty. A college or a university is a fragile, delicately balanced enterprise that rarely can be put on a standby basis for more than a few days. Compared with starting up General Motors or United States Steel after an extended strike, resuming operations at, say, Harvard or the University of Michigan could prove a more formidable and complex undertaking.

College faculties may be tempted to conclude that because public school teachers and professional musicians in recent years have engaged in seemingly successful strikes at the impasse stage of collective bargaining, they, too, can use the strike weapon effectively. The strikes by school teachers in New York City, Newark, Pittsburgh, and countless other cities, and by the members of the symphony orchestras in Philadelphia, Cleveland, Washington, Baltimore, Cincinnati, and other cities appear to have won additional concessions from adversaries as difficult to hurt as will be the governing boards of colleges and universities. To the extent that such strikes have been successful, they may provide some encouragement for faculties unable to win their demands at the bargaining table.

There are differences, however. School boards are under pressure to settle public school strikes by parents who "want the kids back in school" and who will not bear the direct brunt of increased costs, but the parents of college students, more remote from the campus scene, will be less inclined and less well situated to bring pressures on trustees to give in. Some of them may even urge boards of trustees to resist unreasonable demands by a faculty viewed as radical or greedy. A report on faculty collective bargaining prepared by the Committee on Faculty Rights and Responsibilities for submission to the Senate Assembly at the University of Michigan offers this terse warning: "If faculty bargaining should lead to a strike, the people of the state might well react: let them close down!"

The symphony orchestra strike, common though it has become, is difficult to evaluate. The trustees of such enterprises, already burdened with responsibility for meeting annual operating deficits that are all but impossible to eliminate by raising box office prices, nonetheless have often agreed to strike settlements that entail still higher operating costs. They may have done so from a sense of pride and duty to a community to sustain a splendid musical ensemble with a great tradition. But these organizations may be reaching the point where one more strike will lead trustees, however regretfully, to cancel seasons and suspend operations indefinitely. Where is the additional income to meet a costly settlement to be found? Not from increased receipts at the box office where many seats remain unsold because of high prices. Not from wealthy donors, repelled by the combative rhetoric of a strike. Above all, generous strike settlements are unlikely to hasten the coming of talked-about public subsidies for cultural enterprises. Faculties can take little encouragement from the outcome of recent strikes by professional musicians. Indeed, it is probable that musicians will themselves make more sparing use of the strike. The announcement in June 1972 that the Metropolitan Opera had signed a new contract with its orchestra, months before the impasse stage in bargaining would have been reached, with only modest salary increases, suggests that the musicians and their union leaders had recognized that they would not have enjoyed a strong position in a new strike.

If the faculty strike is likely to prove ineffective, what happens to faculty collective bargaining? The classic rationale for collective bargaining has stressed the strike and the lockout (or, more properly, the threat to use these weapons) as forces that keep the adversaries at the bargaining table until they reach agreement. Can collective bargaining succeed if the strike threat is removed or minimized? No answer is now available except that provided by experience. It is important to note, however, that in private industry there is talk about finding a substitute for the strike without abandoning collective bargaining as the means by which management and labor shape the conditions of employment. When George Meany is heard questioning the continued usefulness of the strike, the time has come to consider such talk seriously.[29]

Over the years many proposals to end impasses in industry without resort to strikes have been made, and the literature examining them is extensive. Bills have been introduced in Congress and the state legislatures to implement one proposal or another, but thus far no significant statutory changes have been made. Professor Sands suggests that the situation in higher education is "wholly different" from private industry and thus it becomes desirable to develop "a wholly different set of bargaining sanctions in a wholly different frame of reference." He proposes that the fact-finding mechanism might be developed and used in higher education at the impasse stage of collective bargaining in such a way that faculties and governing boards would present their cases as fully and effectively as they can and then let themselves be judged by public opinion: "a meaningful staging of the process might be to postpone the right to strike for a period after publication of the fact-finding report, and then to impose a limit upon the amount of time that a strike may be continued and possibly provide for compulsory arbitration of disputes which survive the permissible duration of a strike."[30]

These and similar proposals for avoiding strikes in higher education have received consideration in recent years without leading to any significant measure of agreement among students of labor-manage-

29. The *New York Times* (Aug. 31, 1970, pp. 1, 52) reported a group interview with six labor reporters in which Mr. Meany stated: "Naturally we wouldn't want to give [the strike] up as a weapon but ... more and more people in the trade union movement—I mean at the highest levels—are thinking of other ways to advance without the use of the strike method. ... we certainly have advocated for years that you have to have the right to strike, but we find more and more that strikes really don't settle a thing. Where you have a well-established industry and a well-established union, you are getting more and more to the point where a strike doesn't make sense."
But see also the *New York Times,* May 27, 1971, p. 52, for a report that Mr. Meany had vigorously attacked compulsory arbitration as a substitute for the strike and had reasserted his strong belief in the right to strike as labor's principal weapon.
30. Sands, "Role of Collective Bargaining," p. 166.

ment relations. A principal difficulty is responsibility for the funding of a costly strike settlement. How can fact-finders and arbitrators, with or without the supporting force of public opinion, force a strike settlement on the governing board of either a public or a private educational institution if the board believes that it does not possess the means of implementing an overly generous settlement?

Since the right to strike is so closely associated with labor's right to organize and bargain collectively, both in law and practice, a spread of faculty bargaining will probably be accompanied by an increasing number of faculty strikes. At private colleges and universities the faculty strike will be legal, but it will be waged against an adversary hard to pinpoint and difficult to hurt. At public colleges and universities, the political setting may mean that governing boards will prove somewhat more vulnerable and thus ready to give ground in order to end work stoppages promptly, even though such strikes are unlawful. This is a dubious assumption at best. If the faculty strike does prove to be an ineffective weapon, only time and experience can then show how faculty bargaining will be affected.

RATIFICATION OF THE CONTRACT

Customarily in collective bargaining in industry, the contract that emerges from the bargaining table is submitted to the union membership for ratification. Collective bargaining statutes, however, do not require this. So far as the law is concerned, the bargaining agent, once selected, speaks for all members of the bargaining unit, and it is entitled to decide for itself what forms shall be observed in reaching agreement with management. Presumably the members of the labor organization designated as bargaining agent can determine at an open meeting how their negotiating team is to be selected, what instructions, if any, it shall be given, and how the contract is to be ratified when agreement is reached at the bargaining table by the two teams. Bok and Dunlop note that, in industry, when the Federal Mediation and Conciliation Service has been called in to help break impasses at the bargaining table, the resulting contract has been rejected by labor in 10–15 percent of the cases.[31] So far as we have been able to ascertain, all contracts involving faculty members at four-year institutions have been submitted for approval either to the membership of the bargain-

31. Bok and Dunlop, *Labor and the American Community*, p. 244.

ing unit or to the entire faculty. Bok and Dunlop's proposal that labor's negotiating teams be given greater authority to reach binding agreements at the table seems unlikely to find favor in faculty bargaining. A faculty decision to turn to bargaining does not mean that all members of a faculty are confident that the agreement reached at the table will be to their advantage. In some instances the first vote on an agreement has been negative and the faculty's negotiators have had to return to the table and seek further concessions from management.

The issue of who should be allowed to vote in a ratification election is serious and as yet unresolved. To the extent that the union or agency shop is now common in industry, the distinction between the employees who have joined or pay dues to the union and the entire work force included by law in the bargaining unit has largely disappeared in practice. But thus far this circumstance does not hold for faculty collective bargaining. We know of no four-year institution where the faculty is subject to an agency shop agreement. Certainly none has a union shop. The bargaining agent typically enrolls as members something less than all members of a faculty. Indeed, if payment of dues is regarded as the test of agency membership, at many of the institutions where collective bargaining is taking place, less than half of the members of the faculty are actively associated with the labor organization. This being true, it does make a difference whether a contract is submitted for approval to an entire faculty or to the more restricted membership of the labor organization.

At the small group of four-year colleges and universities where contracts are now in effect, the bargaining agent has sometimes found it politically desirable to seek ratification of the contract by all employees in the bargaining unit. Thus, at Central Michigan University the NEA bargaining agent voluntarily submitted the contracts negotiated in 1970 and 1971 to the entire faculty. The local AAUP chapter followed the same policy at Rutgers and Oakland, as did the AFT local at Southeastern Massachusetts University. But at such institutions as CUNY, SUNY, Boston State College, and the Long Island University Brooklyn Center, the contracts were submitted for approval only to those employees—faculty members and nonteaching professionals alike—who were dues-paying members of the bargaining agent. Where the bargaining agent is unsure of its strength within the faculty, or is faced with the threat of a challenge by another labor organization at an early date, it is likely to seek the support and approbation of the entire faculty by allowing everyone to vote in a ratification election. But where it is encountering financial difficulties, the bargaining agent is likely to restrict the voting to union members as a means of bringing pressure on other persons in the unit to join the labor organization and begin paying dues.

The great majority of the contracts that have emerged from the bargaining table have been readily ratified.[32] There are some exceptions. At Central Michigan University, the contract that emerged from the second round of negotiations was at first rejected by the faculty by a narrow margin. The negotiators then returned to the table and made one or two changes, the most important of which provided that the salary adjustment scheduled for the third year of the contract period would be subject to reexamination, at the request of either party, if the consumer price index changed by 15 percent or more between 1971 and 1973. This modification seemed to satisfy the faculty, and the contract was then ratified by a substantial majority.

At Boston State College, negotiations proved unusually difficult and protracted following the certification, in November 1969, of AFT as the bargaining agent. The faculty in May 1971 rejected the first contract that emerged from the table after more than a year of negotiations. The institution, however, was passing through a troubled period; a new president was about to come on the job, and there was some feeling that further negotiations were appropriate. Moreover, since Massachusetts law excluded the salary issue from the bargaining process, faculty members were able to vote to reject an unsatisfactory contract without affecting their salary increase prospects one way or the other. In this instance, a fresh start was made at the bargaining table and a quite different agreement was approved nearly a year later, in March 1972.

Faculties and governing boards are still in the early stages of encountering and coping with the dynamics of bargaining table negotiations. In most instances the two adversaries have worked their way to

32. Ratification elections are conducted by the bargaining agent rather than by the public labor board. Therefore, among other things, a public record of the outcome is not necessarily made. There is no requirement that the voting be by secret ballot, and in theory, at least, the contract can be approved by a show of hands at an open meeting. We have not been able to make a systematic survey of the methods used in faculty contract voting or the margins by which they have been approved.

some kind of satisfactory agreement the first time around, albeit often in ways which suggest that the amateur approach has enabled the negotiators to avoid pitfalls that professionals have learned to be wary of. The serious difficulty encountered at CUNY in negotiating a second-round contract does not mean that the bargaining process at other colleges and universities will necessarily become more complex, contentious, and professional as time goes by. But there is more reason than not for faculties and governing boards to tell themselves that reaching agreements at the table will become harder, not easier, as the full impact of the reality of collective bargaining—both in law and in practice—is felt in higher education.[33]

33. The dynamics of the bargaining process at the table in higher education are thus far inadequately reported, either through published accounts of the process or through data obtained from interviews and questionnaires. An important exception to the paucity of material is Ray A. Howe, "The Bloody Business of Bargaining," 48 *College and University Business* (March 1970), reprinted in *Collective Bargaining on Campus II: What To Do When the Petition Is Filed*, pp. 7–11. Mr. Howe has had considerable experience as a negotiator in collective bargaining at the community college level, having represented at one time or another both management and labor. He is currently director of labor relations for Henry Ford Community College and the Dearborn (Michigan) Public Schools.

CHAPTER SEVEN

Administering the Contract:
Consultation and Conflict

THE CONTRACTS THUS FAR NEGOTIATED AT FOUR-YEAR COLLEGES AND universities are short, considering the range and complexity of issues that are troubling faculties, administrators, and governing boards today. Even at the two great multicampus universities, State University of New York and City University of New York, the first contracts were relatively brief, uncomplicated documents.[1] Each reflects in some significant degree the needs of a situation and a way of dealing with those needs. It is too soon to try to classify or generalize, and there are no model contracts, either for types of institutions or for different bargaining agents.[2]

Two reasons for the brevity of the contracts are readily identified. The first bears out the experience of collective bargaining in industry. In negotiating the early contracts, the bargaining teams are frequently unable to get beyond the most pressing issues. Time and the margin for maneuverability and compromise get used up in reaching agreement on basic matters and specific issues that have been particularly troublesome.

The second reason is more nebulous and less pervasive in its influence. The negotiating teams sometimes share a belief or expectation that, in higher education, management and labor can continue to deal

1. At CUNY, the contract with the Legislative Conference contains thirty-five articles on forty small pages of large type; the contract with AFT has thirty articles covering twenty-six pages. The SUNY contract is longer—forty-nine articles, thirty-nine pages. There is as yet no norm for detail and length of a faculty contract, but at CUNY and SUNY the contracts are shorter than might be expected from the size and complexity of the institutions and the number and diversity of the bargaining unit employees.

2. The AFT contracts at Boston State College, Southeastern Massachusetts University, and the Brooklyn Center of Long Island University differ in significant ways, as do the AAUP contracts at St. John's University, Rutgers University, and Oakland University, and the NEA contracts at the State University of New York, Monmouth College, and Central Michigan University.

with many of their usual problems outside the scope of the contract, either through existing mechanisms of institutional governance or on an ad hoc basis. An outstanding instance is the Rutgers experience. There the contracts have been exceedingly brief, for the parties have agreed to engage in continuous problem solving as their preferred *modus vivendi*. The claim is made that this approach is working well and that the substantive results of such problem solving are implemented as university policy rather than through language in the labor-management agreement.

This combination approach to collective bargaining is an attractive one in the university setting. But it may not adequately recognize that in collective bargaining under law *everything* pertaining to wages, hours, and conditions of employment is sooner or later negotiable, as mandatory bargaining subjects, depending on the inclination of the two adversaries and the force of circumstances. Both parties can, of course, voluntarily refrain from bargaining on mandatory subjects. As at Rutgers, this joint position can be sustained over a period of time. It is probable, however, that at most institutions successive contracts will grow longer and more complex. As both parties discover that the reality of collective bargaining requires a good deal of "going by the book" in carrying on the institution's business, there will be strong pressures to pin things down, "to spell out the rules," more carefully each time the contract is renegotiated.

A tendency toward increasing complexity in successive contracts will be encouraged, among other things, by the grievance-arbitration method of resolving disputed issues involving specific persons and situations. Both parties to a contract often discover that the grievance case load is heavy, costly in time and money, and of a nature to exacerbate working relations between the faculty and the administration and governing board. Under these circumstances, one or both parties may want to write the "case law"—created through rulings in individual grievance-arbitration proceedings—into subsequent contracts, or to change it where there is dissatisfaction with it. We were told by administrators at CUNY that if the first contract had thirty-five articles, the second was likely to have three hundred fifty articles. This prediction undoubtedly reflected some despair and exaggeration, but nothing that we learned from the Legislative Conference's spokesmen suggested that they disagreed with the outlook.

As this book goes to press in February 1973, the second three-year faculty contract at Southeastern Massachusetts University has been made available to us. Time and circumstances have not permitted us to examine the new contract with care or to make appropriate references to it throughout the book. It can be noted, however, that it is considerably more detailed than was the first contract. Institutional governance receives increased attention, particularly at the level of the organization and operation of departments. Policy statements with respect to initial faculty appointments, promotions to higher ranks, the awarding of tenure, and the granting of salary increases are spelled out with care and at some length. A new faculty salary schedule is established, with rank and grade levels stated at substantially higher figures than those in the first contract. The range for full professors in the new contract, for example, runs from $23,023 to $30,516, whereas in the first contract the range was $12,079 to $21,000. The large increases that would have to be made to individual faculty members to bring them to appropriate levels in the new salary schedule will necessarily be dependent on adequate funding of the university by the state legislature. It is probable that the schedule can be fully implemented only over a period of several years.

The new contract appears to be a notable achievement and suggests that collective bargaining between the faculty and the governing board at Southeastern Massachusetts is working well. For one thing, it was negotiated, approved by both the faculty and the board, and put into operation some five months before the expiration of the first contract. This is in contrast with the situation at CUNY where, five months after the expiration of the first contracts, an impasse at the bargaining table still stood in the way of agreement on a second contract.

The Provisions of a Faculty Contract

Although the twelve to fifteen faculty contracts now in effect at senior institutions differ substantially in their details, they share a pattern of sorts. The fundamental working relationship between the institution and the bargaining agent is described or specified. Certain understandings of the university's purposes and principles, such as its educational goals and standards or its adherence to the "1940 Statement of Principles of Academic Freedom and Tenure" and the 1966

"Statement on the Government of Colleges and Universities,"[3] are acknowledged in general terms or are spelled out. The exclusive status of the bargaining agent as the employees' labor organization in all dealings with management is recognized. An economic package dealing with wages and fringe benefits is agreed upon, and other "conditions of employment" are specified. A grievance-arbitration system for the handling of individual worker complaints is established. Commitments are made by labor not to strike and by management to refrain from the lockout.

Compensation

Faculty demands for improved compensation and working conditions usually provoke the most aggressive and difficult bargaining at the table. The need for the bargaining agent to demonstrate to its members that it has "brought home the bacon" is no less acute in higher education than industry. Nonetheless, the economic package provisions of faculty contracts vary greatly. Some contracts simply provide for an overall percentage increase in faculty salaries each year during the life of the agreement. Thus, the salary provision in the SUNY contract is both modest and simple: a straight 6 percent increase for all "incumbents of positions in the professional service of the university" for 1971–72, with a stipulation that the bargaining agent (the Senate Professional Association) has the right to reopen negotiations with respect to salary increases for the second and third years of the contract. In a brief oblique reference to merit increases in salary, the contract reserves to "the university" the discretion to grant "further upward salary adjustments to individual employees." Nothing is said about who exercises this discretion or what standards are to be applied. The SUNY contract stipulates that any provision requiring legislative implementation or additional funds shall not take effect until "the appropriate legislative body has given approval." (The two CUNY contracts contain identical stipulations.)

3. In 1940, following a series of joint conferences begun in 1934, representatives of the American Association of University Professors and of the Association of American Colleges agreed upon a restatement of principles set forth in the 1925 Conference Statement on Academic Freedom and Tenure. This restatement is known to the profession as the "1940 Statement of Principles on Academic Freedom and Tenure." The 1966 "Statement on Government of Colleges and Universities" was jointly formulated by the American Association of University Professors, the American Council on Education, and the Association of Governing Boards of Universities and Colleges. See *AAUP Policy Documents and Reports*, 1971 ed., pp. 1, 33.

The CUNY contract with the Legislative Conference, on the other hand, though brief overall, contains ten pages of closely detailed salary schedules for the different types of institutions within the university, for the several faculty ranks and professional grades, and for each of the three years of the contractual period. Although no provision is made for merit increases of any kind, the across-the-board increases are substantial. The CUNY contract, in a unique provision, also establishes a table by which the Board of Higher Education agrees to "increase the percentages in academic rank" over the three-year period, with full professors, for example, rising from 19 percent in September 1969 to 30 percent by January 1972, and instructors falling from 24 percent to 10 percent in the same period. This provision was viewed by the Legislative Conference as one of its principal gains in the first contract at CUNY. But its implementation has been the subject of much controversy. The CUNY administration asserts that what was promised was an increase in budgeted positions in the upper ranks, not persons holding these positions. It claims that the number of faculty members qualifying each year for promotion to higher rank has not been sufficient to meet the percentanges set in the contract. Although the contract is silent on the matter of the number of faculty members who might be granted tenure each year, there has been sharp conflict between the CUNY administration and the Legislative Conference over this issue. The administration has announced what it calls "tenure guidelines." These have been bitterly attacked by the Legislative Conference as "tenure quotas," unfairly and improperly established without consulting the conference.

An unusually complex method of measuring faculty salary increases is found in the Oakland University contract. Careful reading of the contract appears to show that each faculty member's salary for 1971–72 was arrived at by multiplying his "regular annual salary" successively by three factors: "an adjustment factor of 1.0419"; a "department-school factor" ranging from a low of 1.000 (speech and library) to a high of 1.180 (School of Economics and Management); and a "merit factor" ranging from 1.000 to 1.454. The formula has been described by one faculty member as "aimed to raise everyone's salary, while those below the median received an even greater boost."[4]

---

4. Jesse R. Pitts, "Strike at Oakland University," *Change*, February 1972, p. 18. An Oakland administrator told us that the formula for determining salary increases calls for a veritable computerized mixing of "longevity, market value, merit, experience, and cost of living."

The contract at Boston State College is entirely silent on the issues of faculty salaries, for the Massachusetts public employees bargaining statute does not authorize bargaining with respect to wages and salaries. The contract does contain an article on "Faculty Fringe Benefits," but it does little more than commit the Trustees of the State Colleges to provide members of the bargaining unit with all of the benefits authorized by state laws.

Work Loads and the Productivity Issue

The statutory language authorizing bargaining about "hours" translates in faculty contracts into "work load" provisions. In the CUNY contract with the Legislative Conference this article is brief and broadly worded. It is worth quoting in its entirety:

> Employees on the teaching staff of the City University of New York shall not be required to teach an excessive number of contact hours, assume an excessive student load, or be assigned to an unreasonable schedule, it being recognized by the parties that the teaching staff has the obligation among others to be available to students, to assume normal committee assignments, and to engage in research and community service.

The AFT contract covering lecturers and teaching assistants contains an identical provision except that the "obligation . . . to engage in research" is omitted. The similar wording of the two contracts indicates that management either suggested much of the language at the beginning of the bargaining with the two unions or was successful in insisting that the two contracts be largely uniform in the final versions.

When administrators at CUNY were questioned about this provision, they revealed uncertainty of mind about it. They defended the provision as allowing great flexibility in fixing faculty work loads in the face of the sharply increased burdens placed on the university under its open admissions program. But they agreed that it gave them a weak basis for negotiating increased teaching loads year by year. It is significant that only one of the 122 grievances that reached the chancellor's office during the first two years of the contract raised a work load issue. This fact suggests either that the faculty has had much the best of work load arrangements under the contract, or that policy and practice have been set in this respect outside the reach of the contract and that individual dissatisfaction with work loads has been resolved by other means than resort to the collective bargaining grievance process.

The SUNY contract contains no language dealing with the work loads of any of the several classes of employees in the bargaining unit. At Southeastern Massachusetts University, a detailed "Faculty Work Load" schedule is prescribed: a teaching load of up to twelve hours a semester is set, faculty members are required to be available during an academic year running from September 1 to June 30, and provision is made for the assignment and scheduling of courses and for non-teaching faculty responsibilities. Our interviews at SMU suggest that these provisions set outer limits only and have had minimal effect in improving the working conditions of the faculty.

The AAUP contracts at St. John's, Rutgers, and Oakland Universities differ greatly in the matter of faculty work loads. The St. John's contract is detailed. It sets a "maximum teaching load" of "twelve semester hours of credit or its equivalent" at the undergraduate level, nine hours at the graduate level, and fifteen hours in the School of General Studies. "By mutual agreement" these limits can be exceeded, but the teacher is to receive extra compensation. Other clauses fix a "normal office-hour responsibility" (two hours per week for most faculty members), prescribe a system for the "assignment of courses," limit the number of preparations for different courses to three per teacher (exceptions permitted), and set a "standard work week for professional librarians" of five days. The contract also creates a Faculty Responsibilities Committee to conduct a study and make recommendations to the president concerning "other professional responsibilities" of faculty members. The Rutgers contract is entirely silent on the faculty work load issue. The Oakland contract deals with it only in oblique fashion: nothing is said about teaching loads, but the academic calendar for 1971–72 is prescribed, a student-faculty ratio of 21.4:1 is set, and it is agreed that the professional librarians covered by the contract will continue to work on a twelve-month schedule "under established procedures," with one month of vacation.

These faculty contracts suggest that at most institutions the work load issue has not led to a serious confrontation between management and labor in the first round of negotiations. There is little evidence that any hard bargaining has occurred at the table on this issue. The specific work load requirements or limitations in the contracts at such institutions as Southeastern Massachusetts University and St. John's University are said not to depart significantly from precontract practices. However, as time goes by, the work load issue will probably become a much more troublesome one at the bargaining table. In industrial bargaining, labor traditionally hopes to make gains in the "hours" as well as the "wages" category. "Shorter hours and more pay" sums up a good part of what labor seeks in each new round of bargaining. There are strong indications that in higher education the "hours" issue may become one where management will expect to make the gains in a trade-off for higher salaries. With or without collective bargaining, trustees and administrators are already contending that improvements in compensation will have to be balanced by increased productivity—by heavier teaching loads in terms of hours and courses, larger classes, more out-of-class student counseling, and perhaps longer school years.

The first reaction of members of the academic profession has been to resist this line of reasoning and to contend that improvements in productivity in higher education are not properly measured by such means as heavier course and student loads for individual teachers.[5] The issue is certain to remain troublesome throughout the decade and to provoke a series of confrontations between faculties and governing boards and administrators at many institutions. It will undoubtedly strain the relationship at the bargaining table at those institutions where the balance between compensation and work loads is being worked out through collective bargaining. On the other hand, bargaining could be the means by which institutions succeed in working their way through an otherwise virtually hopeless problem, for it does enable the representatives of faculty and trustees and administrators to sit down at the table and analyze together accurate data concerning such interrelated matters as the size of the student body, the size of the faculty, institutional income, faculty compensation, and teaching loads.

5. The report of Committee Z on the Economic Status of the Profession submitted at the 1971 annual meeting of AAUP argues that increasing class sizes and course loads "would surely reflect a decline in the quality of education offered, other things being equal." And it argues that "the real (but hidden) increase in productivity of college professors is the increased productivity of the students they train, not the visible increase in numbers of students met" ("At the Brink," 57 *AAUP Bulletin* [June 1971], 229).

This sharing of information, which is an integral aspect of collective bargaining, may make it easier for faculties, trustees, and administrators to share also the task of devising hard answers to a hard problem than will be possible under other systems of institutional governance.

Other Conditions of Employment

The statutory authorization to bargain over "other conditions of employment" has resulted in contract provisions ranging all the way from better parking facilities for the faculty, snow tires on college cars during the winter months, keys for faculty offices, and time off for jury duty, to improvements in staff housing, office space, secretarial assistance, and research opportunities and facilities. Many of the first faculty contracts deal at some length with the matter of faculty leaves. Thus, the SUNY contract, while giving the salary issue only a few sentences, contains many pages setting forth policy on vacation leaves, sick leaves, maternity leaves, disability leaves, sabbatical leaves, and holidays. Much of the detail on leave policy in the SUNY contract reflects the demands of the several thousand nonteaching professional employees in the bargaining unit (to whom NEA felt strongly obligated) for concessions in an area of great importance to them.

Management and Faculty Rights Clauses

In most instances faculty contracts contain clauses reserving to management and the faculty all existing rights and authority not covered or affected by the express language of the contract. A typical management rights clause is the following in the Boston State contract:

> All management rights, and functions, except those that are clearly and expressly abridged by this Agreement, shall remain vested exclusively in the Board of Trustees. Nothing contained in this agreement shall be deemed or construed to impair or limit the powers and duties of the Board under the laws of the Commonwealth.

A quite different clause in the Oakland contract seems intended to produce the same result.

> Oakland has the legal responsibility and, subject to the terms of this Agreement, the right to manage its operations, including but not limited to the right to (a) hire, assign, promote, demote, schedule, discipline, and discharge faculty members; (b) determine and schedule the aca-

demic year; (c) locate or relocate its physical facilities and equipment; (d) control all its property.[6]

Clauses reserving rights to the faculty are somewhat more ambiguously worded. Thus, the St. John's contract provides that:

> The presently constituted agencies within the University (e.g., the University Senate, faculty councils, departmental personnel and budget committees, etc.) or any other or similar body composed in whole or in part of the faculty, shall continue to function at the University provided that the actions thereof may not directly or indirectly repeal, rescind or otherwise modify the terms and conditions of this Agreement.

Neither of the CUNY contracts contains a typical management rights clause. Both, however, contain language that may be viewed as protecting existing faculty rights not covered by the contracts, as they have been recognized by the Board of Higher Education in the university's bylaws:

> Nothing contained in this Agreement shall be construed to diminish the rights granted under the Bylaws of the Board to the entities and bodies within the internal structure of CUNY so long as such rights are not in conflict with this Agreement. If provisions of this Agreement require changes in the Bylaws of the Board, such changes will be effected.

Management rights clauses in faculty contracts are a carry-over from collective bargaining in industry, where management has traditionally desired to underscore the fact that it retains full authority over the operation of a business with respect to all policy issues not touched on in the contract. Faculty rights clauses have no counterparts in industrial contracts, for in industry labor does not come to the bargaining table already in possession of the same large measures of authority for

---

6. In Article I of the agreement, entitled "Definitions," "Oakland" is stated to mean "the Board of Trustees of Oakland University, Rochester, Michigan, a state institution chartered by the State of Michigan, and the administrative agents of said Board." Both in legal terms and for purposes of collective bargaining, this is correct. But it is nonetheless surprising that AAUP as the bargaining agent should so readily agree, even for purposes of a definition, that the governing board and its administrative agents *are* the university. In entering the business of collective bargaining, AAUP may be expected to try to have the best of both worlds. Thus, to protect the old notion that professors "are the university," AAUP might insist that the "employer" or "management" in a collective bargaining contract be defined as "the governing board." But it is probable that AAUP and professors will find it necessary, as they turn to collective bargaining, to abandon the contention that the faculty *is* the university.

the operation of the enterprise that many faculties have. In any event, the theory behind all of these reserved rights clauses is that, while all issues of wages, hours, and conditions of employment are negotiable, not everything has in fact been negotiated. What, for one reason or another, has not been negotiated remains outside the agreement and thus is subject to existing policies and to the agencies that have authority to change those policies. This is the theory; in practice, as at CUNY, controversy can develop over the extent to which policies, not covered by contracts, can be changed through the traditional authority structure, particularly where there is unilateral action by trustees, administrators, or faculty agencies.

Institutional Governance

Reserved rights clauses serve to underscore the problem inherent in faculty collective bargaining of whether a line should or can be drawn between conditions of employment and matters of institutional governance and educational policy. It might be supposed that the former is the proper subject of a collective bargaining contract and the latter of institutional bylaws and regulations and faculty policies and practices. As already noted, collective bargaining in industry has not generally encompassed worker participation in policy making on business issues. Management retains control over the operation of the business itself, in particular the designing, manufacturing, pricing, and marketing of the product or service. It has been said that "the American worker has given very little evidence that he cares at all about participating in the running of the business that gives him his livelihood."[7] In higher education, the bargaining process must be superimposed on an existing arrangement under which the faculty often already has much to say about "the product." Through such mechanisms of governance as the department, the faculty educational policy committee, other standing committees, and the faculty senate, professors are usually already exercising large measures of control over institutional policies with respect to the substance of the curriculum, degree requirements, teaching methods, the admission of students, the reward-penalty system by which student academic performance is measured, and faculty personnel determinations.

7. Derek C. Bok and John T. Dunlop, *Labor and the American Community*, p. 345.

The relationship between the two contracts at CUNY and the university's bylaws illustrates a problem that is likely to pose difficulties for many institutions where faculty bargaining takes shape. The CUNY bylaws—more properly the "Bylaws of the Board of Higher Education of the City of New York"—are a voluminous, complex collection of regulations dealing with the organization and work of the board itself, the organization and duties of the faculty, and the governance system of the university and its separate colleges, with particular emphasis on the faculty departments. The bylaws deal with many matters that might under law be dealt with at the bargaining table and become part of the contractual agreement. Accordingly, much is left out of the CUNY contracts that might be there. The two contracts negotiated in 1969 had almost nothing to say about the university's governance system, which is either described in the bylaws or is continuing to take shape through decisions arrived at by administrators and faculty members under the supervision of the university's governing board. As has already been seen, both contracts contained provisions to the effect that all rights and arrangements under the bylaws which "are not in conflict with this Agreement" remained operative.

The attempt to establish a workable relationship between the bylaws and the two contracts left unresolved a large number of matters that promptly became subjects of controversy at CUNY between the bargaining agents and the university administrators and trustees. For example, policies with respect to the appointment and removal of department chairmen and the granting of tenure to faculty members were not covered by the contracts. They were either determined by the bylaws or established by university officers and agencies exercising authority under the bylaws. But such issues are typically of concern to a faculty bargaining agent and at other institutions often become part of the agreements reached at the bargaining table. At CUNY the Legislative Conference argued that its contract with the Board of Higher Education did provide, both expressly and by implication, that important changes in policy with respect to such matters would not be made unilaterally by the governing board or administration without consultation (and some measure of agreement) with the officers of the conference. The conference stirred up enough controversy to lead the chancellor and the Board of Higher Education to back away from certain changes in policy that they deemed necessary. At best, an uneasy peace was maintained between the conference and the governing board and administration which was certain to be broken at the bargaining table when the second contract was negotiated.

Faculty governing agencies at CUNY are still evolving. The growth of the university, as a collection of scattered and diverse colleges, has outstripped the ability of the faculties of the separate colleges or of the entire university to establish strong faculty governing mechanisms above the level of the departments. This CUNY experience suggests that when an institution lacks an adequate system of governance, or there is dissatisfaction with the way the internal machinery is operating, or a power struggle begins to take shape between regular faculty agencies of governance and the labor organization or the new agencies it spawns, bargaining will become more complex and intensive as time goes by. As a result, contracts will become increasingly concerned with issues in institutional governance.

At institutions where a governance system is nonexistent or unsatisfactory, particularly with respect to faculty participation, or where there are no bylaws, the initial round of collective bargaining may be expected to provide for the establishment of agencies and processes of governance. The contracts at Southeastern Massachusetts University and Boston State College are examples. The former contract provides for the creation of several new faculty agencies, such as a series of "Academic Councils" to formulate recommendations concerning faculty tenure appointments for submission to the deans of the several colleges. It spells out the procedures to be employed by these councils but leaves the fixing of standards for substantive determinations to them. The contract also creates an Academic Review Committee "to review changes in academic programs which directly affect wages, hours, and conditions of employment" under the contract. This committee is directed to submit recommendations to the parties to the contract for their consideration.

The Boston State College contract, in a long section entitled "Participation in Decision Making," creates a whole new system of institutional government. A complex interlocking arrangement of committees at the departmental, divisional, and "campus-wide" levels is provided for "to insure substantial participation of all faculty in the formulation of decisions affecting the conditions of their employment and related professional interests as provided in this Agreement." Moreover, provision is made for student membership on certain of these committees and also for the creation of student committees on faculty evaluation, both at the departmental and campus levels, which would be advisory to a parallel series of faculty committees on evaluation. The contract provides that before this arrangement can take effect the students of Boston State College must vote affirmatively in a referendum to "participate in the governance of the College as set forth in this contract." Only 305 students out of a student body of 5,500 took part in the election, and the vote was 217 to 88 to participate in the new governance system. This contract may well be the only one thus far at a four-year institution that expressly recognizes a student role in the administration of the agreement reached by management and labor at the bargaining table.

Where the governance system is prescribed in the contract, changes can only be made when a new contract is being negotiated or through invoking some kind of amendment procedure. This arrangement can make for less flexibility than exists where the faculty and the governing board are free to change the system at any time in the light of experience or new needs. Similarly, the bargaining agent may insist on language in the contract giving it some measure of control over the selection of personnel and the work of campus agencies, both of which should properly be free from any influence external to the institution in its formal or collegial sense. Thus, at both Southeastern Massachusetts and Boston State the AFT local is granted some control over the selection of the persons serving on faculty committees. It is reported in each instance to have sought complete control, arguing that this authority would be consistent with standard labor relations practice in industry.

Local Issues: Retrenchment Policy

Faculty contracts always in some measure reflect local conditions and problems and the differing ways in which trustees, administrators, and faculty members react to them. For example, the SUNY contract contains a section, entitled "Retrenchment," that in effect establishes a rigid seniority system if "termination of employment of incumbents of positions which are subject to retrenchment" becomes necessary. It requires that any terminations made necessary by a retrenchment program must be made "in the inverse order of original appointment" rather than on any selective basis the university might use to retain those faculty members deemed most satisfactory or useful.

The retrenchment section in the SUNY contract, with its rigid expression of seniority rights, probably reflects the approach that NEA and AFT will take to the problem of cutbacks in personnel and programs at institutions where either is the bargaining agent. The St. John's contract, where AAUP is the agent, also has a section, called "Reduction or Elimination of Programs," that provides for a slightly more flexible cutback program. It authorizes the administration to "abolish programs and reduce the size of the faculty in a particular program . . . because of bona fide financial exigency," provided "it consults with the faculty" and follows a series of guidelines set forth in the contract. These require that reductions must "first take place among adjunct faculty members, then superannuated faculty members, and then non-tenured faculty members in the department affected," although within each of these three categories the reductions "shall be on the basis of worth to the department and to the University." Only then may reductions be made among tenured faculty members, "on the basis of a combination of seniority and worth to the department and to the University." An elaborate mechanism is spelled out for the possible "retention" of a faculty member by reassignment to another unit within the university.

Retrenchment clauses are likely to appear in collective bargaining contracts on a more regular basis in view of the budgetary difficulties and staff reduction needs that many institutions will be facing in the next few years. Bargaining agents—including AAUP, if the St. John's contract is an indication—will argue for substantial implementation of the traditional labor union "seniority rule." But applying the rule may not be simple. On most compuses, nontenured faculty have become much more aggressive in identifying and defending their interests, and, as members of the bargaining unit and as dues-paying members of the bargaining agent, will quickly learn to exert pressure within the labor organization for a different stance at the bargaining table. Trustees and administrators are likely to argue for a flexible policy that will enable the institution to retain the services of its most useful faculty members, with minimal regard paid to seniority.

Retrenchment clauses may also bring institutions into conflict with the federal government under the affirmative action and compliance requirements of federal education grant programs specifying equal employment opportunities for women and minority groups. Since women and members of minorities are often "the last hired" at institutions that are pushing to improve their faculty profiles in these respects, contracts like those at SUNY and perhaps even St. John's will result in the automatic dismissal of (failure to reappoint) these persons if retrenchment becomes necessary. There is a pressing need in retrenchment situations to choose between a system that retains the "best qualified" people and one that retains those who have the most seniority (or who belong to the right minority or sex). A collective bargaining contract may impose one of these choices on an academic community without adequate examination of all the options.

COLLECTIVE BARGAINING: THE CONTINUING PROCESS

For a faculty to have negotiated a contract with the governing board of its institution may seem like the battle won, particularly if a pleasing salary increase has been gained. Negotiating a contract, although the task of a few persons working in private, is a dramatic business which, in traditional collective bargaining theory, involves a confrontation that tests the strength of position and bargaining ability of the two adversaries. All members of the governing board, the administration, and the faculty eagerly await the outcome of the negotiations; the attention of all is certain to be sharply focused on the contract that emerges from the sessions.

Collective bargaining is, of course, more than the negotiation of a contract: it is a continuing process. The contract establishes relationships that are thereafter ever present and must be implemented—administered—if the benefits and obligations it imposes are to be fully realized by both parties. In addition, the parties will encounter continuing business that supplements the contract or takes shape outside its scope.

A contract will be self-enforcing to the extent that its provisions are recognized and enforced by university administrators as routine duties. If, for example, the contract provides for across-the-board salary increases, the treasurer or personnel officer will have the purely ministerial task of preparing the payroll and issuing the proper salary checks to faculty members each month.

But a contract is never wholly self-enforcing. Doubts and disagreements are bound to arise concerning some of the clauses which, because of their nature, have to be applied on a selective basis to specific situations and individuals. If, for example, a contract provides for a merit component in salary increases and indicates the means and standards for granting them, some recipients will be disappointed with the amount and complain that the contract provisions were not followed in an even-handed way in their cases. Or again, pressing problems and needs are likely to arise concerning which the contract is either silent or ambiguous. Means must thus be available for enabling the parties to deal with these difficulties with some hope of preserving the harmonious relationship that collective bargaining is intended to foster. Otherwise, the good will and satisfaction that marked the signing of the contract can be readily dissipated during the contract period.

Collective bargaining in industry has witnessed the development of a variety of ways of administering a contract. In significant measure the industrial pattern has been taken over in higher education. But at many colleges and universities, collective bargaining has also been superimposed on existing patterns of running the institution—patterns that already involve the faculty, the administration, and the governing board in complex relationships and activities. Thus, administering a contract necessarily becomes an aspect of the daily routines, the ongoing life of the academic community, particularly when the contract expressly or by implication assigns the administration of certain of its provisions to existing officers and agencies. For example, a contract may spell out a sabbatical leave system and then transfer its administration to department chairmen, faculty committees, deans, the president, and the governing board in accordance with their usual ways of doing business, but also, of course, in such a way as to carry out the terms of the contract. On the other hand, the contract may require that other provisions be carried out through agencies or means established by or responsible to the bargaining agent. The Boston State College contract creates an "All Campus Committee" to coordinate the activities of three principal "campus-wide" committees (on curriculum, college development, and budget consultation) and a committee on governance review. This coordinating committee consists of nine faculty members, five students, and one administrator. The faculty members are appointed by the president of the Faculty Federation (the bargaining agent) with the approval of the federation's executive council. Thus, the personnel of this key faculty committee in the college's governance system is substantially determined by the bargaining agent.

CONTRACT ADMINISTRATION THROUGH CONSULTATION

Many of the contracts negotiated in higher education make formal provision for some kind of regular consultation between officers of the bargaining agent and administrators or trustees of the institution. Thus, the two CUNY contracts provide for consultations at both the university and college levels. Under each contract the chancellor "or his designee" is to meet twice each semester with representatives of the labor organization to discuss "legitimate and proper subjects of collective negotiations," as well as "other matters" that may be placed on the agenda at the chancellor's discretion. Similar provisions are made for "the President or Provost or his designee" at each CUNY college to confer regularly with representatives of each union.

The Southeastern Massachusetts University contract, "recognizing the importance of frequent communications in maintaining good relationships," provides for regular monthly meetings between the president and the officers of the bargaining agent, called the "Faculty Federation," and also between the deans of the several colleges within the university and the "local officers" of the federation. Issues pertaining to wages, hours, conditions of employment, as well as individual grievances, are expressly excluded from these discussions; instead, the meetings "shall be for the purpose of discussing and resolving mutual problems affecting the overall relationships between the parties." Agreements have been reached from time to time on specific matters concerning which the contract is silent, such as setting up the means by which faculty appointments, reappointments, promotions, and tenure grants will be made, and working out the criteria by which "merit money" salary increments will be determined. These agreements are then approved by the trustees, the administration, and the bargaining agent, as may be necessary.

At Rutgers, joint consultation on a continuing basis has been viewed as the very essence of collective bargaining. The formal contract is, as already indicated, exceedingly brief. Substantively, it does little more than provide for a salary increase and establish a grievance processing system. But the two parties have conferred from time to time and have reached agreement on a number of matters. Where a solution has been arrived at, it has either been implemented by means of a letter or memorandum of agreement between the parties, or been adopted through appropriate action by the faculty, the administration, and the

governing board. At its best, then, such continuing consultations between the administrative officers of an institution and the faculty
officers of a labor organization can help implement the shared authority
concept of university governance.

Another common means of consultation in collective bargaining
practice is the ad hoc or study committee established by agreement
between the institution and the bargaining agent to examine certain
issues or problems that could not be dealt with in the contract or that
have arisen since it was negotiated. At Central Michigan University,
through letters of agreement between the president and provost of the
university and the president and secretary of the labor organization,
called the "Faculty Association," such committees have been authorized to study "the teaching load policy of the university," the institution's salary policy "with respect to internal consistency, relationships
to comparable institutions, and approaches to equitable faculty compensation," the fringe benefit program of the university, and "opportunities for women faculty." These committees report to both the
university and the association. While it has not been possible to determine the exact outcome of each of these study projects at Central
Michigan, the ad hoc committee device provides a promising means by
which a variety of matters of mutual concern to the institution and the
faculty's labor organization can be kept under study during the contract term. The findings of such a study group may enable the two
parties to reach agreement on the matter in the next contract, or they
may permit an interim agreement to be put into effect under the existing contract. This means of making collective bargaining a continuing
consultative process may well prove more effective than the provisions
for regular meetings between administrators and bargaining agent
officers to discuss whatever matters either party may place on the
agenda. Apart from situations such as the one at Rutgers, where the
brief contract makes regular consultations a necessity as a means of
coping with inescapable problems, we have not encountered convinc-
ing testimony that regular meetings are being used by administrators
and bargaining agent officers as an effective problem-solving mechanism. There is no evidence that at CUNY, for example, the numerous
tensions and conflicts that arose between administrators and the Legislative Conference under the first contract were abated through the
prescribed regular meetings of the chancellor and the college presidents with LC representatives.

The device of continuing consultation between administrators and the faculty bargaining agents carries the danger that problem solving may take shape in such a way as to undermine the regular instruments and processes of governance. If a problem could have been solved just as readily, although perhaps differently, through existing means, the consultation approach may represent a successful attempt by the bargaining agent, and the faculty members identified with it, to wrest authority and responsibility away from such an agency as a faculty senate and the faculty members identified with it. There is reason to doubt whether such parallel or dual systems of faculty representation and authority can continue to survive at an institution over the long pull, even where the intentions of the leaders and members in both groups appear to be complementary and noncompetitive. The principal officer of the bargaining unit at one institution has summarized his opinion on this issue:

> The real question is, who is going to run the place? The issue is *power.* Can a faculty senate survive when another faculty organization has become the bargaining agent? I would like to see someone pull that off! When collective bargaining comes in, the faculty senate is finished! I repeat, finished!

ADMINISTRATION THROUGH GRIEVANCE PROCESSING

The contract states the standards—the rights and commitments agreed to by management and labor. Through grievance processing these standards are applied to specific situations and particular individuals. It is, of course, only one of the means by which contract provisions are carried out. At some institutions with faculty contracts, grievance processing is not yet a major aspect of contract administration. At other institutions, however, grievance processing has been so extensively utilized that it has been described to us as "the name of the game" in faculty collective bargaining.

Although the term "grievance" was largely unknown in higher education as recently as half a dozen years ago, many educational institutions are now using the word and devising systems of grievance processing even in the absence of formal collective bargaining between faculties and governing boards. To some extent this development is an extension (under a new name) of the older concept of "academic due process," although the latter has generally more narrowly described an obligation that the institution must meet when it takes an unfavorable action against a faculty member, such as dismissing or failing to reappoint him.

What exactly is a grievance? In standard collective bargaining practice, it is often understood to include any complaint by an employee or by the bargaining agent on behalf of itself or of one or several employees that the terms of the contract have been violated. Almost all faculty contracts make provision for a grievance system of resolving disputes, and most faculty contracts define a grievance narrowly. The definition in the Central Michigan contract (NEA) is terse:

> A grievance is an alleged violation of this agreement.

Some contracts are more broadly worded to suggest that the grievance procedure is available as a means of settling miscellaneous disagreements that may arise between a worker and his employer, whether a grievance alleges specific violation of language in the contract or not. Thus, the contract at Oakland University (AAUP) seems to provide that any "problem" can become the basis of a grievance:

> any grievance . . . any faculty member may have in relation to his employment at Oakland arising from a problem, or from an application or interpretation of this Agreement, will be adjusted as stated in this Article.[8]

In taking over the patterns of collective bargaining from private industry, colleges and universities have committed themselves to an elaborate system of resolving the grievances of individual workers that can include as many as five or six "steps" at successively higher levels. In general these steps encompass three different kinds of effort, starting with informal discussion and attempt at settlement between the worker and his immediate supervisor within the enterprise and culminating in binding arbitration by an outside professional expert.

The first level of negotiation is informal and is designed to settle routine complaints that are likely to be everyday occurrences but can quickly be disruptive to the business unless they are dealt with promptly and effectively. In industry, the worker first takes his complaint to the lowest level of managerial authority, the first-line super-

---

8. This wording may be more a matter of careless drafting than a deliberate intention by the parties to broaden the scope of the grievance process at Oakland. Careless drafting of such a clause in a contract can later prove troublesome, particularly in the processing of grievances on campus and in third-party arbitration. We have not ascertained Oakland's experience under this grievance clause.

visor, commonly a foreman. A foreman is a salaried worker, but, as a supervisor, he is an agent of management and thus ineligible for membership in the bargaining unit. In turning to the foreman, the complainant worker may seek the assistance of the man at the lowest level of union authority, the union steward. The steward, too, is usually a salaried employee with regular work to perform. Under the collective bargaining contract, the employer recognizes that the steward represents the union in helping other workers obtain satisfactory adjustment of complaints through negotiations with the foreman. In a large or complex business, a necessary expectation is that the vast majority of all complaints will be adjusted at this level; otherwise, both management and labor would be overwhelmed with the task of dealing with complaints in more formal and elaborate ways.

This expectation is carried over into higher education in the language of many faculty contracts. In both contracts at CUNY, the Board of Higher Education and the Legislative Conference or the AFT agree "to use their best efforts to encourage the informal and prompt settlement of complaints and grievances." The Central Michigan contract states, "Faculty members are encouraged to work out claimed violations of this agreement within their department or through their department chairmen without resort to the informal or formal grievance procedure wherever possible."

The department chairman and the dean are the persons to whom faculty members have in the past typically turned with their complaints. The former have always been heavily relied on to resolve routine difficulties. But under collective bargaining, is the chairman a foreman or a steward? Both administrators and faculty members are apt to continue to regard chairmen as their agents. Administrators who have to live with a collective bargaining contract count on the chairman, as the first-line supervisor, to see that the provisions are adhered to at the department level and that, thereby, only a minimum number of situations get out of hand and cause trouble up the line. The chairman must observe all contract provisions that assure faculty members certain rights or procedures in, among other things, personnel decisions, the assignment of courses and class schedules, the fixing of work loads, and the granting of sabbatical leaves. He can go to the dean for instructions and counsel, but then he must try to satisfy his sometimes unreasonable colleagues by protecting their rights under the contract without conceding more than the contract allows.

But faculty members have traditionally viewed the department chairman as their agent—their shop steward. They have chosen him, under good academic practice, to serve their interests in managing the most important unit in the institution, the department. He is to negotiate for them, individually and collectively, with all other levels of institutional authority—the dean, the provost, other departments, and even the faculty at large.

In hard fact, the chairman is both foreman and steward. This dual role explains why, in determining composition of faculty bargaining units, the status of department chairmen has caused so much difficulty to faculties, governing boards, labor organizations, and labor relations boards. It also suggests that the role of the chairman may become more difficult and thankless under collective bargaining.

The second effort to settle grievances takes place in an internal series of hearings, in ascending steps, that may be quite formal. At some institutions all such hearings are held before administrative officers. Thus, the Southeastern Massachusetts contract provides for four levels of opportunity to settle a grievance beyond the informal departmental effort. They are, in order: the dean of the respective college, the dean of the university faculty, the president, and the board of trustees. The two CUNY contracts specify only two levels of formal institutional grievance processing above the department level. The hearings are conducted by the college president and the university chancellor (or their designees). Similar provisions for a successive series of hearings before administrative officers and sometimes the governing board are found in the contracts at SUNY (Senate Professional Association-NEA), St. John's University (Faculty Association-AAUP), and Boston State College (AFT).

At other institutions, a quite different model for processing grievances is used: the grievance committee is composed of an equal number of representatives of the institution and the labor organization. At both Rutgers and Oakland Universities this agency is known as the "University Appeals Committee" and is made up of six persons. At Oakland, when this committee can reach an agreement, "the adjustment is final and binding upon all parties." At Rutgers, the decision "shall be considered advisory to the President and to the Board of Governors." At Central Michigan the arrangement is somewhat more complex. The agency is the University Conference on Contract Grievances and comprises two representatives each of the university and the bargaining agent. If these four persons cannot reach an agreement, they are authorized to choose "a mutually acceptable person from the academic community-at-large" who is then empowered "to render his written decision and opinion." The contract is not entirely clear whether this decision is binding on both parties.[9]

A tentative version of the contract at Boston State College provided for a joint management-labor committee to hear grievance cases. However, in the final contract, the more usual step system was adopted, providing for a succession of administrators and ultimately the board of trustees to hear and decide grievances. We were told that the change was made at the insistence of the AFT bargaining team, which argued that in industry employees are not expected to pass judgment on their fellow worker's grievances. A shop steward, for example, negotiates with the shop foreman for a satisfactory settlement of a worker's complaint, but he does not serve as half of a two-man tribunal that judges the complaint. AFT at Boston State did, however, argue aggressively at the table for a third-party binding arbitration provision in the contract. Refusal by the governing board to agree to such a provision almost resulted in an impasse on the negotiations.

Under most contracts, if an individual faculty member or a group of faculty members has a complaint that qualifies as a "grievance" within the contract definition, and if the complainant is not satisfied with the outcome of the informal-level effort to settle the matter, then he has the right to carry the complaint to the grievance process level. Most contracts also allow the bargaining agent to initiate a grievance proceeding, which enables the agent to act for a group of faculty members (or an entire faculty) where the disputed issue is broader than the interests of a single individual. Contracts also generally allow the bargaining agent to be present at a grievance hearing held at the request of an individual teacher (who may not even be a member of the labor organization) and to offer objection if the settlement appears to be inconsistent with the terms of the contract.

9. The grievance procedure at Central Michigan is further complicated by an alternative proceeding under university regulations. The grievance of a faculty member can be considered and adjusted by the University Grievance Review Committee (a standing committee of the university senate). The second contract, negotiated in 1971, seems to provide for a Formal Hearing Committee that can decide a grievance regarding nonreappointment, the granting of tenure, or a promotion in rank, if a Committee on Contract Grievances (an agency of the labor organization) has examined the grievance and decided it deserves consideration at a higher level. An outsider cannot readily understand these intricate mechanisms for processing grievances; they may be part of a power struggle between the senate and the faculty association.

An occasional contract gives the bargaining agent a larger measure of authority to supervise or monitor the use of the grievance system at an institution. At Central Michigan, a faculty member may not carry a grievance beyond the level of an informal conference in the Office of the Provost without the approval of the bargaining agent's Committee for Contract Grievances. In giving such approval, the committee is directed to determine whether (*a*) the grievance arises out of a violation of the contract, (*b*) the bargaining agent wishes "as a matter of policy" to pursue the grievance to the formal stages provided for in the contract, and (*c*) "there may be other ways to resolve the grievance."

The Arbitration of Faculty Grievances

The third kind of effort to adjust the complaints of workers is referral of the dispute to a third party, external to the institution, for a finding that will be binding on both parties. This final effort is known as "arbitration." In faculty bargaining contracts the process provided for comes more or less intact from industrial bargaining, where it has long been practiced. The arbitrator is usually an experienced person, either provided under the contract by the American Arbitration Association, or selected from a panel of professional arbitrators agreed upon by the parties to the contract.

The faculty contracts thus far negotiated differ substantially in the provision they make for arbitration. Some, such as the contracts at Rutgers and Boston State, make no provision at all for outside arbitration. At Boston State there was doubt whether state law permitted resort to binding arbitration by state agencies or institutions, and at Rutgers the parties to the contract were apparently unwilling to let their internal disputes be settled by outsiders. At St. John's and Southeastern Massachusetts only the labor organization has the right to carry a complaint to arbitration.[10] At Oakland either the labor organization or the university may decide to go to arbitration from an unsatisfactory ruling at the highest step of the grievance process within the university. At none of these institutions is the individual

10. Since the Southeastern Massachusetts contract provides for arbitration and the Boston State contract does not, there is a difference of judgment about the propriety of arbitration under Massachusetts statutes providing for collective bargaining by public employees. We have been told that the Trustees of the State Colleges takes the position that the law does prohibit resort under a faculty contract to binding third-party arbitration. The Southeastern Massachusetts University Board of Trustees obviously does not agree.

grievant permitted to make the decision to go to arbitration. He does have the right at CUNY, as does the labor organization. But the governing board does not have the right. Where a contract does not recognize the right of the institution to carry a dispute to arbitration, it is usually an administrative officer or the governing board that makes the ruling at the highest step of the internal grievance process. Under such circumstances the institution can be assumed to have no wish to appeal the ruling to an arbitrator. Where the highest level of internal grievance processing involves a committee on which the institution and the labor organization have equal representation, the possibility of a deadlock exists. The Oakland contract thus permits either party to carry the case to arbitration. At Rutgers, where no arbitration is provided for, both sides must accept the ruling of the internal grievance committee or, if that agency is deadlocked, presumably find a way out of the dilemma on an ad hoc basis.

Where the individual grievant is allowed to ask for binding arbitration, as at CUNY, he must meet half the cost of the arbitration, except that if the labor organization joins him in the decision to go to arbitration, it bears the cost. Since arbitration can be expensive, the grievant with a routine complaint may conclude that an unsatisfactory ruling internally is not worth the cost of an appeal to an external arbitrator unless he has the support of the labor organization.

Although both administrators and bargaining agent officers complain that arbitration is expensive, few hard data are available showing the cost of arbitration to educational institutions. For management, arbitration costs become part of the expense of collective bargaining incurred in additions to the administrative staff and increased use of outside legal counsel. No institution has yet made public the total costs of collective bargaining, but clearly they are becoming substantial at several institutions.[11]

Faculty labor organizations, almost always short of funds, must be selective in choosing cases to carry to arbitration. Agents are influenced by such considerations as whether they think they can win,

11. In a paper read at the 1971 annual meeting of the Association of American Colleges, a member of the Central Michigan University administrative staff, Neil Bucklew, examined with care the direct and indirect costs of the collective bargaining process that an institution is likely to incur. He suggested that these costs must be carefully identified by management, a series of "costing models" developed, and all pertinent information about costs readily shared with labor's negotiators. His remarks, however, were perhaps directed to the hidden as well as actual costs of policy concessions made to the faculty in the contract, more than they were to the hidden and actual costs of administering a contract.

the importance of the precedent that may be set, the need to satisfy political pressures within the bargaining group, and the wish to see justice done the individual.

The two CUNY contracts illustrate an attempt to place limits on the use of third-party binding arbitration. Both contain *nota bene* clauses providing that all grievances relating to faculty appointment actions "which are concerned with matters of academic judgment" may not be processed beyond step two in the grievance system, the point at which the university chancellor holds a hearing and makes a ruling. An exception is allowed when there is an allegation of "arbitrary or discriminatory use of procedure." In such situations, however, the arbitrator at step three is limited to a ruling on the disputed procedural point. If he finds in favor of the grievant, the case must then be returned to the university for a decision on the disputed substantive issue in compliance with the prescribed procedure.

The contract at St. John's University, where AAUP is the joint bargaining agent with a local faculty association, goes one step beyond the CUNY contracts. It excludes from grievance processing (as well as from arbitration) complaints relating to the appointment, promotion, removal, or suspension of faculty members, and also complaints relating to academic freedom and tenure. The contract notes that complaints in these areas are "governed exclusively" under the university's "statutes" and "other written practices of the Administration." The contract also notes that the trustees of the university have agreed to observe the standards and procedures set forth in the "1940 Statement of Academic Freedom and Tenure" and the 1966 "Statement on Government of Colleges and Universities." In addition, the contract states that where grievances are carried to arbitration,

> The arbitrator shall limit his decision strictly to the application and interpretation of the provisions of this Agreement and he shall be without power or authority to make any decision contrary to, or inconsistent with, or adding to, or subtracting from, or amending, or modifying or varying in any way, the terms of this Agreement or the Statutes or written practices of the Administration.

The Oakland contract excludes the merit salary increase granted to a faculty member from the grievance process. It also states that an arbitrator

> will have no authority to (a) add to, subtract from, or in any way modify this Agreement, (b) interpret any policy, practice, or rule which does not relate to wages, hours or conditions of employment,

(c) formulate or add any new policy or rule, and (d) substitute his judgment for academic judgment in the establishment of the classification or change in the classification of any faculty member.

These contract provisions at institutions where AAUP is the bargaining agent reflect the association's concern that arbitration and grievance processing within the institution will result in rulings which depart from certain basic principles of academic freedom and tenure that the association regards as beyond negotiation or compromise.

Apart from the qualifications in an occasional contract, such as those at CUNY and St. John's, collective bargaining in higher education has taken over the grievance-arbitration system of the industrial model virtually without change, in spite of the probability that this is one of the points where the industrial model is not well suited to serve the needs of higher education. There is reason to fear that the traditional grievance-arbitration system will disrupt the processes by which academic communities have attempted to control faculty appointments, promotions, and dismissals in ways that are fair to faculty members and yet serve the educational needs of the institutions with respect to both the substance of programs and the quality of faculties. Reputable institutions have developed evaluative processes through which they endeavor to measure faculty members for competence and quality of performance and to distribute rewards and penalties in accordance with the results of these measurements. The processes and the results have never been free from controversy. Any system for the awarding of tenure, for example, that incorporates a true element of selectivity or discrimination is certain to produce a number of unhappy persons who conclude that they have not been fairly judged. Under traditional institutional arrangements, opportunities for informal appeal and review have usually been available. Yet the principal response to the dissatisfied individual has necessarily been made in the form of a reminder that the institution is entitled to be selective in recruiting and maintaining a strong faculty and that the judgment in each case is the product of an evaluative process in which the individual's own peers have done their best to act wisely and fairly.

Under a collective bargaining contract, the dissatisfied individual is invited to lodge a "complaint" or "grievance" and to have this processed through a series of appellate steps or agencies, culminating in a judgment by an outside arbitrator that is binding on both sides. Moreover, the bargaining agent typically gains authority to monitor the process, and, in particular, to encourage (or, if it will, discourage) the individual to claim every right and opportunity available to him under the contract in pressing for review of his dissatisfaction. In any event, it is apparent that the grievance and arbitration processes will produce results that are in some measure incompatible with the goals and processes worked out by the academic profession both at the national and institutional levels.

Grievance-Arbitration Patterns at Southeastern Massachusetts University

What, in fact, have been the results of the grievance-arbitration processes provided for in faculty contracts? It is too early to answer this question definitely, for the few four-year institutions with faculty contracts are just beginning to gain experience with grievance processing and arbitration. That limited experience has not been well reported up to now. In only two or three instances is there any basis for evaluation or judgment. Thus, at Southeastern Massachusetts University we were told that during the first two years under the contract some ten faculty grievance cases required rulings at one of the four levels of the grievance process that are internal to the institution (dean of the college, dean of the faculty, president, and board of trustees). Eight were reported to have been settled more or less to the satisfaction of the grievant and the bargaining agent.[12] Two cases were appealed by the bargaining agent to an arbitrator (under the Southeastern Massachusetts contract only the bargaining agent can carry a case to arbitration). Both resulted in rulings favorable to management. In one of these cases the arbitrator declined to take jurisdiction, ruling that the contention of a nontenured faculty member that his academic freedom had been violated by the university's failure to reappoint him was not arbitrable.[13]

12. The information here reported was obtained through interviews with faculty members and administrators. We believe it is essentially correct, although it was offered on an informal basis.

13. Board of Trustees, Southeastern Massachusetts University v. S.M.U. Faculty Federation, Local 1895, AFT, AAA Case No. 1139–0528–70 (April 6, 1971) (Zack, Arbitrator). The contract at Southeastern Massachusetts provides that a tenured professor who has been dismissed may not take his case to arbitration but, instead, shall have access to an internal hearing, which he may then follow with an appeal to the courts. The arbitrator reasoned that if a nontenured teacher were given access to arbitration to challenge the university's failure to reappoint him, he would be granted greater rights under the contract than would a tenured professor.

In the second case the president of the university had ordered a faculty member transferred from the education department, where he had been the acting chairman, to the English department. The faculty contract was entirely silent about such transfers. The contract did contain a management rights clause. Moreover, there was evidence that the governing board had previously recognized the right of the president to make such transfers. The faculty member filed a grievance and, following failure to gain satisfaction internally, the bargaining agent carried his case to arbitration. The arbitrator ruled against the faculty member on the ground that:

> The Administration is not required to prove "just cause" for transferring a professor. It is a management right and as a result action under it does not require a defense.

But the arbitrator noted that the professor had also alleged that the transfer violated a provision in the contract guaranteeing academic freedom to faculty members. He indicated that, had the faculty member produced evidence showing that the transfer had actually been made "for the purpose of denying [the teacher] the freedom to discuss controversial . . . issues," he could properly have ruled in the faculty member's favor. The right to transfer a faculty member from one department to another as a reserved management right would not permit a president to violate another section of the contract (here the academic freedom clause) in the process of ordering a transfer.[14]

Grievance-Arbitration Patterns at CUNY

A second institution at which experience with grievance processing and arbitration has been sufficient to support an effort at analysis and

14. SMU Faculty Federation Chapter 1895 AFT v. Board of Trustees, SMU, AAA Case No. 1139–0490–70 (March 10, 1971) (Kennedy, Arbitrator). This analysis of arbitration at Southeastern Massachusetts University and the City University of New York draws on a prepublication draft of an excellent paper by Matthew W. Finken, "The Arbitration of Professorial Grievances." Mr. Finken is acting general counsel in the Washington office of AAUP.

The outcome of the two arbitration cases at SMU, referred to here and in the preceding footnote, was reversed by the university's governing board when, in 1972, it voted (1) to reinstate with tenure the faculty member who had not been reappointed and (2) to return to his original department the professor who had been transferred by action of the university's president. These somewhat curious actions, by which a governing board renounced the favorable rulings it had won through arbitration, are probably explained by two intervening developments: there had been several changes in the board's membership, and the president of the university at the time the two cases took shape had been dismissed by the **board.**

comment is CUNY. The contract with the Legislative Conference states:

> A grievance is an allegation by an employee or the Conference that there has been:
> (1) a breach, misinterpretation or improper application of the terms of this Agreement; or
> (2) an arbitrary or discriminatory application of, or a failure to act pursuant to, the Bylaws and written policies of the Board related to the terms and conditions of employment.

A grievance can be filed by an individual employee or by the conference on behalf of an employee or group of employees in the bargaining unit. Three steps are provided for in the filing and settlement of grievances. At step one, the grievance is heard by the president, or his designee, of the college where the grievant works. If the case is not settled at this step satisfactorily to the grievant, an appeal at step two is made to the chancellor of the university, or his designee. If the case is not satisfactorily resolved at this level, the grievant or the conference may at step three request arbitration.

There was a substantial flow of faculty complaint cases through the three steps of the grievance-arbitration system at CUNY under the first contract between the Board of Higher Education and the Legislative Conference. It is not possible to examine the cases in which grievances were satisfactorily settled at step one, for these are not regularly reported to the office of the chancellor in such a way that the data can be examined and analyzed by an outsider. During the first two years of the contract, 122 grievances were carried by individual employees (or the conference on behalf of individuals) to step two. We have had access to information about these cases and their disposition.[15]

The 122 cases did not include ten class action grievances filed by the Legislative Conference on behalf of groups of bargaining unit members with a common complaint. All of the class actions involved such matters as work loads, salary schedules, and office equipment. Only seven of the 122 grievances filed by individuals, or by the Legislative Conference on behalf of individuals, were concerned with such matters. The other 115 cases involved academic personnel issues of re-

15. Vice-Chancellor Timothy Healey was particularly helpful in providing us with information about the 122 step two grievance cases. An unpublished report, "The Impact of the Legislative Conference Grievance Procedure on Academic Affairs," prepared for internal use in the CUNY chancellor's office in the summer of 1971, was made available to us and was helpful.

appointments, promotions, and tenure grants. The categorical breakdown of the 122 cases was: tenure, 78; reappointment without tenure,
27; promotion, 10; sabbatical leave, 2; salary, 2; faculty research grants,
1; work load, 1; schedule and grading, 1.

Grievances reached the chancellor's office from 16 units of the CUNY
system, with a high of 18 from Lehman College and a low of two from
Richmond College. Forty-three percent of the cases came to the
chancellor's office from CUNY community colleges. Ninety-two of the
grievants were instructors or assistant professors, 17 were associate or
full professors, seven were technicians and specialists, and seven occupied other nonteaching posts which had been included in the bargaining unit. Nearly one-third of the grievants were women.

Fewer than half of the 122 cases reaching step two were satisfactorily settled at that level. There were rulings favorable to the grievant
in seven cases; 32 grievances were denied, and seven were remanded
to the colleges for further proceedings there. In 74 cases (61 percent
of the total) arbitration was demanded by the grievant or the Legislative Conference. This percentage appears to be excessive and suggests
either that the internal grievance system at CUNY is not working well
or that the parties to collective bargaining at CUNY are unusually
militant and intransigent.[16]

As of September 1971, rulings by an arbitrator had been made in
only six of the cases; 24 had been withdrawn from arbitration by
either the individual or the Legislative Conference, and 44 were still
awaiting a hearing or an arbitrator's ruling. The six cases in which
rulings had been made all presented a claim of tenure by the grievant.
In two of these cases the arbitrator ruled against the grievant. In four
cases the arbitrator ruled that there had been procedural deficiencies
in the evaluation of the faculty member. Of the four, three were remanded to the university for correction of the deficiencies, and in one
case the arbitrator ordered that the grievant be reappointed and
thereby granted tenure.

The significance of the *nota bene* provisions in the two CUNY contracts may now be noted more carefully. They are identical in wording:

16. If statistics are the test, the grievance system under the CUNY contract
with AFT is not working well either. The number of employees in the unit is
substantially less than the number in the LC unit. Yet in the first sixteen months
under that contract, 125 grievance cases were processed at step two. Arbitration
was then demanded in 24 of these cases.

Grievances relating to appointment, reappointment, tenure or promotion which are concerned with matters of academic judgment may not
be processed by the Conference beyond Step 2 of the grievance procedure. Grievances within the scope of these areas in which there is an
allegation of arbitrary or discriminatory use of procedure may be processed by the Conference through Step 3 of the grievance procedure.
In such case the power of an arbitrator shall be limited to remanding
the matter for compliance with established procedures. It shall be the
arbitrator's first responsibility to rule as to whether the grievance relates to procedure rather than academic judgment. In no event, however, shall the arbitrator substitute his judgment for the academic
judgment. In the event that the grievant finally prevails, he shall be
made whole.

As noted above, in three cases at CUNY, arbitrators found procedural
mistakes and accordingly remanded the cases to the university for
consideration under proper procedure. In one case that has become
the center of much controversy and litigation, the arbitrator found
that the grievant had been denied reappointment (which would have
carried tenure) as a result of procedural mistakes, and then concluded
that the grievant could "be made whole" only by his ruling that she be
reappointed with tenure.

The Perlin Case

Zalmar Perlin served as a nontenured instructor in the art department at Brooklyn College of CUNY on a series of three one-year
appointments beginning with the academic year 1967–68.[17] During
the preceding three years she had served as a lecturer, both on part-
time and full-time appointments. In October 1969, at the beginning of
her third year as instructor, and shortly after the collective bargaining
contract had taken effect, she was notified that her department was
not recommending her for reappointment for 1970–71. Under the university's regulations, an appointment for a fourth year would necessarily have carried a grant of tenure. Instructor Perlin filed a grievance
within a month. She alleged violation of the collective bargaining con-

17. Information about the Perlin case was obtained through interviews with
officers of the Legislative Conference and CUNY administrators. The arbitrator's
ruling is cited as Board of Higher Education v. Legislative Conference, AAA
Case No. 1339–07060–70 (Dec. 1, 1970) (Roberts, Arbitrator). In the two New
York Supreme Court rulings, the citation of the case is Legislative Conference of
the City University of New York v. Board of Higher Education of the City of
New York (New York County [June 1971]); 38 App. Div. 2d 478, 330 N.Y.S.
2d 688 (1st Dept. [1972]). See also 80 LRRM 2340 (April 11, 1972).

tract, the regulations and bylaws of the Board of Higher Education, and the tenure procedure rules established by the dean of faculties at Brooklyn College. She also alleged that the art department at Brooklyn regularly discriminated against women in its recommendations for appointments with tenure.

Instructor Perlin's allegation that the contract and the bylaws had not been followed depended on a contention that the elaborate provisions at CUNY for an observation-evaluation-discussion system of judging nontenured faculty members during the three-year probationary period had not been faithfully observed in her case. In effect the record showed that Instructor Perlin had been properly "observed" by department colleagues in her teaching, but that her department chairman had failed to "evaluate" in writing the results of these observations, or to "discuss" with her the substance of the evaluations, thereby giving her a chance to respond or to attempt to correct weaknesses in her teaching. About a month after the grievance was filed, the art department notified the dean that its appointments committee had met again and had concluded that, since some of Instructor Perlin's complaints were justified, "it therefore could not in good conscience deny her reappointment." The committee was reported as still feeling that "more qualified candidates were available," but it nonetheless unanimously recommended her reappointment with tenure. This amended recommendation of the art department was rejected by the Brooklyn College Personnel and Budget Committee, which voted to sustain the original recommendation. This decision was submitted to the president of Brooklyn College and subsequently approved by the Board of Higher Education.

The step one hearing of the grievance by the president of Brooklyn College resulted in an adverse ruling. At step two the chancellor's designee rejected as unsubstantiated the allegation of discrimination based on sex. A finding was made, however, that the art department had failed to communicate negative criticism to the grievant which might have provided direction for her own effort at improvement. This failure was found to violate BHE bylaws and written policies and, in effect, the contract with the Legislative Conference, although the procedural errors had occurred before the contract took effect. The demand for reappointment with tenure was nonetheless denied, but a proposal was made that Instructor Perlin resign her instructorship at the end of the current year and then be appointed as a full-time lecturer for 1970–71 on a terminal basis. (Apparently, then she could start again as a faculty member seeking tenure at Brooklyn College, for, while the lectureship appointment would have been terminal after one year, it could have been renewed, or she could later have been offered an instructorship, depending, of course, on new evaluations of the quality of her work.)

This proposed settlement was rejected by Instructor Perlin, and the case was taken to arbitration. Arbitrator Roberts reviewed the case carefully and, in December 1970, ruled that it was properly before him because, even though it concerned reappointment and tenure, it challenged "procedure" rather than "academic judgment" at Brooklyn College. Having satisfied himself that procedural errors had indeed been committed, the arbitrator then concluded that merely to remand the case to the university for compliance with correct procedures "would be a meaningless exercise."

> It would not give any redress to Miss Perlin for the arbitrary denial of her procedural rights that clearly are substantive. To accede to the University's pro forma position assuredly would result in a repetition of this type of proceeding no matter how many times her case is remanded in the vacuous context suggested by the University. . . .
> It is true that for Miss Perlin the procedural decision requiring reappointment automatically means tenure for her. But this cannot justify a denial of her contractual rights or impair the validity of this remand as the only available remedy for the arbitrary denial of . . . established procedures.

The arbitrator then suggested that if Miss Perlin were in truth unqualified for tenure at Brooklyn College, the university could attempt to remove her from her tenure post "for cause" under Article XIX of the contract, dealing with "Disciplinary Actions."

The university's reaction to this ruling was that the arbitrator had exceeded his authority and that it was accordingly not bound by the ruling. The Legislative Conference then sought and won an order in June 1971, in the New York Supreme Court, New York County, directing the university to implement the arbitrator's ruling. This decision was appealed by the university to the Appellate Division of the Supreme Court. By a three-to-two vote the appellate division in April 1972 reversed the lower court ruling. The majority held:

> . . . in our view, the determination of the Arbitrator exceeded the purview of his power, as the power to grant tenure is vested exclusively

within the province of The Board of Higher Education; and, thus, when the Arbitrator arrogated this power unto himself, he violated the *nota bene* . . . of the Agreement. . . . That tenure should not be conferred by a "back-door" maneuver is obvious because of the intrinsic value the courts attach to tenure.

The majority recognized that the case presented a puzzling situation, but it concluded that "the only fitting solution is that offered by the Board," which was "improvidently rejected by the respondent," namely that she resign her instructorship and accept a full-time lectureship for 1970–71 on a terminal basis.

In a sharply worded dissenting opinion, the minority judges stated their belief that the arbitrator had acted properly in ordering reappointment so that the grievant "shall be made whole."

> We do not pass upon the instructor's qualifications, although it may be pointed out that she was employed at the College for a long time, and that it was only within reach of the finish line that she was brought up short. . . . The offer made by the Board, while possibly satisfactory from a settlement point of view, gives no assurance that procedures will be followed and it would require the instructor to retrace her employment route. What's more, she does not accept the offer, which leaves us with no alternative other than to direct a reappointment or to adopt the default of the Board of Higher Education in following its own rules as a natural concomitant of its existence.
>
> When criminal law standards of justice and due process are not followed, even malefactors go free.

The Legislative Conference has appealed this adverse ruling by the Appellate Division of the New York Supreme Court to the highest court in the New York State judicial system, the Court of Appeals. As of November 1972, that court had not made a decision.

Even though the university may yet win final reversal in the courts of the arbitrator's ruling in the Perlin case, the ruling has left an aftermath of bitterness which emphasizes that at CUNY the adversary quality of collective bargaining appears to have overwhelmed the cooperative quality. Thus, the vice-chancellor for academic affairs at CUNY, addressing the annual meeting of the Association of Departments of English in December 1971, offered the following observations about collective bargaining at CUNY:

> It is . . . an axiom of union negotiations, that what the union failed to get at the bargaining table it must strive to get via the grievance procedure. . . .

If at this point I seem to be saying that "a union is a union is a union," even when it is made up of professors, I agree that I am. Several serious attacks on academic process in its broadest sense are underway.... Traditionally unions are interested in two major accomplishments: job security and money. The City University's faculty union has won its point on money. But its current course in pursuing job security places the union, in my judgment at least, on the collision course with the university itself....

... That the academic world bears at best a limited likeness to the industrial model is an idea that neither side has yet been able to communicate to the panel of arbitrators. Thus the union fights to entrust the single most important decision that any university faculty makes (the award of tenure), the decision by which it lives and grows or stagnates and dies, to the hands of an outsider in an outside forum, bound and governed by rules never designed for universities....

... I would do anything in my power to prevent the steady invasion of the academic world by arbitrators, the police, the courts, and the legislatures.[18]

In one of the grievance cases under the AFT contract, which also took shape at Brooklyn College, part-time lecturers had been notified that they would not be reappointed because their departments had decided to limit such appointments to persons holding or working toward a doctor's degree. A provision in the CUNY contract with AFT could be read as limiting nonreappointment of part-time lecturers to reasons of "insufficient registration, financial inability, or changes in curriculum." The arbitrator ruled that these reasons should be regarded as exclusive except for an evaluation report showing unsatisfactory performance and misconduct, "commonly recognized by courts and arbitrators as reason for dismissal or nonreappointment, because it involves a lack of fitness to teach, a failure to meet standards of conduct, express or implied." The university had used a new reason, not mentioned in the contract, to justify the nonreappointments. The arbitrator accordingly ordered the reappointment of the complainants. That he was prepared to disagree with "academic judgment" is indicated in the following words:

> The philosophy of hiring the best personnel available is of course commendable, and it is presumed whenever anyone is hired, at the time of such hiring, he is the best available. The upgrading of a faculty is also desirable but may not be done at the expense of violat-

18. Timothy Healey, "The Future of Tenure," *ADE Bulletin* (Association of Departments of English), May 1972, pp. 3–6.

ing a contract. The term "upgrading" is, of course, a subjective term. The mere holding of a doctorate, or taking courses toward a doctorate, does not of itself mean that such an individual would make a good lecturer or professor, nor that a faculty would necessarily be upgraded by having such an individual become a member of the faculty.[19]

AN EVALUATION OF ACADEME'S EXPERIENCE
WITH ARBITRATION

There is considerable dissatisfaction at CUNY on the part of administrative officers with the institution's arbitration experience and the problems that have arisen under the *nota bene* clauses.[20] What lessons can be learned from this unhappy experience of CUNY with its grievance-arbitration system? One is the need to draft collective bargaining contracts in more careful langauge. The *nota bene* clauses in the two initial contracts were certainly poorly drafted and perhaps unwisely conceived. But when the need in contract drafting is to draw a line between issues of procedure (which may properly go to arbitration) and substantive issues of academic judgment (which an academic community may well wish to settle finally inside the institution), hitting upon the right words will not prove easy.

A second lesson is that the role of department chairmen is crucial from management's point of view when it comes to making certain that the contract is being administered in such a way as to minimize individual grievances arising under it. The department chairman in the Perlin case seemingly did blunder badly. Thus, at an institution where chairmen are elected by their department colleagues and are viewed by the faculty as shop stewards, it is understandable that administrators should want the system changed to bring chairmen under a much larger measure of administrative supervision and discipline.

On the specific issue at CUNY of "making a grievant whole," following a denial of procedural rights, an institution might create still another personnel review agency with the means and the authority to take a fresh look at a personnel case where an arbitrator has ruled that

19. City University of New York v. Local No. 1460, U.F.C.T., AFL-CIO, AAA Case No. 1330–0207–70 (May 25, 1970) (Wildebush, Arbitrator).

20. As early as 1970, Vice-Chancellor Mintz wrote, "one begins to have doubts about the wisdom of placing academic contract dispute adjudication in the hands of industry oriented professionals" ("The CUNY Experience," 1971 *Wisconsin Law Review* [no. 1], 112, 122). These "doubts" were strongly reaffirmed thereafter at every meeting we had with CUNY administrative officers.

an earlier decision is fatally flawed for procedural reasons. In this way, an arbitrator could reasonably be expected to remand the case to the institution for final action by that additional agency, rather than to claim that he must settle the case himself lest the review on campus by the officers and agencies that were responsible for the original judgment be a "meaningless exercise." This new agency would carry a price in the sense of a further proliferation of governance machinery in an academic community and of the time and energy required of the people who staff such agencies. But this may be the price, in turn, of a faculty's decision to turn to collective bargaining, including the use of binding third-party arbitration. Moreover, if the original error was truly procedural only, this new agency might well find that the first judgment was sound on substantive grounds. Would that "make the grievant whole"?

Finally, the CUNY experience demonstrates that arbitrators (and judges) cannot necessarily be counted on to bring good understanding of educational institutions and of academic ways to their decisions in cases concerning faculty appointments, promotions, and tenure grants. The seven outside experts who have thus far had their say in the Perlin case at Brooklyn College have divided four to three in their judgments in the matter, a fact that suggests a high degree of unpredictability when academic matters are disposed of finally by such persons. It may be, as some friends of arbitration are asserting, that, with time and experience, certain arbitrators associated with the American Arbitration Association and with state labor and mediation boards will develop a good understanding of the ways of higher education and will bring both wisdom and justice to their rulings. That day is not yet at hand. And it may be doubted that trustees, faculty members, and administrators will ever reach the point where they will be truly content to have many of the crucial decisions of the faculty evaluation process made by third parties, however expert.

The grievance-arbitration process under a collective bargaining contract has been described by Mr. Justice Douglas, speaking for the United States Supreme Court, as being

> at the very heart of the system of industrial self-government. Arbitration is the means of solving the unforeseeable by molding a system of private law for all the problems which may arise and to provide for their solution in a way which will generally accord with the variant needs and desires of the parties. The processing of disputes through the

grievance machinery is actually a vehicle by which meaning and content is given to the collective bargaining agreement.

... The grievance procedure is, in other words, a part of the continuous collective bargaining process.[21]

Experience in industry reveals that a union may use arbitration in an attempt to keep the bargaining process continuous and thereby win concessions that it was not able to obtain at the bargaining table, or to prepare the way for strong demands at the next round of negotiations. In this respect, persons concerned with collective bargaining in higher education must recognize the existence of the two schools of thought concerning the arbitral process. One, sometimes described as the judicial approach, limits arbitrators to rulings that go no further than is necessary to resolve the uncertainties of contract language. The other accepts Justice Douglas' contention that collective bargaining is a continuous process. This approach regards arbitration as a legitimate means of extending an agreement to answer policy questions on which the contract is silent or needs revision during contract time in the light of experience or changed circumstances. Pushed to an extreme, this approach makes arbitration, not an attempt to reach a decision consistent with the contract, but a means to an innovative settlement that in effect revises or extends the contract.

Attorney William P. Lemmer, of the University of Michigan staff, who has considerable experience in collective bargaining, urges trustees and administrators to encourage and insist on the judicial approach in the arbitration of cases arising under university collective bargaining contracts.[22] In particular, he argues, the governing board's team should strive for contract language at the negotiating table that is as precise and detailed as possible at every crucial point. The phrasing of the contract should be done, he advises, with thought given to the arbitrator who may later be called upon to interpret and apply the language in grievance cases. Similarly, he recommends a carefully drafted formulation of the "reserved rights philosophy" to forestall rulings by arbitrators that will erode management rights and prerogatives which have been inadequately covered in the contract. He might well have stated, although he did not, that a faculty in its collegial

21. United Steelworkers v. Warrior and Gulf Navigation Co., 363 U.S. 574, 581 (1960).
22. "Arbitration, Use, Value and Precautions in Institutional Labor Contracts," *College Counsel*, June 1970, pp. 209–44.

being also has strong and similar reasons for wanting to confine arbitrators to the "judicial approach" where collective bargaining exists.

Attorneys for labor organizations frequently view arbitration as a creative process: a collective bargaining contract, like the law itself, becomes a living thing, a progressive force, capable of growth and adaptation, not only to take care of new problems and unforeseen needs, but also to provide an ever-larger measure of industrial justice. This position seems to assume that arbitration will frequently result in rulings more favorable to labor than to management. Whether this assumption is borne out by the facts—administrators at CUNY would say it is—is beyond our ability to judge.[23]

Some students of the arbitral process in collective bargaining argue that the two approaches described above really differ in degree rather than kind and that the arbitrator as policy-maker and the arbitrator as contract interpreter merely occupy slightly different points on a continuous spectrum. All agree, however, that the contract which emerges from the bargaining table should be as carefully drawn as possible, and that when the contract is well drawn, any principled arbitrator will endeavor to follow its mandate.

The experience with collective bargaining in higher education thus far does not permit a final judgment of the gains and losses to the academic community under a grievance-arbitration system. In its justification, such a system is a manifestation in academic life of the widespread and commendable concern that the society has been showing for individual rights, particularly for the need to be scrupulously fair in the treatment accorded an individual accused of an offense, or

23. See "The Final Word: A 'New Breed' Emerges in Conservative Field of Labor Arbitration," *Wall Street Journal*, Sept. 20, 1972, p. 1, on approaches employed by contemporary arbitrators:

"Arbitrators are torn between two contrasting codes of professional behavior. In a field still dominated by a shrinking band of aging men, the traditionalist code holds that an arbitrator should be almost as cloistered as a judge—aloof, majestically impartial, limiting himself strictly to the narrowest interpretation of the problem at hand.

"Arbitrators 'often get too close to the parties and thus risk losing their impartiality,' grumbles Philip Carey, a longtime New York pro. 'So they shouldn't try to be nice guys or do-gooders—just umpires.'

"At the other extreme are Mr. Carey's nice guys and do-gooders, mostly younger men who take a decidedly activist approach to their profession. They think arbitrators should be a force for good, as they define it. They contend that an arbitrator's ruling should always square with equal hiring laws and other social reform legislation—even when the dispute at hand could be settled strictly on the contract."

denied an opportunity or reward that he had reason to expect. There are serious costs, however, to the academic community that commits itself to the grievance-arbitration system as a means of reaction to allegations that individual faculty members have suffered injustices in the course of the community's daily business. Where deans, provosts, presidents, and governing boards are the formal agents for the settlement of grievances, their place, authority, and relationships in the community may well undergo troublesome changes. A governing board that is called on to hear and settle a wide range of grievances will necessarily be drawn further into the business of running the institution. This enlarged role may be desirable and appropriate, but will most administrators and faculty members view it thus? Where administrators settle grievances, the law of collective bargaining may compel them to be less open, informal, and helpful in their routine relations with faculty members. The president of one institution complained to us, "An administrator can no longer talk to an individual teacher except in the presence of a representative of the union, unless he is prepared to risk being charged with an unfair labor practice." An administrator at another institution made much the same point: "No dean can have a serious talk with a faculty member without a stenotypist at his side and a lawyer in front of him." Whether these assessments are accurate is beside the point; this is how some administrators perceive their place and responsibility under collective bargaining.

Where faculty members serve on internal grievance committees of the kind provided for in the Rutgers, Oakland, and Central Michigan contracts, the cost to them in terms of time and energy can be enormous if these committees are called on to hear and settle a significant number of grievances. The burden on administrators serving on these same committees is equally great, but more readily justified as another facet of administration. A concomitant effect might be an increased reluctance of faculty members to take their turns serving as deans and provosts.

This analysis may overstate the adversary relationship—and the impact of "law" and "adjudication"—that will be sensed or felt by the members of an academic community in the process of living with a collective bargaining contract. No one in higher education yet has extended experience with what it means to find familiar relationships and ways of doing one's work affected, and in some degree controlled, by a contract and by the agencies, internal and external, that may be called on to enforce that contract. At some institutions administrators and faculty members alike testify that the collective bargaining relationship is proving to be a harmonious and constructive one, that it is proving to be the means by which problems are defined and their solution made easier. They testify also that they are aware of the threat posed by "creeping legalism" and by external intrusions on institutional autonomy. The same point is sometimes made a bit differently by emphasizing the idea that the problems, conflicts, and even the basic adversary relationship were there on the campus to start with. Collective bargaining did not create them; instead, it is a way of coping successfully with difficulties that already existed. Such testimony, where it is forthcoming, is encouraging. But it suggests a more favorable view of the grievance-arbitration aspect of faculty bargaining than the actual experience at some institutions will support.

CHAPTER EIGHT

An Evaluation of Faculty Bargaining:
Problems and Prospects

THE EXPERIENCE OF FACULTIES WITH COLLECTIVE BARGAINING IS STILL SO limited that any identification of trends or balancing out of gains and losses can be only tentative. One thing *is* clear: a good deal of experimentation is going on. Contracts differ greatly, and experience under them is far from uniform. A number of models are becoming discernible, ranging from some that closely follow industrial patterns of collective bargaining to others that, whatever their faults, do represent significant attempts to adapt the bargaining process to the needs of higher education. If institutional autonomy and uniqueness are viewed as sources of strength in American higher education, this experimentation with different forms and processes of bargaining is healthy. Out of the trials and errors, preferred models may emerge that will be suited to different segments of the academic profession and to different types of institutions.

Whatever the consequences of collective bargaining for a faculty, the decision to turn in this direction tends to be irreversible. Experience in the industrial sector indicates that it is easier to take the step to collective bargaining than it is to get disentangled from this form of labor-management relations if a labor group finds itself dissatisfied with its experience.[1] A faculty may find it feasible, both in terms of formal process and political realities, to review the situation and make a new decision when its contract runs out, but no faculty at a senior institution has yet voted to give up collective bargaining after a period

1. Far more elections are conducted to decide whether to engage in bargaining and to choose an agent than are held to change agents or give up bargaining. Thus, in the fiscal year ending June 30, 1970, the NLRB conducted a total of 7,311 representation elections of all types. Of these, only 301 were elections in which a previously certified union was challenged as the bargaining agent. In 210 of these elections the union was ousted and the workers voted to give up collective bargaining. See *Thirty-fifth Annual Report of the National Labor Relations Board*, pp. 16, 178–81.

of experience. A more likely development is that one labor organization will supplant another as bargaining agent through a new representation election.[2]

A faculty is thus well advised to inform itself fully concerning the options open to it, and the probable consequences associated with each option, before it decides to engage in collective bargaining and selects a bargaining agent. A few faculties have had studies that may prove useful to other faculties as time goes by. At three institutions in Michigan—the University of Michigan, Michigan State University, and Western Michigan University—faculty committees prepared excellent reports on the meaning and significance of collective bargaining for their colleagues to consider well in advance of any movement on the campus to bring about a representation election.

Even at institutions where the movement toward an election comes swiftly, the case for and against the options open to the faculty can be developed with considerable care. Though the dialogue or debate must necessarily be carried on largely through the admittedly partisan presentations of the persons or organizations supporting each of the available options in the election, a faculty can insist that the presentations be thorough and responsible. This appears to have happened at the University of Rhode Island in 1971 and at Rhode Island College in 1972. At the former, a faculty group was organized in support of the "no bargaining" option and saw to it that the case against collective bargaining was presented to the faculty in a responsible way. Some of the campaign literature and speeches contained exaggerated rhetoric, but the level of the debate was not noticeably below that prevailing at faculty meetings at most institutions. In the end, the faculty at the University of Rhode Island voted to engage in bargaining, but it had had the benefit of a reasonably fair and thorough examination of the case against the step.

2. The merger of the Legislative Conference (NEA) and the United Federation of College Teachers (AFT) at the end of the first contract period in 1972 at City University of New York may well have warded off a successful challenge of LC-NEA by AFT as the bargaining agent for the full-time faculty unit.

According to the AFT *American Teacher,* January 1973, the faculty at the eight campuses of the New Jersey State College system voted in December 1972 to supplant NEA with the AFT affiliate. The first two-year contract, negotiated by NEA, had expired in June 1972. In the election, AFT received 1,173 votes to 1,090 votes for NEA from approximately 2,800 eligible faculty members in the unit.

THE EFFECTS OF FACULTY BARGAINING
ON THE ACADEMIC COMMUNITY

There is still time for the academic profession, as a whole, to weigh the further usefulness of collective bargaining with care. The spread of collective bargaining up to the middle of 1972 has been slower than had been widely predicted when the first faculties turned to bargaining in the late 1960s. Also the results of bargaining have been less significant than many observers predicted. The gains to faculties have almost everywhere been modest in character. The costs of these gains—the trade-offs—have also been modest in terms of increased teaching loads, damage to faculty participation in institutional governance, and the endangering of academic freedom and tenure. Collective bargaining has not yet revolutionized the academic profession or higher education. If it comes to encompass most of higher education, the consequences probably will become much more significant, although even then faculty bargaining may be absorbed into the existing system without materially changing that system. Such a result might disappoint the friends of faculty collective bargaining and confound its critics. But it is a possibility.

Have Faculties Won "More"?

The first question that a faculty is likely to raise as it weighs the desirability of turning to collective bargaining is: Will it bring us more money and better working conditions? Have salaries and fringe benefits risen more significantly at institutions where faculties are using collective bargaining than elsewhere or than they would have without any bargaining? Can faculties expect to make gains with respect to "hours" as well as "wages," as workers in industry have done, or does experience with bargaining in higher education carry a warning that governing boards may insist on heavier teaching loads, in one form or another, as a trade-off for increased faculty compensation?

Among the community colleges, the evidence suggests that significant gains in compensation have been won through bargaining that might not otherwise have been forthcoming. How much the gains amounted to in precise dollar or percentage figures is difficult to state, for in every instance there are variables and uncertainties to take into account. Many public school teachers won sharp improvements in their salaries through collective bargaining during the second half of the

1960s. Because of the close ties community colleges have to public school systems, their faculties seem to have benefited as a part of this same trend. In Michigan, for example, it is generally agreed that the faculties at the twenty-four community colleges that are engaging in collective bargaining have won substantial salary gains.[3]

Among four-year institutions, it is less clear that faculties engaging in collective bargaining have won significant salary improvements beyond those they would have received in any event. The two contracts negotiated at CUNY in 1969 with the Legislative Conference and the United Federation of College Teachers are widely believed to have established the most handsome faculty salary schedules to be found at any American college or university. But CUNY administrative officers contend that essentially the same schedules would have taken shape without faculty bargaining. They maintain that for some forty years faculty salaries at the New York City colleges have been determined by a formula which sets them at a fixed point above the salaries of the city's public school teachers. This contention, if correct, may affirm only that CUNY faculty members, like those at many two-year colleges, were benefiting from the salary gains won through collective bargaining by public school teachers in the same community.

The contract at the State University of New York, in sharp contrast with that at CUNY, provided for a seemingly modest increase of 6 percent in the basic salaries of all persons in the professional service of the university for 1971–72, with a provision for subsequent negotiation of salary adjustments for 1972–73 and 1973–74. The contract also recognized the right of the university "in its discretion" to make "further upward salary adjustments to individual employees," but it contained no commitment by the state to fund such merit increases. The 6 percent increase, according to one judgment, was about the same as members of the state civil service were receiving at that time,

3. President William B. Boyd of Central Michigan University asserts that a 1969 study "dramatically revealed" that seven of the ten state institutions having the highest faculty salaries were junior colleges ("Collective Bargaining in Academe," 57 *Liberal Education* [October 1971], 306, 310). He gives no authority for this statement. The Faculty Association at Northern Michigan University, in a memorandum sent to all faculty members on March 22, 1971, used data from AAUP and NEA salary surveys demonstrating that in Michigan between 1967–68 and 1969–70, faculty salaries rose at twenty-four two-year institutions much more rapidly, both in dollar totals and on a percentage basis, than they did at eleven four-year institutions. Many of these two-year institutions were bargaining with their faculties during this period.

but "a good deal less than most faculty members, in the light of campaign literature and general aspirations, had been led to expect."[4]

It is difficult to put dollar values on the various fringe benefits provided for in faculty contracts. Contract language does not usually distinguish new fringe benefits from those that carry over from prebargaining days, nor does the language always reveal dollar or percentage increases where an improvement in an existing benefit is provided for. The CUNY contract with the Legislative Conference (National Education Association), for example, provides for such fringe benefits as sick leaves, sabbatical leaves, staff housing, a faculty welfare fund, and retirement annuities, without making clear what improvement has been achieved. The retirement-pension system is presumably strengthened, but only to the extent that the Board of Higher Education and the Legislative Conference agree jointly to support bills in the New York legislature implementing the terms of the contract. The board agrees to increase annual support of the sabbatical leave program from $500,000 to $1,000,000. The staff housing provision is an innocuous one in which the board "recognizes the housing problem on each campus" and agrees to request each college president to establish a committee "to chart specific progress toward the solution of the problem." No such "progress" has been reported on during the life of the contract. It is probable that the progress, if any, has been modest.

The CUNY contract with LC also provides that the university will make the sum of $1,500,000 available annually in support of faculty research. This does appear to have been a new fringe benefit. The Legislative Conference has taken some satisfaction in this product of the bargaining process at CUNY. So, too, has the CUNY administration, although we were told in the chancellor's office that "the same number of dollars would have gone into faculty salaries had the research program not been established."

The fringe benefit provisions of the SUNY contract are surprisingly inconsequential. The contract states that "all present benefits" are to be preserved, and it establishes "new" death benefits of up to $20,000 for each employee, and "new" dental insurance. As already noted, the contract makes elaborate provision for a variety of leaves, including

---

4. Since this judgment was made by an AAUP officer, it was not necessarily wholly dispassionate, but it probably expressed the general reaction to the salary provision in the SUNY contract.

sick leaves and maternity leaves (which undoubtedly represent significant costs), but there is no reference whatsoever to the retirement-pension system. Presumably retirement annuities (and other fringe benefits) are provided at SUNY under state law or prior university programs, but the silence of the contract on this matter suggests that no improvement in these fringe benefits had been won through collective bargaining.[5]

The contract with the American Association of University Professors at St. John's University, the contract with the American Federation of Teachers at Boston State College, and the NEA contract at Central Michigan University all make systematic and detailed provision for such standard fringe benefits as retirement annuities, regular and major medical insurance, life, accident, and disability insurance, and tuition remission (at St. John's for faculty children, and at Central Michigan for members of the bargaining unit). The indications are that at all of these institutions the stated fringe benefit provisions represent some degree of economic gain but also in some measure merely affirm policies already in effect.

The experience at Central Michigan University provides one of the strongest cases among four-year institutions for claiming that significant faculty compensation gains have been won through collective bargaining. For each of the four years covered by the two contracts—1970–71 through 1973–74—each faculty member received an across-the-board increase in his salary over the previous year: for the first year this figure was 7.1 percent and for each of the next three years it was 6.5–6.6 percent. There were also provisions for some modest merit increases and for improvements in fringe benefits. Officers of the NEA bargaining unit at Central Michigan publicly claimed that the increases in total compensation (salaries plus fringe benefits) obtained in the second contract, agreed to in May 1971, were 8.2 percent for 1971–72, 9.25 percent for 1972–73, and 10.5 percent for 1973–74. Administrative officers at the university agreed that these figures were correct, but pointed out to us that they were obtained by measuring the increases in total compensation for each of the three years against

5. That trivia can find a place in a contract at a great university is suggested by the following provision in the SUNY contract:

"Article XXXVI, Medical Assistance: A. It is agreed that in the event of a medical emergency resulting from an injury to an employee on the campus, the injured employee shall be given emergency first aid by a qualified staff nurse during the normal working hours of the nurse."

the salary, rather than the compensation, base for 1970–71. Measured against the compensation base for 1970–71, the percentages of increase were significantly lower. These lower figures were not publicly identified by either the labor organization or the university. In any event, the improvements in compensation at Central Michigan may well have constituted better increases than were being granted faculties at most other four-year state institutions in Michigan at the same time, among which only the faculty at Oakland University was also engaging in collective bargaining.

There are difficulties about all such efforts to measure the economic gains of faculties through collective bargaining by percentages of improvement. The individual faculty member can, if he wishes, calculate year by year the percentage increases in his own salary and, with a bit more difficulty, in his fringe benefits. Similarly, where access can be had to an institution's total compensation budgets year by year, total increases in salaries and fringe benefits for an entire faculty can be determined in both dollars and percentages. Such statistics do undoubtedly throw some light on the effort that an institution is making (or is being forced to make) to improve the compensation of its faculty.[6] But these total dollar or percentage increases in faculty compensation are not then readily translated into average compensation increases for faculty members, for, to obtain meaningful figures, account must be taken of yearly fluctuations in the size of a faculty, the number of individuals in each faculty rank, and the number at each level of the salary schedule within a rank. The number of promotions to higher rank, of faculty members retiring or resigning each year or going on leave, and the nature and cost of their replacements, as well as the number of additional appointments reflecting institutional expansion or new programs are all variables that enter into any measurement or evaluation of annual increases in an institution's total faculty compensation program. Some of these factors or variables can be and are manipulated so that substantial increases in individual faculty salaries can be granted without an accompanying significant increase in an institution's total faculty compensation budget. Con-

6. As time goes by, the AAUP annual salary surveys ought to provide a basis for determining whether faculty bargaining is providing greater economic gains then are being granted at institutions where bargaining is not taking place. We have studied the Committee Z reports of the last three or four years to see whether any such pattern was emerging, but were forced to conclude that it was too soon for the evidence to show up in the surveys.

versely, an institution may be compelled by built-in commitments to increase its total compensation budget substantially without managing to grant significant increases to individual faculty members.

For reasons such as these, public claims about the economic package provided for in a collective bargaining contract, whether in industry or in higher education, and whether made by labor or management or both, must usually be viewed with some skepticism. Such claims may be presumed to be honest and accurate and to demonstrate that collective bargaining does result in economic gains for a labor force, but a labor organization can usually be counted on to announce the gains it has won in whatever way gives the strongest impression that these are substantial, better than was expected, or greater than have been won elsewhere. Moreover, management often has reasons of its own not to challenge labor's claims by engaging in public argument concerning the correct way of measuring gains. At Northern Michigan University one of the pieces of literature distributed to faculty members in March 1971, immediately preceding the election in which that faculty voted to reject collective bargaining, asserted that at Central Michigan University the average "faculty increase" (whether in salary or compensation is not indicated) during the first year of collective bargaining was 7.5 percent, whereas the figure at Northern Michigan for the same year was said to have been 12.2 percent without any bargaining.

The compensation provisions of the Oakland University contract, effective for 1971–72, are so complicated that, by some reports, they are fully understood only by the faculty member who devised the formula governing them. Oakland administrative officers have estimated that the increase in compensation was at an annual rate of 7.5 percent. However, the contract did not take effect until mid-November 1971. It was thus possible to "load" all of the increase in compensation into the seven and a half month period between that date and the end of the fiscal year on June 30, 1972. For that period the rate of improvement was said to be 14 percent.[7]

Neither Central Michigan University nor Oakland University appears to have obtained a single additional dollar from the state legis-

7. In a supplementary "Letter of Agreement" entitled "Duration of Salary Structure" the university appears to have protected itself against any understanding that the compensation levels established for the seven and a half month period would be continued beyond the duration of the contract.

lature because it is engaging in collective bargaining.[8] For fiscal year 1971–72, the legislature appropriated funds for each of the thirteen four-year state institutions based on an expectation that all of them would thereby be enabled to improve faculty compensation by 6.5 percent measured against the compensation base for the previous year, or 8.1 percent measured against the salary base. However, each of these institutions receives its state appropriation on a largely unrestricted basis. Although the legislature may expect the funds it appropriates to be used in accordance with the budgetary estimates submitted to it by the institutions, the latter are free, within broad limits, to use their appropriations as they see fit. Therefore, a faculty can bring pressure on its governing board to increase the percentage of institutional income assigned to faculty compensation by changing "institutional priorities." In this respect, it appears that the Central Michigan faculty has fared better under collective bargaining than did other Michigan faculties in persuading its governing board to assign additional income to the improvement of faculty salaries.

Faculty Work Loads and the "Productivity" Trade-off

When collective bargaining comes to a campus, a reasonable expectation is that the governing board will make strong demands at the bargaining table concerning faculty work loads and productivity. The evidence does not suggest that faculties have thus far suffered much through aggressive trading of "wages" against "hours." A number of contracts use the kind of vague language found in the CUNY contract to state an expectation that work loads will be "normal," and not "excessive" or "unreasonable." It is not wholly clear which adversary expects to gain from such a provision. Other contracts are more specific about standard teaching loads, faculty-student ratios, and the length of the academic year, but we have encountered no contract under which the faculty had to accept heavier work loads, however described or measured, as part of the price for gains in wages.

Faculty bargaining agents are likely soon to encounter a much more aggressive position by management on the trade-off between salaries and work loads. Almost all institutions, public and private, will be

8. For a highly critical examination of the way the annual state appropriation to the four-year institutions was determined in Michigan in 1967–68, see "The State of Higher Education in Michigan," 54 *AAUP Bulletin* (December 1968), 473–84. The report was prepared by a special committee of the AAUP Michigan Conference.

facing financial difficulties for several years to come. The rate of growth in income will be much reduced during at least the first half of the 1970s from that of the 1960s. At some—perhaps many—institutions, income will reach a plateau or actually decline in absolute terms. Under these circumstances further improvements in compensation, particularly those of the order that have come to be expected of collective bargaining (or that the academic profession is still entitled to in terms of equity with other professions, if not by market conditions), will have to be associated with some measure of productivity gain. This is the principal conclusion reached in an essay on faculty collective bargaining by Joseph W. Garbarino, director of the Institute of Business and Economic Research at the University of California, Berkeley. He calls attention to the "productivity agreements" that are becoming a part of collective bargaining in industry and that involve "a dramatic break with traditional practices." He writes that the

> essence of a productivity agreement is the trading of major concessions on both sides, with the final settlement ideally including machinery for joint action to improve efficiency in the future. Prospects for success are greatest when both parties realize that major changes are needed and are probably inevitable if conditions do not change.[9]

The first major test of the ability of a university management to demand and obtain such a productivity agreement with a faculty bargaining agent will come at CUNY in the summer of 1972, as the university endeavors to negotiate a new contract with the Professional Staff Congress (the bargaining agent created through the merger of the Legislative Conference–NEA and the AFT local), which now represents all of the university's "instructional staff." The need for such an agreement will be acute. The university is under strong pressure to increase the size of its instructional staff to meet the heavy burden imposed by its open admissions program. But it also is up against the bleak reality that its appropriations from the city and the state will not continue to rise at the spectacular rates of recent years. The bargaining agent is certain to insist on further improvements in all of the salary scales in the present contracts, but it will be particu-

9. Garbarino, "Precarious Professors: New Patterns of Representation," reprinted by the Carnegie Commission on Higher Education from 10 *Industrial Relations* (February 1971). The author states that "highly publicized examples in the U.S. are the West Coast longshoremen's agreements and the Kaiser Steel agreements" (Carnegie reprint, pp. 19–20).

larly insistent about gains for its "underprivileged members"—for the lecturers and teaching assistants, who have come into the new unit from the old AFT unit, and for the nontenured faculty members and numerous nonteaching professionals from the old Legislative Conference unit. There will be much militancy on both sides of the table and easy agreement is unlikely. It will be surprising, indeed, if the bargaining agent wins significant improvements in compensation without accepting at least the beginnings of a true productivity agreement.[10]

THE EFFECTS OF FACULTY BARGAINING ON GOVERNANCE

The influence that faculty collective bargaining will have on institutional governance is receiving almost as much attention as is the basic issue of whether it is producing economic gains for faculties engaging in bargaining. Usually attention is focused on what is happening to the faculty role in the running of a college or university. Here the interest and speculation run from apprehension that the adversary character of collective bargaining may prove to be incompatible with a faculty's part in a shared authority system of governance, all the way to the expectation that bargaining may prove to be the means by which an institution's governance system will be altered to give the faculty a stronger and more appropriate role. In any event, it must be recognized that collective bargaining can also affect the roles in governance of an institution's board of trustees, its president, and its students.

An Expanded Role for Boards of Trustees?

Collective bargaining will increase the authority and influence of the members of an institution's governing board at a time in higher education when many observers are questioning the continuing usefulness of lay boards and have been noting signs that their role has been declining. The reason for this countertrend is basic. Collective bargaining is a relationship between two adversaries—management and labor. The governing board is management. It possesses and must exercise the responsibility at the institutional level of deciding what is

10. These words written in June 1972 have not been contradicted by events through January 1973. Nonetheless, predictions of this kind are chancy. Management at CUNY may take a "soft" stand if city and state political leaders intervene in the negotiations on the employee side and allow a mounting university deficit to become a further item in the already desperate budgetary difficulties faced by the city and the state. Similar developments have occurred in New York in collective bargaining with other public employee groups.

acceptable to management regarding the very wide range of issues that are negotiable at the bargaining table. The law requires that both sides negotiate in good faith; it does not require the reaching of an agreement and it certainly does not require the reaching of any particular agreement. There is much discretion to be exercised on both sides of the table. The governing board must decide how far it will go in meeting the faculty's demands and also whether it will make demands of its own and insist on some degree of trade-off in the final contract. Here negotiations concerning productivity standards and modifications of the tenure system can prove significant. At some multi-campus institutions, such as the Massachusetts state colleges and CUNY, management may be a statewide or systemwide board of higher education, but it is nonetheless a governing board.[11] In any event, the emerging patterns of faculty collective bargaining show that boards of trustees are exercising authority and making decisions on many issues and problems that might otherwise have been left to administrators and faculty members to decide within the campus academic community.

The increased board role is unlikely to be affected by the fact that trustees seldom serve on the management negotiating team. The evidence shows that management's negotiators are significantly influenced by guidelines established by the board and that the agreement reached at the table must be acceptable to the board. Thus, at Boston State College the state governing board insisted that the contract contain no provision for binding arbitration, whereas its negotiators were prepared to give a little ground to the bargaining agent on this point.

The contract administration aspect of collective bargaining is also likely to encourage increased involvement by trustees in the day-to-day business of the academic community. Many contracts, for example, bring the governing board into the grievance process, as the final agency on campus that hears and decides individual grievances before binding third-party arbitration is resorted to. It is too early to try to measure the extent to which trustees are in fact assuming an

11. At SUNY the agreement is between the Senate Professional Association and "the Executive Branch of the State of New York," and the SUNY board may have lost rather than gained importance with the coming of faculty collective bargaining to the institution. Other governing boards of public institutions may also lose some of their authority to state government as time goes by. In private higher education, collective bargaining seems certain to enhance the role of governing boards in the actual operation of institutions.

administrative role under collective bargaining, but there is good reason to believe that they will help administer as well as help make policy in such areas as faculty appointments, reappointments, promotions, and tenure grants, teaching loads, sabbatical leaves, and the supervision of department chairmen. There is a distinct danger that the coming of faculty bargaining will play into the hands of those trustees, of which every institution seems to have one or more, who have an irresistible desire to help run things on campus.

The Faculty Role in Governance under Bargaining

Is collective bargaining proving to be an effective means of strengthening a faculty's place in the power structure of its institution? To put the question the other way around, can a shared authority system of institutional governance survive where a faculty elects to engage in collective bargaining? In industry, any group of employees that turns to collective bargaining expects thereby to improve its wages and working conditions. Such groups, at least in the past, have not been presumed to be much interested in power structure issues. For a faculty, this interest may be as strong a motive in collective bargaining as is the expectation of economic gain. It might be thought that the governance issue has been a strong consideration at many of the two-year colleges whose faculties have turned to collective bargaining, for these institutions have in many instances been slow to develop the shared authority governance systems found at four-year colleges and universities. But these faculties do not appear to be more dissatisfied with their roles in institutional governance than are their counterparts at four-year institutions. Instead, when they turn to collective bargaining, usually the expectation of economic gains is a more dominant motive than it is with faculties at four-year institutions.[12]

The development of faculty collective bargaining in the four-year

12. For example, a study of faculty contracts at public community colleges in Michigan in 1969–70 does not even discuss changes in governance systems brought about by the contracts. The closest the study comes to the governance issue is in a summary of the extent to which contracts recognize the right of trustees to set policies on such matters as teacher evaluation, tenure, academic freedom, creation of new academic programs, and reductions in work forces. Only under the "new programs" heading is any reference found to faculty participation in the decision-making process. It may be inferred from this study that these contracts do not deal with issues of institutional governance to any significant extent. See *Analysis of Faculty Contract Information at Public Community Colleges in Michigan 1969–70.*

public institutions in Massachusetts may well provide the strongest available evidence that the governance issue is a significant one for faculties, for the Massachusetts statute authorizing collective bargaining by state employees is generally viewed as excluding salary negotiations from the bargaining process. In spite of this limitation the faculties at eight of the eleven four-year state colleges and also at Southeastern Massachusetts University have voted to engage in collective bargaining. Moreover, in the contracts negotiated at Southeastern Massachusetts University and Boston State College, institutional governance questions receive major attention.

Virtually all faculty contracts create or designate agencies to handle grievances and in that sense are concerned with institutional governance. But no contract at a four-year institution creates a faculty senate or similar basic agency of faculty governance where none had existed. The closest approach is found in the Boston State College contract. Its three "Campus-Wide" committees on curriculum, college development, and budget consultation may come to play much the same role that a faculty senate does elsewhere, and its All-Campus Committee may come to resemble the community type of senate established in recent years at many institutions, such as Colby College and Columbia and Cornell Universities. In the "community" senate, all segments of the academic community come together on a "participatory democracy" basis "to govern" the institution.

Many contracts, such as those at CUNY, SUNY, Rutgers, St. John's, and Oakland, are almost silent about institutional governance systems or agencies and the faculty role therein, being almost wholly problem- or policy-oriented. The reason is not always easy to determine. Perhaps the faculties at these institutions are satisfied with existing governance systems and their place therein, and have concentrated their energies on winning substantial economic gains. In so doing, they may unconsciously have been following the advice of Myron Lieberman, a long-time observer of collective bargaining in education, who is highly critical of using bargaining to strengthen the faculty role in running the institution. Running the business, he argues, is the responsibility of management—of trustees and administrators. When a faculty turns to bargaining, it should, in his view, keep its sights firmly fixed on the economic gains that can be won, forgoing other possible benefits.[13]

13. Lieberman, "Professors, Unite!" *Harper's Magazine,* October 1971, pp. 61–70.

Another possibility is that in the negotiations leading to these initial contracts, it did not prove feasible, for one reason or another, to give a high priority to problems of institutional governance. The same situation may prevail in the second or later rounds of negotiations at some places. If rivalry between a faculty senate and the bargaining agent—now discernible at Central Michigan and Southeastern Massachusetts Universities—does take shape as a full-scale power struggle, the subsequent contract will necessarily reveal a larger concern with the faculty role in the governance system.

How much difference it makes whether the authority of a faculty is exercised through a traditional agency of governance, such as a senate, or through a bargaining agent and its substructure cannot be answered from experience, for there is no institution where faculty bargaining has yet led to a spectacular transfer of function and authority. One can speculate that such transfers will begin to occur and that they will have significant consequences because a bargaining agent will have a different power base from that of a senate. The members of a faculty senate are usually chosen on some kind of representational basis, with seats assigned to departments, divisions, schools, and colleges on a proportional basis deemed fair and appropriate to the diverse educational elements that make up the total academic community. The bargaining agent is much more likely, both for reasons of compliance with law and with political strategy, to follow the one-man, one-vote principle on a unitwide basis in the selection of officers and negotiating teams and in the approval of a contract. Such practice is likely to bring about a significant shift in authority and influence away from senior tenured professors and associate professors toward untenured assistant professors and instructors and toward part-time teachers and nonteaching professionals who have been included in the bargaining unit.

Even where a senate and a bargaining agent might encompass and speak for identical populations, on closely contested policy issues, a majority vote could produce different determinations, depending on which type of governance system is being used. The fair representation doctrine in the law of collective bargaining places the bargaining agent, which may have been chosen in a representation election by a bare majority of the workers, under obligation to represent the interests of all of the workers in the unit fairly. Accordingly, in the negotiation of a contract, the agent must not reach an agreement that discriminates against some members of the unit on an invidious or irrelevant basis. (It also requires the bargaining agent to play its role in the processing of grievances in an even-handed way.) But the doctrine cannot, and does not, prevent the agent from making a contract that has more favorable effects on some employees in the unit than on others.[14] Labor unions in industry have not always been conspicuous examples of democracy, in principle or in practice. They frequently are quite authoritarian in organization and operation, and are characterized by one-party rule and long tenure for officers. "Faculty unions" need not be equally authoritarian: when faculty members under collective bargaining discover how much is at stake in contract negotiation and administration, they may well become more active and aggressive participants in the politics and business of the bargaining agent organization. Yet a labor organization does provide a different setting from that of a faculty organization. Faculty organizations have not always been free from authoritarianism, disinterest, and inertia, but at many instutions the faculty organization—power system—is viewed as providing a balancing out of competing interests and of majority power and minority rights. Whether such a delicately balanced and workable equilibrium can be established in a faculty labor union, only experience will tell.

A major risk is that the transaction of institutional business through collective bargaining mechanisms will alter existing working relationships within the academic community and thus threaten the shared authority concept. These relationships are often somewhat strained under existing governance mechanisms even at the best institutions. The adversary relationship in collective bargaining, both at the bargaining table and in the administration of a contract, may well exacerbate the stresses to a point where essential patterns of trust and cooperation are severely damaged. A conclusion that this danger is already being widely encountered in practice would be premature. At some institutions, trustees and administrators have stated publicly that they accept and support collective bargaining with the faculty, and evidence in some places indicates that these three components in the academic community are gaining improved understanding of their separate and common functions and responsibilities through collective bargaining. This may be happening at Boston State College and Rut-

14. See Charles J. Morris et al., eds., *The Developing Labor Law*, chap. 27, "The Duty of Fair Representation," pp. 726–56.

gers and Central Michigan Universities. But there is evidence that at other institutions, CUNY in particular, collective bargaining is accentuating old strains and conflicts and creating new ones.

The Uneasy Role of the President under Bargaining

Collective bargaining may, even under the best circumstances, complicate the lives of presidents (and provosts and deans) and make their jobs more intolerable than many chief executives have found them to be in recent years. There are three postures that a president may take or be asked to take when faculty bargaining comes to his campus: (1) He can be a direct participant in the process, serving as a principal negotiator for management and taking charge of the administration of a contract. (2) He can keep off the firing line, but, as the institution's chief executive, help shape policy and instructions for the guidance of management's bargaining team and for his colleagues in the administration who enforce the contract. (3) He can try to free himself entirely from any involvement, direct or indirect, in faculty collective bargaining.

The choice among these alternatives is not easy. Agreement is quite widespread that the president should not be a member of management's negotiating team and that he should not take charge of contract administration. He may well be tempted to leave the latter to the business manager, on the theory that collective bargaining concerns only wages, hours, and conditions of employment, and that the major interests of a president lie elsewhere. Even then, he will have difficulty in disclaiming any interest in or responsibility for the compensation of his faculty and its conditions of employment. But faculty bargaining patterns show that issues of educational policy and institutional governance—matters of major interest to the president—do become intertwined with issues of employment standards. No president, unless he is a figurehead, can stand aside and let others shape these policies through the process of collective bargaining. There remains only the choice of avoiding direct, highly visible involvement while trying to provide the indirect leadership and supervision expected of a president. Here a president must walk a fine line. His governing board will expect and demand that he identify and protect all of management's interests. If the faculty drives too hard a bargain on salary increases, work loads, fringe benefits, and other perquisites, or if grievance procedures are frequently invoked during the life of the contract (and rulings by outside arbitrators go against management), trustees will blame the president and conclude that firmer leadership could have prevented some of these unfortunate results. But if the president plays the role of the governing board's agent faithfully, aggressively, and effectively, he is sure to find himself deep in controversy with the faculty on a steady succession of issues. Faculty members will say that he "stood with the trustees rather than with us" or that he "was an ineffectual spokesman of our position." This will be a particularly unhappy development at institutions where the president has good academic credentials and has in the past identified himself more closely with the faculty than with the governing board on many issues.[15]

Some presidents have accepted collective bargaining as an understandable and appropriate development in labor-management relations and institutional governance, and have managed to live comfortably if not happily with the process. But no president we know is without apprehensions about the consequences of collective bargaining nor does any seem truly to enjoy his part in the ongoing business of bargaining. At some institutions the impact on the president has been more decidedly negative.

In leaving the City University of New York for the Berkeley campus of the University of California, Chancellor Albert Bowker can hardly be said to have gone to a trouble-free university. But collective bargaining at CUNY did prove to be an abrasive relationship for all of the principal parties. And this is one trouble from which Berkeley is

15. For a decidedly contrary point of view concerning the academic credentials of administrators, see Sheila Polishook, "Collective Bargaining and the City University of New York," 41 *Journal of Higher Education* (May 1970), 377–83. A faculty member at one of the CUNY community colleges, Professor Polishook writes, "like the managers in the industrial sphere, many university officers are often trained as administrators, coming with degrees from graduate schools in educational administration. They have not risen from the ranks, offer little in the way of customary scholarly achievements of the academic world, and are seen, therefore, as an alien element without faculty orientation" (p. 383).

Although no documentation of this judgment is offered, Professor Polishook may be speaking correctly about community college administrators. We do not offer documentation of our contrary belief that college and university administrators (presidents, provosts, and deans, in particular) more often than not have good academic credentials and have come up through the academic ranks. It is our impression, certainly, that recent chancellors and presidents of the senior colleges in the CUNY system have had quite impressive "academic" credentials. Professor Polishook's article, written shortly after faculty bargaining went into effect at CUNY, is itself significant evidence of the troublesome, even abrasive, relations prevailing at CUNY among trustees, administrators, and faculty members.

still free! At Southeastern Massachusetts University, the trustees, the president, and the faculty were already involved in unusually serious conflict when the first contract went into effect in 1970. Collective bargaining certainly did not reduce the intensity of that conflict. At the end of the contract's first year, the board of trustees asked the president to resign. The institution had an acting president during 1971–72, the second year of the contract. However collective bargaining affects the work of a new president, his assignment at Southeastern Massachusetts will be challenging.

At Oakland University, where a brief faculty strike occurred in September 1971 at the impasse stage of negotiations, the president and other administrators found themselves, as part of management, in an unusually tense adversary relationship with "labor." Oakland in its early years was a much-admired experimental college which seemed an almost ideal environment for faculty members, and the faculty and administration had shared a strong sense of commitment and coopera- tion. In little more than a decade, the institution became a multipur- pose university faced with serious educational and budgetary prob- lems and increasing faculty discontent. At the time of the strike, many of the administrators, including the president, were former faculty members, but this potential element of strength seemed to ebb away as collective bargaining took effect. These unfortunate changes may have been made inevitable by the drastic change in character of the institution,[16] but collective bargaining did not noticeably help matters.

Any Governance Role for Students under Bargaining?

Will collective bargaining jeopardize the governance role students have gained in recent years at many colleges and universities? Is the suggestion correct that some faculties are turning to collective bar- gaining as an indirect means of checking student participation in gov-

16. Professor Jesse R. Pitts, "Strike at Oakland University," *Change,* February 1972, pp. 16 ff., attributes some of the conflict between the president and the faculty members to the fact that the president had "supported massive and expen- sive recruitment of black students." He is said to have been "pushing for the development of remedial and applied programs which are in opposition to the traditional liberal arts orientation of Oakland's talented faculty." Professor Pitts also criticized the president in more personal terms, calling him "an opinionated man," a member of "the McGeorge Bundy school of administrators, caustic and not suffering fools gladly." For a picture of more idyllic days at Oakland, see David Riesman, Joseph Gusfield, and Zelda Gamson, *Academic Values and Mass Education: The Early Years of Oakland and Monteith* (Garden City, N.Y.: Doubleday, 1970).

ernance systems? Such questions are easier to ask than answer. Up to now faculty collective bargaining has had little effect on the place and influence of students in the operation of an institution. Faculty collective bargaining and student participation in governance may, however, be on collision courses. The initial reaction of students to faculty bargaining has been favorable. Faculty members voting to participate in collective bargaining are seen by students as at long last recognizing and asserting their valid interests and claims against a common enemy. But students may yet discover that they get the short end of the stick when the administration and faculty play games together at the bargaining table.

At many institutions students are now voting members of traditional faculty senates and also of new-style community senates. Students have also gained voting memberships on faculty committees, particularly those concerned with "student life" and educational policy. Students are also seeking a voice and a vote in those agencies that make faculty personnel decisions, although their gains in the latter area have been minimal.

The naïveté of the first student reactions to faculty bargaining will not persist if faculty bargaining patterns reveal to students that control of educational policy is shifting from the governance agencies on which they have representation to the bargaining agent substructure, where they have none. In their initial reactions, students do not recognize that collective bargaining is a particular process defined by statute and supervised by public administrative agencies and the courts. The law and practice of collective bargaining have developed over a forty-year period, but the process at bottom remains what it has always been—a two-way confrontation in which management and labor argue their way through to a series of acceptable, short-term agreements concerning wages, work loads, and other conditions of employment.

The exclusion of students from faculty collective bargaining resembles the exclusion of the consumer from industrial collective bargaining (or the taxpayer from public employee bargaining). Two parties, absorbed in reaching agreement concerning their own interests, do not hesitate to bargain away the interests (and the money) of third parties with valid interests in what is being decided. The statutes, administrative rulings, and court decisions that dictate collective bargaining patterns can conceivably be changed to overcome this sacrifice of third-party interests. But if collective bargaining comes to be viewed as an unsatisfactory mechanism for reconciling all relevant social interests, it will probably give way to a system by which, under law, the control of not only wages and hours but also product quality and prices will be sought through more direct means. Such a development might have been considered under way in 1972 in the wage-price control program of the federal government, which gave an administrative board authority to set aside wage agreements in private industry reached through collective bargaining. Whether the business of the academic community is increasingly controlled by collective bargaining or by statutes, the student role in institutional policy making is likely to be weakened.

It is difficult to visualize the conditions under which students might one day sit at the bargaining table and help shape the agreement reached there by the governing board and the faculty. Students—or their parents—pay the tuition or the taxes that provide some of the revenue necessary to sustain a wage increase. Students certainly have an interest in the productivity of the work force, with respect to both quantity and quality of the education they receive. But they do not share the direct interest in deciding the basic conditions of employment that trustees, administrators, and faculty members have. The law certainly does not help them gain a place at the bargaining table. And they have no sanction, beyond their freedom to take their business elsewhere, through which they can try to influence the agreement indirectly. Students can, however, exert pressures on their own campuses in such matters as curricular design, course content, teaching method, academic calendar, and, in the end, "the nature of the product"—the relevance of a higher education. These pressures may, and perhaps should, be sufficiently strong to prevent management and labor from fixing the policies that control such matters at the bargaining table. In industrial bargaining the consumer and the shareholder seldom have any direct role or influence at the bargaining table. But there is much in which they are validly interested that is not bargained about at the table and, instead, is settled in other ways—ways that may still leave the consumer and the shareholder with weak voices, but voices nonetheless. Product design, quality, price, and advertising are examples.

This analysis of difficulties that militate against direct and formal participation of students in faculty contract negotiations may be qualified if the presence of students at the bargaining table at the Brooklyn

Center of Long Island University sets a pattern (as opposed to their exclusion from the table at the second round of negotiations at CUNY). Even under the best of circumstances it is difficult to see the student role at the bargaining table as extending much beyond that of interested observers to whom a measure of polite attention is given by the two main adversaries. Those who negotiate a collective bargaining contract must make a commitment to the parties they represent. They commit management to pay certain wages to the organization's employees and they commit the latter to perform work under certain conditions. Moreover, the negotiators will be around long enough to be held accountable for what the contract turns out to mean in practice. How would students who helped shape an agreement be held accountable to those having a direct personal interest in the balance struck at the table? What could be done about the student bargainer who conceded too much, or too little, but was no longer even identified with the enterprise when the consequences of a bad agreement became apparent?

It is easier to conceive of students having a direct and official involvement in the administration of a contract, or—put differently—of their playing a role in the governance system provided for under a contract. Where a contract is silent about the governance system, as at CUNY and Rutgers, collective bargaining imposes no barrier to whatever student participation in the work of faculty agencies may be agreed to by trustees, administrators, and faculty members through the usual means by which such arrangements are made. The contract at Boston State College makes express provision for student participation in the administrative aspect of collective bargaining through membership in agencies concerned with budget determinations and in faculty personnel decisions. This experiment at Boston State College deserves to be watched with interest by the academic profession. (As of January 1973, it is reported that the second contract at Southeastern Massachusetts University, as negotiated at the table but not yet approved by management or labor, will give students a significant role in the faculty evaluation process at that institution.) There are difficulties inherent in the arrangement. A collective bargaining agreement *is* a contract. It establishes certain rules; administering it requires "going by the book." Failure to do so typically results in grievances being lodged by individual faculty members who are dissatisfied with the effect that deviations from the rules have on them. They are unhappy with the salary adjustments they receive or with the failure to give them reappointment, promotion, or tenure, or to award them a sabbatical leave or a research grant. And they are prepared to argue that conditions laid down in the contract for the control of these decisions have been violated in their cases. If students serve on agencies that review the performance of individual faculty members but have had no part in shaping the collective bargaining contract, they may not feel bound by the contract specifications with respect to wages, hours, and conditions of employment. They may feel free to pursue a straightforward course of rewarding the teachers they like and punishing those who have failed to win their favor, without too close attention to what the contract says or requires by way of adhering to standards. And insofar as student votes may swing the balance in individual cases, the result may be a larger number of grievance cases where higher authorities (including, at the final stage, outside arbitrators), in adhering to contractual requirements, will have to reverse decisions that students helped shape through their participation in the regular processes of institutional government.

The above analysis is necessarily theoretical, for there has been no experience to show whether or not collective bargaining that is confined to management and labor can coexist with, or be integrated into, new forms of university governance in which students play significant roles. The difficulties that might emerge from such an arrangement are sufficiently numerous and serious to give everyone pause before decisions are made that collective bargaining and increased student participation in institutional governance are compatible and desirable goals or processes. There is reason to be apprehensive that these two developments are fundamentally inconsistent and, if experimented with at the same time, very likely to set the stage for new campus confrontations.

One thing is clear. It is dangerous to use the term "collective bargaining" as a euphemism for "participatory democracy," where everyone on campus has a say about almost everything until a consensus is reached that enables everyone to live together happily, if not forever after, at least as long as the students who help make up the consensus are still around. This tendency to appropriate the term to describe something quite different from established usage is illustrated when some student activists assert that they are going to insist on their right to a new form of collective bargaining through which they will negotiate with their institutions concerning *their* interests and *their* rights. Presumably they have in mind a wide range of rights and interests running all the way from control of student social life and discipline, the shaping of course content, and examination, grade, and credit systems, to fundamental alterations in the very brick-and-mortar existence of a university. Such changes may be desirable and they may ultimately be effected in American higher education. But they cannot come about through any process that is properly called "collective bargaining." Who will sit on the other side of the bargaining table with students? And what sanctions will students use when the impasse stage is reached in the negotiations? Who will process their grievances? In sum, it is likely to prove folly of the most dangerous kind to romanticize the term "collective bargaining" by using it as though it referred to a universal process by which great goals can readily be achieved, if well-intentioned people will only use it.

The Effects of Bargaining on the Professional Status and Values of Faculty Members

The concept of "profession," although very old, remains inexact. In claiming membership in professions, lawyers, physicians, and professors have usually stressed such characteristics as a high level of general learning and precise competence achieved through rigorous training programs that are offered at the graduate level by the leading universities; a limiting of the right to practice to those able to meet exacting standards imposed through a licensing mechanism, formal or otherwise; a service motivation that takes precedence over the desire for personal gain; and the enjoyment of a substantial group autonomy that encompasses, among other things, the authority to set performance standards and professional values and to monitor adherence to them by members of the profession.

Unlike the medical and legal professions, the academic profession, dating back to the first universities in the Middle Ages, has carried on its work in an institutional setting. The relationship between the professor and his college or university has varied greatly from time to time and place to place and has never been easy to define. He is at the same time a practitioner of a profession, an employee of an organization, and a manager who helps set and administer the organization's policies and programs. This threefold status is largely a pragmatic condition; it has never received a widely accepted rationalization.

Thus, in their roles as professionals and managers, faculty members assert, particularly in times of crisis at their institutions, "We are the university." At the same time they also speak of themselves as "hired" by their institutions and readily condemn "the administration" for treating them badly. Granted this initial ambiguity concerning the academician's employment status, it is difficult to assess the influence of collective bargaining on his professional values. Three issues must be considered, even if the hard information brought to bear is limited.

The Issue of Faculty Integrity

The first question is whether collective bargaining will so dilute faculties, through the addition of nonfaculty people to the bargaining units, as to threaten the professional cohesion and integrity of academic communities. The assumption has always been that the academic profession has at its center the teaching and research faculties, which determine its character and quality and shape its values, principles, and work patterns. The certifying system under which it operates has never been as strict as those for the medical and legal professions; the Ph.D. or an equivalent degree is viewed as the professor's license to practice. Moreover, the shaping of the training that leads to this degree and the decision to award it to successful candidates have been almost entirely entrusted to the profession itself through those of its members who staff graduate school faculties.

As faculty collective bargaining comes to an institution, if the central teaching faculty is compelled to include sizable elements of so-called supportive professional personnel ("regular, part-time teachers" and "nonteaching professionals," who are subject to separate training and certification processes) and if essentially all of the institution's policy making and administrative processes can be encompassed in the bargaining operation, the control base for institutional business will have been extended far beyond the ranks of the traditional faculty. At many institutions which have collective bargaining, the broadened base is already a reality. What remains speculative is the extent to which supportive professional personnel, by their votes, will divert educational programs, teaching methods, and institutional resources into paths designed by "the labor organization" rather than by "the faculty." Part-time teachers and nonteaching professionals will not necessarily attempt to influence educational policy and methodology directly. But in using their voting power in the bargaining unit to shape policies on wages, hours, and conditions of employment to their liking, they may well compel the teaching faculty to adjust its professional goals and programs to the realities of an altered institutional situation. If the faculty senate (or "the faculty meeting") gives way to the bargaining agent as the dominant employee organization, where, how, and by whom will educational policies be made? Will the department remain a viable agency of educational policy making and administration? Will the individual teacher exercise less control over what happens in his own classroom? Or is it possible that the typical academic community will soon be finding it appropriate and even necessary to absorb or accommodate supportive professional people under any circumstances and that collective bargaining will thus prove to be no more than one of the mechanisms by which this change is effected at educational institutions?

The Issue of Quality versus Egalitarianism

The second and closely related question concerns the influence of faculty bargaining on academic excellence. Every profession commits itself to quality. Practitioners must meet certain basic standards of performance in order to gain admission to and (in theory at least) to remain in the profession, and, beyond the basic standards, the individual is challenged to make a unique contribution to the total effort and achievement of the profession. Every useful definition or description of a profession stresses the importance of the individual in the life and work of the group. Doctors and lawyers receive standard training, but as practitioners they are not viewed as readily interchangeable or replaceable. Indeed, the line between the professions and the so-called semiprofessions is said to depend in significant degree on the replaceability factor. It is argued, for example, that library science, nursing, and public school teaching constitute semiprofessions rather than professions because the training and performance in each instance have been standardized to a point where the practitioner is quite readily replaced. Individual quality and excellence are not totally lacking, but a good nurse, or a good librarian, or a good fifth-grade teacher can be replaced by another practitioner whose training and work standards warrant an assumption that the replacement's job performance will also be good.[17]

17. See Amitai Etzioni, ed., *The Semi-Professions and Their Organizations: Teachers, Nurses, Social Workers.* The concluding chapter, by William J. Goode, "The Theoretical Limits of Professionalization," provides a useful analysis of the distinguishing characteristics of a profession.

The academic profession clearly places a high value on individuality—on the belief that at least the best of its practitioners are not readily interchanged or replaced. In the main it believes that there are different levels of quality and excellence which individuals can aspire to and reach. This belief is much more evident in some parts of higher education than in others. Not all institutions, for example, make a serious attempt to measure individual merit in granting salary increases to their faculty members. The personnel policies of the two-year community colleges and of the four-year state colleges and state universities that emerged from teachers college or vocational school backgrounds do not usually include a merit-measurement factor. Such institutions can be assumed to have set a standard for a "good teacher" than can be reached by many individuals. A "good" faculty member is replaceable.

There is, furthermore, a strong egalitarian movement pervading all of higher education today which views with disfavor traditional efforts to encourage and reward quality and achievement in students, faculties, and institutions. "Elitism" and even "excellence" have become pejorative terms to adherents of this movement.

Collective bargaining has long been recognized as exerting a leveling influence. Nearly three decades ago, the U.S. Supreme Court observed that collective bargaining takes precedence over individual bargaining and thus discourages selective rewards for members of a work force. Speaking for the Court, Justice Jackson called attention to the leveling effect in these words:

> The practice and philosophy of collective bargaining looks with suspicion on . . . individual advantages. Of course, where there is great variation in circumstances of employment or capacity of employees, it is possible for the collective bargain to prescribe only minimum rates or maximum hours or expressly to leave certain areas open to individual bargaining. But except as so provided, advantages to individuals may prove as disruptive of industrial peace as disadvantages. . . . The workman is free, if he values his own bargaining position more than that of the group, to vote against representation; but the majority rules, and if it collectivizes the employment bargain, individual advantages or favors will generally in practice go in as a contribution to the collective result.[18]

Many of the early students of faculty collective bargaining have concluded that bargaining will have a negative impact on faculty

18. J. I. Case Co. v. NLRB, 321 U.S. 332, 338–39 (1944).

salary differentials and merit increases and even on selectivity in promotions and tenure grants. Donald Wollett observes that "collective bargaining agents tend to favor policies that treat all employees alike." In regard to the salary advantages that have traditionally been enjoyed by university faculty members in such areas as law, medicine, and engineering, he notes:

> Collective negotiations is a system of representative government pursuant to which decisions are made on the basis of compromises which survive the test of majority rule in the appropriate bargaining unit. It seems unlikely that the majority will long tolerate adverse differentials. They will either want their salaries and work loads improved to the level of the professional schools or they will want those differentials removed and distributed throughout the group.[19]

Joseph Garbarino sees collective bargaining as "a vehicle for positive gains" only "for the occupational groups on the lower rungs of the academic ladder." The overall prospect is for "a process of 'homogenization' or 'rationalization' of the total academic labor market in the sense of a reduction in differential privileges between occupational sectors of the academic labor force." And again:

> The paradox of faculty unionism to date is that the greatest gains have accrued to the teaching faculty on the margin of the core faculty, to the faculty of the institutions in the integrated systems that have been lowest in the academic hierarchy, and to the nonfaculty professionals.[20]

Experience with faculty collective bargaining does not yet provide overwhelming evidence of a leveling, homogenizing effect on faculty salaries. At most institutions where the contract stage of bargaining has been reached, salary policies seem to have remained much as they were in prebargaining days. The contracts at Central Michigan, Oakland, Rutgers, and Southeastern Massachusetts Universities all make some provision for merit increases as well as across-the-board increases. Indeed, they may reflect some slight movement at these institutions toward the introduction of a selectivity factor in the evaluation of faculty members, where past practice was more nearly a

19. Wollett, "The Status and Trends of Collective Negotiations for Faculty in Higher Education," 1971 *Wisconsin Law Review* (no. 1), 18.

20. Garbarino, "Creeping Unionism and the Faculty Labor Market," pp. 2, 33 (draft MS prepared for *Higher Education and the Labor Market*, forthcoming publication of the Carnegie Commission on Higher Education).

straight across-the-board increase. Whether such a movement would have occurred in any event and might have been more pronounced in the absence of collective bargaining is, of course, an unknown. The two contracts at Central Michigan University reveal a continuing although limited effort to develop a merit salary increase program acceptable to both management and labor. In the first contract, the modest sum of $65,000 was made available to the deans of the five schools for use in "rewarding meritorious service" in accordance with criteria set by the council of deans and the provost. The second contract authorized an indefinite number of "distinguished professional awards" drawn from a fund equal in 1972–73 to 0.5 percent of the base salary figure for all members of the unit, and 1 percent for 1973–74, the distribution to be made in accordance with procedures and criteria developed by a "University Achievement Increase Committee," made up of equal numbers of administrators and faculty members. The latter are appointed by the faculty labor organization, an NEA local.

At Southeastern Massachusetts University, an ingenious plan was agreed to for the distribution of "merit monies" for 1972–73. The plan is an example of continuing bargaining on details of the contract between the faculty labor organization and the administration and trustees. The problem at Southeastern Massachusetts was essentially that faced at Central Michigan and all other Michigan public four-year institutions: how to divide among the instructional employees the money appropriated by the legislature for salary increases (or whatever other funds might be available for faculty salary increases). At Southeastern Massachusetts it was first decided that "merit monies shall be divided proportionate to the groups that generated them"; that is, subtotals would be set for administrators and faculty members in the separate colleges of the university in direct ratio to the number of employees in each of these subgroups. It was then agreed that every faculty member who had "concluded twenty-five years of service at the University" would receive a flat increase of $1,092. (This may be an indication of the power wielded by older faculty members in the bargaining unit at this university.) Next, every faculty member being promoted in rank would receive a flat increase: promotions to professor would carry $600, to associate professor $400, and assistant professor $300. Finally, the remainder of the "merit monies" would be divided into ten equal parts, nine parts to be distributed by the faculty labor organization, "in procedures developed by them," in such a way that both "general merit" (across-the-board increases) and "special merit" would be recognized. One part would be held in contingency against successful "merit appeals" and "adjustments deemed appropriate by the Dean of each college" to correct inequities in individual salaries.

The agreement stated "that General Merit shall only be awarded through a positive recommendation of the tenured faculty members within a department, the department chairman and the Dean of the college." The college dean was also authorized to veto general merit increases in individual cases, but if the tenured members of his department recommended such a faculty member for a general merit increase the following year, he would receive it.

The agreement listed four criteria to be considered in awarding "special merit" increases, but it was silent about the size and number of such increases and the method of choosing recipients. The four criteria were: superior teaching, scholarly or professional activities, service to the academic community, and service to the community at large, with the first two receiving "priority."

No provision for merit increases is made in the contracts at CUNY, SUNY, and St. John's University. The elaborate salary schedules in the first CUNY contract with the Legislative Conference established step increases within each faculty rank, but each faculty member moved through these steps automatically, in accordance with prebargaining practice at CUNY. The salary schedules for the two-year community colleges in the CUNY system provided strikingly large increases for all persons affected by them. Although this provision confirms the observation that collective bargaining will benefit persons on the margin rather than at the center of the "core faculty," salaries at CUNY were so substantially improved for everyone in the two bargaining units that there was little reason for anyone to be unhappy with the result.

The SUNY contract provided a straight 6 percent increase in the salaries of all members of the bargaining unit for 1971–72.[21] But it

21. Joseph Garbarino reports that as of December 1971, six months after the SUNY contract went into effect, the New York legislature had not yet appropriated the additional money to implement the 6 percent increase and that no salary increases had actually been paid. He indicated that the administration would eventually "find money for the increase" even if the legislature failed to provide it. See his "Faculty Unionism: From Theory to Practice," 11 *Industrial Relations* (February 1972), 7.

also expressly recognized the right of "the University, in its discretion," to grant "further upward salary adjustments to individual employees." Provision was also made for the creation of a joint management-labor committee to study the adequacy of the salary schedule for "full-time academic employees ... at the colleges of medicine and dentistry at the University Health Sciences Centers."

The SUNY contract appears simply to postpone decisions about whether in the university as a whole there is to be a single salary schedule or a series of differential schedules and also whether yearly increases are to be uniform or include a merit factor. Because the university is such a conglomeration of different types of schools and colleges, and the employees in the bargaining unit perform such differing types of work, it is probable that later contracts will either include a series of detailed salary schedules for different types of employees, following the CUNY model, or authorize the establishment of such schedules as an aspect of continuing bargaining or contract administration. Whether a merit factor of any consequence will be approved and made a part of the institution's compensation program remains to be determined. If it were to prove possible to raise all salaries at SUNY on an across-the-board basis as handsomely as was done at CUNY in 1969, merit increases might be avoided or be quite minimal. The income limitations that a university with SUNY's aims and purposes is likely to experience for the next few years will create strong pressures to compensate faculty members on a selective basis, in recognition that professors in certain disciplines and professional areas (like medicine) can command premium salaries, as can also professors of recognized distinction, regardless of discipline.

CUNY may experience these same pressures, unless its open admissions program reduces its faculty overall to the level of post-public-school teachers offering standardized instruction on a universal education basis to a large standardized student body. If this eventuality becomes the essential character of the CUNY operation, "standard pay for the same work" will be the rule that determines the pay of all teachers.

The preceding analysis suggests that such institutions as SUNY and CUNY will shortly face a hard choice: they can try to build and maintain strong faculties and quality educational programs which will require some movement toward recognizing and rewarding individual merit, or they can pursue strictly egalitarian policies in compensating faculty members at the risk of encouraging a trend toward uniformity and mediocrity. Some observers of collective bargaining trends in higher education are predicting that the choice will inevitably be made in favor of equality and mediocrity. We are somewhat more hopeful that selectivity and quality in both personnel and programs can survive under collective bargaining. At many institutions, both teams at the bargaining table will be under pressure to recognize differences of function and quality in the work performed by bargaining unit members. The employee bargaining team will also show sensitivity to the idea that the "majority rules" within a bargaining unit, to which Justice Jackson referred, and this tendency will nudge labor's agents at the table toward an egalitarian compensation program. But "the majority" is made up of subgroups, or "minorities." Thus, a faculty bargaining agent, in fashioning and sustaining its basis for control and power, must pay some attention to the special needs and claims of the subgroups that support it, including those with strong claims for top compensation, as measured by market conditions and individual merit. Moreover, as long as the bargaining agent represents professionals only, it will experience and give some expression to pressures to seek or maintain quality in both the institution as a whole and on a down-the-line basis. Finally, there is always the threat that "elitist," professional school components in a general faculty will continue to seek recognition as separate bargaining units, despite their knowing they must overcome traditional labor board prejudices in favor of broad units.

That even AFT, with its traditional opposition to salary differentials and its ties to a national labor movement which has never encouraged the measurement of individual worker merit, will experience and respond to the pressures to reward merit and quality in higher education is suggested by the posture of the AFT local at Rhode Island College during the 1972 campaign that led to its selection by the faculty as the bargaining agent. Prior to the faculty's decision to turn to collective bargaining, the college's salary program had included a merit dimension by which some faculty members were awarded "outstanding performance increments" in addition to the "satisfactory performance increments" (the latter were essentially across-the-board increases). The AFT local announced during the campaign that it would support a continuation of the merit type of increase, at least for the next year.[22] This policy was one means used by AFT, which had run a poor second to the NEA in the first election, to make a successful appeal for the support of senior members of the faculty and win the bargaining agent designation in the second election. AAUP, on the other hand, as the bargaining agent at St. John's and Oakland Universities, did not take as firm a stand for a true merit system of granting faculty salary increases as might have been expected of an organization that seeks to advance excellence and quality in the academic profession. This is not to say that AFT, or NEA, will end up favoring special rewards for excellence more than will AAUP, as these organizations compete to become faculty bargaining agents, but rather to suggest that all will be subject to strong pulls in both directions: toward merit rewards for the members of a community committed to individuality and excellence and toward uniform rewards for the members of a community committed to standardization and egalitarianism.

Compensation Differentials in Symphony Orchestra Bargaining: A Model for Faculty Bargaining?

The experience of the nation's major symphony orchestras strongly suggests that collective bargaining need not have a leveling effect on

---

22. An AFT newsletter, sent to the faculty during the period between the two elections entitled "Values," asserted:

"The members of the Executive Committee favor the principle that professional performance should determine rewards in form of salary. Professional competition is the essence of college teaching and research, and should be considered healthy. Continued growth and activity with demonstrable scholarly productivity should be encouraged and rewarded. . . .

"Contracts for the immediate future should contain: (1) a cost-of-living 'elevator clause' tied to the rate of increase incurred in the prior year; (2) provision for true annual merit increment consisting of a sum of $1,000 for instructors, $1,500 for assistant professors, $1,800 for associate professors, and a sum of $2,200 for professors; (3) additional funds for outstanding merit increments amounting to $500 per unit with a limit of three units for any one faculty member, and no more than 1/3 of the faculty receiving outstanding merit increments; (4) an adjustment budget to be used by chairmen to enable faculty members to retain their same relative salary positions when inequities are identified."

This was, of course, only a campaign promise. How aggressively AFT would bargain for a significant merit component in the faculty salary program remained to be discovered at the bargaining table, but it was unlikely to win everything referred to in its newsletter. Management, on the other hand, would almost certainly welcome agreement on a merit component. AFT, having thus committed itself during the campaign, would be likely to work out such an agreement at the bargaining table even though it discovered it could not win its total salary program.

compensation policies within the work force of an enterprise, even over a long period of time. Professional musicians have long been organized. A single union, the American Federation of Musicians (AFL-CIO), enjoys a virtually unchallenged monopoly in this field. Since most music ensembles, including symphony orchestras, operate on a union shop basis, a young professional musician must join AFM and maintain his status as a dues-paying member if he expects to make his living as a musician.[23] The collective bargaining contracts between the associations that operate the major orchestras and AFM provide a model that is useful to the parties to collective bargaining in higher education. Among other things, these contracts have by no means brought an end to compensation to individual players on merit and market bases. Typically the contract sets a standard salary scale, which, while often announced to the public as though it provided orchestra members with their principal means of support, is known within the profession as the "minimum scale." In recent years, as the major orchestras have extended their seasons toward the goal of a fifty-two-week year, annual salaries under these minimum scales have been raised to a $14,000–$16,000 range.[24] But many members of an orchestra are paid salaries well above the minimum. The manager of one leading orchestra estimates that at least half of its members are paid higher salaries. These salaries above the union scale are almost never announced to the public or even to a player's colleagues. It can be assumed that among the players receiving higher salaries are the concertmaster, the assistant concertmasters, the first and second chair players in each section, and many members of the woodwind, brass, and percussion sections.

23. The Boston Symphony Orchestra was the last major symphony orchestra to operate on a nonunion basis. Its first contract with AFM was negotiated in 1942.

24. Orchestra members have vacillated on the issue of a fifty-two-week year. In the mid-1960s they favored such a policy, and at each new round of negotiations the bargaining agent sought an extension of the season. But with the fifty-two weeks won in the major orchestras, some players changed their minds and argued for the right to work a shorter season, in particular, to be excused from playing during a summer season or from making overseas tours. In fact, many members of major orchestras have other income sources, such as teaching and summer engagements deemed more attractive than the orchestra can provide. The change in attitude is reflected in the latest contract of the Cleveland Orchestra, which offers members a choice between working a full fifty-two-week season (with a minimum five-week paid vacation and a six-week vacation for members with twenty or more years of service) and asking to be released during so-called optional weeks. The latter option plus the vacation weeks would enable a member to miss ten weeks each year.

To describe this arrangement in slightly different terms, collective bargaining in the symphony orchestra setting has been successfully superimposed on an older system of individual bargaining. The collective bargaining contract contains the standard language that its provisions take precedence over the provisions of any individual contract where there is a conflict. But the collective contract does not supplant or supersede the individual contract; it complements it, and takes precedence over it where necessary. Indeed, the typical collective contract expressly recognizes the continuing legitimacy of individual bargaining. Thus, the first article in the contract between the Musical Arts Association (which operates the Cleveland Orchestra) and the Cleveland Federation of Musicians states:

> It is recognized that the Association has entered into, and will in the future enter into, individual contracts of employment with the Musicians. . . . All individual contracts . . . shall in all respects be subject to the terms of this Agreement, although any such individual contract may include terms and conditions in addition to those, so long as they are not in conflict with this Agreement.

This dual bargaining is not a tension-free process. At times rivalries and jealousies within an orchestra threaten to be disruptive of the arrangement. Moreover, since the bargaining in the major orchestras has tended to become more aggressive each time a contract is renegotiated, often with strikes by the players at the impasse stage, it might be supposed that the musicians union would bring pressure on management to use an ever larger percentage of its total income to improve the minimum scale. This does not appear to be happening. Orchestra members have sought and won higher minimum scales with each new contract, but they have not tried to compel orchestra managements to put all of the income available for salary payments into this form of compensation. This suggests that the rank and file of an orchestra's membership and the leaders of the AFM, nationally and locally, accept the idea that a strong orchestra cannot be built and maintained on a strictly egalitarian basis. Moreover, if, in the typical orchestra, half or more of the members are paid above the scale under individual contracts, it is quite possible that a majority of the members of the bargaining unit would vote in favor of continuing the existing arrangement in the event minimum scale players tried to force the elimination of higher salaries for some players.

In a study of the Philadelphia Orchestra that is critical of both its social character and musical goals. Edward Arian suggests that, among the players, there exists a subgroup that feels disadvantaged and alienated and that seeks to advance its interests through collective bargaining and any other means available to it.[25] Arian describes the nonegalitarian character of the Philadelphia Orchestra in the following words:

> There exists in the Orchestra a carefully differentiated allocation of benefits wherein first chair players have been singled out by the management for special treatment in a variety of ways: they receive higher salaries than other Orchestra members; they receive bonuses for the making of records; they are occasionally allowed to perform as soloists at concerts or on records; they are invited to social functions of the Association from which other Orchestra members are excluded; they are mentioned or featured from time to time in Orchestra publicity; they are assigned preferential travel facilities and hotel accommodations; organization rules, in many instances, are waived for them; and, in certain cases, their students are shown preference in hiring.

Arian refers repeatedly to a "most-alienated group" of players in the Philadelphia Orchestra which, he states, comprises 25 percent of the players. He describes one attempt to force the merging of the individual bargaining for salaries above the minimum scale with the collective bargaining process as follows:

> Orchestra members, in recent negotiations for a new labor contract, asked for a voice in a formalized and impersonal promotional procedure. They also asked that a specified salary for each chair in the Orchestra, regardless of the occupant, be placed in the union contract. This was vehemently refused, however, by the Association [management] attesting to the importance which it places upon these control mechanisms.[26]

Arian fails to indicate whether this was a "most-alienated group" proposal or had the support of a majority of the orchestra members and of the Musicians Union.

There are other tensions in a symphony orchestra indicative of an

25. Arian, *Bach, Beethoven, and Bureaucracy: The Case of the Philadelphia Orchestra.* Mr. Arian was a member of the Philadelphia Orchestra for twenty years. At the time his book was published, he was teaching political science at Drexel University.
26. Ibid., p. 37.

egalitarian mood. Thus, the latest Cleveland Orchestra contract contains new language requiring the conductor to notify the members of the orchestra by May 1 each year of the seating in the string sections for the following season. It is stated, however, that this provision does not preclude reseating during the season "for artistic reasons determined by the conductor." There is also a requirement that the conductor invite the principal player of a section to be present if he "holds auditions." An attempt was apparently made to secure an agreement that players in the string sections would advance from the rear chairs toward the first chairs as vacancies occurred, but management successfully resisted the demand. Whether such an agreement is found in the contract of any other major orchestra has not been ascertained, but the very fact that the demand is being made indicates a reluctance by some part of an orchestra's personnel to let management (and the conductor) measure the competence of players. If the experience with shared authority in higher education can be thought of as providing a pattern for music organizations to follow, it may be that musicians will seek and win agreement that auditions for preferred locations within an orchestra shall become the responsibility of a joint management-labor committee. On the other hand, management may win the argument that a symphony orchestra cannot be successfully operated on a shared authority basis and that the conductor must possess and exercise a larger measure of authority than does a college president (or a provost, dean, or department chairman).[27]

The Issue of Academic Freedom

The third issue is whether collective bargaining will have an adverse effect on certain principles and values that the academic profession prizes, particularly those concerned with academic freedom and tenure and so-called academic due process. The danger is that damage will be done to those principles both substantively and procedurally. Academic freedom and tenure are clearly "conditions of employment" and are thus negotiable at the bargaining table. Most of the existing contracts at four-year institutions expressly identify academic freedom as a condition of employment that management recognizes and agrees to ob-

27. There are other professional employment areas where collective bargaining has proved to be compatible with merit compensation. For example, in journalism, reporters and editorial writers who are members of the American Newspaper Guild (AFL-CIO) are often paid salaries above the minimum scale and thus enjoy the advantages of both collective bargaining and individual bargaining.

serve. Some contracts, such as those at Oakland, St. John's, Central Michigan, and CUNY, specifically adopt the "Academic Freedom" section of the "1940 Statement of Principles on Academic Freedom and Tenure"[28] as part of the agreement, either repeating its exact language or incorporating it into the contract by title only. Other contracts, such as those at Boston State College, Southeastern Massachusetts University, and SUNY, formulate their own definitions of academic freedom, some of which closely resemble the 1940 Statement, or they acknowledge and ratify prior action by the institution's governing board in support of academic freedom. The treatment of tenure in these contracts is less universal and uniform. Some contracts define tenure and prescribe the procedure for its award. The Rutgers and SUNY contracts do not mention tenure, and the CUNY contract refers to it only indirectly. Presumably such institutions have bylaws or statutes establishing formal tenure systems, but these are not always acknowledged in, or made a part of, the contracts. In referring to the 1940 Statement, the two CUNY contracts acknowledge only the academic freedom guarantee.

The academic profession and much of the higher education establishment accept the 1940 Statement as the most satisfactory formulation of academic freedom that has yet been arrived at after years of trial-and-error experimentation. The 1940 Statement, however, is not universally accepted. Many colleges and universities have not formally adopted it, although most institutions probably regard themselves as committed to it in some degree. Not all national organizations having an interest in higher education have endorsed it. One leading organization, the American Association of State Colleges and Universities, voted in 1971 to withdraw its endorsement in favor of a statement of its own devising.[29] This statement resembles the 1940 Statement in many ways, but it differs, among other things, in stressing the idea that academic freedom must carry with it an acceptance of the concept of academic responsibility. Neither the AFT nor the NEA has endorsed the 1940 Statement, although both organizations claim that they support aca-

28. See *AAUP Policy Documents and Reports*, 1971 ed., pp. 1–2. In addition to the original sponsoring organizations, some seventy-five educational associations and learned societies have endorsed the statement. Several hundred colleges and universities have made formal institutional commitments to observe it.

29. "Academic Freedom and Responsibility, and Academic Tenure," "Adopted at the Eleventh Annual Meeting of the American Association of State Colleges & Universities, Denver, Nov. 9, 1971" (Washington: The Association).

demic freedom and tenure. Local affiliates of AFT and NEA, as bargaining agents at the campus level, are clearly free to reach agreements with managements that guarantee academic freedom in language differing from the 1940 Statement, or that ignore the subject entirely.

A survey of the first contracts at four-year institutions reveals that academic freedom (as well as tenure) is dealt with variously. The contract at Southeastern Massachusetts University, while following the language of the 1940 Statement closely, also explicitly recognizes that the determination of course content and the selection of textbooks shall be the responsibility of the faculty. On the other hand, the SUNY contract appears to establish a somewhat narrower right to academic freedom than does the 1940 Statement. The outline of the 1940 Statement is followed, but the enunciation of the right is shorter and more restrictive. Where the 1940 Statement is content to warn the teacher to "be careful not to introduce into his teaching controversial matter which has no relation to his subject," the SUNY statement asserts that the faculty member "may not . . . claim as his right the privilege of discussing [such material] in his classroom." The Boston State College contract couples academic freedom and responsibility. This idea is far from bad, but in fact neither side of the equation is fully developed. A preamble properly condemns "acts of physical force or disruptive acts which interfere with university activities," but the substantive statement on academic responsibility does not go beyond a paragraph in the 1940 Statement which examines the teacher's tripartite role as a citizen, a member of a learned profession, and an officer of an educational institution.

This legitimation of a variety of academic freedom formulations through collective bargaining contracts may or may not prove counterproductive or dysfunctional to the academic profession's sustained effort—dating back to 1915—to win agreement on and adherence to a single formulation of academic freedom. There is no evidence that academic freedom has become less secure because of collective bargaining. There may, nonetheless, be cause for apprehension about the ultimate result. Understanding of the concept of academic freedom, both within the profession and by the public generally, may be weakened if the trend toward a variety of contractual definitions persists. Variety might reflect only the differing attitudes toward academic freedom that already exist at the institutional level. The formalizing of these different attitudes among contracts would, however, probably slow the movement toward widespread acceptance of a single standard—either the 1940 Statement or a new statement worked out and accepted by organizations representing components of higher education, as was the 1940 Statement.

The procedural threat to academic freedom will be encountered in the administration of collective bargaining contracts. One principal means for enforcing a contract and resolving complaints of contract violation is, as noted, the grievance-arbitration process. Most collective bargaining laws allow the individual worker to take a complaint directly to his employer without intervention or assistance by the bargaining agent. But the latter is entitled to have a representative present at any discussion or hearing the employer grants the employee. If the employee decides to ask an organization to help him, he must turn to the bargaining agent, for such assistance is one aspect of that agent's exclusive authority to represent all of the employees in the bargaining unit.

Therefore, if the contract contains language guaranteeing academic freedom, a complaint alleging violation of a teacher's academic freedom must be processed as a grievance. The question then arises: What happens to the traditional arrangement under which AAUP, as the recognized guardian of the 1940 Statement, conducts investigations of cases where faculty members allege that their academic freedom has been violated and, if it finds that the administrations of institutions have committed such violations, it imposes censure on them? Where the local AAUP chapter is the bargaining agent, it and the individual complainant are presumably free not to employ the grievance machinery and to stand aside in favor of the traditional national AAUP approach (an on-campus investigation by an ad hoc committee of outsiders, followed by consideration of the committee's report by the national Committee A on Academic Freedom and a possible vote of censure by an AAUP annual meeting).[30] But there is little likelihood that other bargaining agents, particularly those affiliated with NEA and AFT, will stand aside in this fashion. Where a bargaining agent uses the grievance-arbitration process in an academic freedom case, the administration and governing board will be justified in refusing to cooperate with an AAUP investigating committee if AAUP attempts to intervene. Indeed, the law may compel them to refuse to cooperate in order to avoid the risk of being charged with an unfair labor practice.

AAUP has found itself involved in one such situation. At Camden

---

30. The AAUP contract at St. John's University expressly excludes complaints concerning academic freedom from the grievance process.

County Community College, a local faculty association, as the bargaining agent, had negotiated a contract with the institution. A faculty member on term appointment who had been dismissed in mid-academic year was dissatisfied with the help the bargaining agent gave him in his efforts to obtain redress. He requested the AAUP to intervene, which it did. An AAUP ad hoc committee conducted an investigation and prepared a report, even though the college administration refused to cooperate. AAUP decided not to publish the report, influenced perhaps by the possibility that the institution's "management" might go to court to prevent AAUP's intervening in a matter that the law required be handled in another way.

What happens when a faculty member's complaint involving an academic freedom issue is considered and resolved through the grievance-arbitration process under a collective bargaining contract? There is as yet little hard evidence. If a complaint is satisfactorily settled on campus at one of the levels of grievance processing provided for in the contract, the academic community may be presumed to have used its understanding of academic freedom to reach a solution satisfactory to the grievant, his peers on the faculty, and the administration. But where a situation requires turning to external arbitration for a ruling binding on everyone concerned, there is less assurance that the result will be consistent with academic freedom principles as they are accepted by the academic profession. There is certainly no assurance that an arbitrator will reach the same conclusion that Committee A and an annual meeting of AAUP would have, had the case been handled in the traditional way.

If, in a collective bargaining contract, the academic freedom provision adheres closely to the 1940 Statement, an arbitrator is under a presumed obligation to apply this provision properly in reaching his ruling. But no contract states that an arbitrator shall be controlled by AAUP's view of the 1940 Statement; that is, no arbitrator is bound to observe the extensive "case law" that has taken shape out of the many investigations that AAUP has conducted over the years. The arbitrator is free to arrive at his own ruling and to shape whatever rationale he chooses to offer in support of that ruling. And his ruling is binding.[31]

31. One of the limited grounds on which an appeal can be taken from an arbitrator's ruling to the courts is the allegation that the arbitrator has exceeded his authority under the contract. An allegation that an arbitrator has interpreted and applied an academic freedom principle differently from an AAUP application would not provide a basis for court review of a case.

It does not follow, of course, that an arbitrator's ruling in an academic freedom case will be viewed by the parties as less sound than an AAUP ruling would have been. If the arbitrator rules against the grievant, the faculty members and administrators alleged to have encroached on his academic freedom will almost certainly consider the ruling a good one. But a consequence of the settlement of academic freedom cases through the grievance-arbitration process may well be a substantial localizing and fragmenting, and thus a weakening, of the law of academic freedom.

If agency or union shop provisions are written into faculty collective bargaining contracts, another kind of threat to academic freedom will be encountered. As yet, no contract at a four-year institution contains such a provision, and all faculty members thus retain complete freedom to decide to join the "union" and pay dues to it or to decide not to do either of these things. Bargaining agents at many institutions are not happy with this situation. They find it difficult to meet the costs of bargaining because their dues income depends so heavily on the whim of individual faculty members. They are thus favorably disposed to an agency shop provision in the contract, and are increasingly using the rhetoric that "faculty freeloaders" are taking unfair advantage of the gains the union is winning for them. In the public sector, in those states that now prohibit the agency shop for public employees, the law will have to be changed if this union argument is to prevail. In New York State, organized labor, including AFT and NEA, is lobbying at Albany to bring about such a change. In the private sector, the National Labor Relations Act permits both the agency shop and the union shop (except in states that have enacted right-to-work laws), and the way is open for bargaining agents to try to persuade governing boards to agree to one or the other in the contract.

The academic freedom issue here could become acute. At root is the question: What is to be done with the faculty member who refuses to join the faculty union, or even to pay dues or a "fee" to the union without joining it, because he objects to the compulsory arrangement either on principle or for more practical reasons? The law would require that he be dismissed from his position; yet neither the 1940 Statement nor any other recognized formulation of the principle of academic freedom condones any such reason for the dismissal of a college teacher, tenured or probationary. AAUP's Committee A on

Academic Freedom is aware that this issue in faculty collective bargaining may quickly reach the crisis stage, and it has engaged in long discussions in searching for a way out of the dilemma. The best it has been able to suggest thus far is that some kind of conscientious objector status be accorded the faculty member who demonstrates that he is refusing to join the union or pay dues to it because of a well-founded personal belief.

This proposal may not prove persuasive to some academicians, and the fact that it is seriously made by the responsible leaders of AAUP indicates the difficulty that the association, itself, is encountering as it tries to play the dual role of labor union and professional organization. In the 1971 edition of the AAUP "Red Book" (*AAUP Policy Documents and Reports*), the statement of policy on the representation of economic and professional interests contained the unequivocal warning:

> No person shall be required to become a member of or make any financial contribution to the Association as a condition of his enjoying the benefits of representation.

But in a "Statement on Collective Bargaining," published in the December 1972 *AAUP Bulletin,* this guarantee of complete freedom of judgment and position to the individual faculty member was replaced by the following provision:

> In any agency shop or compulsory dues check-off arrangement, a chapter or other Association agency should incorporate provisions designed to accommodate affirmatively asserted conscientious objection to such an arrangement with any representative.[32]

32. The 1971 statement appears in *AAUP Policy Documents and Reports,* 1971 ed. (p. 41), as III, B, of a policy statement "approved" by the AAUP Council in October 1969. The latest "Statement on Collective Bargaining" appears in 58 *AAUP Bulletin* (December 1972), pp. 423–24. It is identified as having been "prepared" by the association's Committee N on Representation of Economic and Professional Interests and "approved for publication" by the Council in October 1972. The statement also says that "comments from members, chapters, and conferences will be welcome and should be submitted to the Washington Office." This latest statement of policy, then, has not yet been approved by an AAUP annual meeting. But the 1972 annual meeting enthusiastically approved a more aggressive AAUP role in collective bargaining; it is unlikely that any serious objection to the new agency shop position will be made by a large number of members or sustained by a majority of the delegates at a later annual meeting. The pinch will come when individual faculty members find themselves in disagreement with AAUP chapters over the latter's interpretation and application of the "conscientious objection" proviso.

It remains to be discovered in practice what this will mean. AAUP chapters that become bargaining agents at their institutions will continue to encounter the same budgetary difficulties that have plagued virtually all bargaining agents at four-year colleges and universities. Some chapters will be tempted, where the law permits, to enter into agency shop agreements with governing boards and then to interpret the "conscientious objection" loophole as narrowly as possible, even to the point of risking censure by, or expulsion from, the national association. AFT, NEA, and independent bargaining agents will be even less willing to follow the lead of the national AAUP in working out an accommodation between academic freedom and compulsory union membership or payment of dues by faculty members. Where they achieve agency shop agreements and nonconforming faculty members are then dismissed from their jobs, AAUP may well be asked to intervene in its traditional role as the principal academic professional association defending the 1940 Statement. As a labor organization, it has already changed its own policy and moved some distance toward acceptance of the agency shop. At best, it will encounter embarrassment in attempting to put on its hat as a professional association in order to condemn other labor organizations and educational institutions for entering into agreements which compel faculty members to behave in ways that they regard as violating their academic freedom. At worst, AAUP is likely to be turned away at the door where another labor organization has won recognition as the exclusive bargaining agent of the faculty and faculty members have then been dismissed for failure to pay dues to that agent.

EFFECTS OF COLLECTIVE BARGAINING ON EDUCATIONAL INSTITUTIONS

American colleges and universities have long enjoyed a large measure of autonomy, more, perhaps, than institutions of higher learning in any other country. This autonomy is a principal explanation of the diversity that characterizes the American system of higher education. It has also generally been regarded as an element of strength in the system. Private institutions, throughout most of their history, have been almost wholly free from governmental controls. Autonomy and diversity have been most pronounced in the private sector. But even in the public sector, there has been more autonomy and diversity than in other countries: American public colleges and universities have been free from the centralizing influence of a national ministry of education, found in many other nations. Within the fifty different state systems of higher education, many public institutions have been allowed a surprising amount of autonomy and freedom to diversify. A persuasive case can be made that the state institutions that have achieved the highest levels of excellence are also the ones that have enjoyed the most autonomy.

The Erosion of Institutional Autonomy

Institutional autonomy and diversity have undoubtedly been declining during the last decade or two in both the private and the public sectors, as governments at all levels have imposed a wide variety of controls over higher education, particularly as part of the price institutions must pay in accepting more and more assistance from public treasuries. It is too early to say that collective bargaining is contributing to this decline. Yet faculty bargaining must be recognized as subjecting colleges and universities to the threat if not the reality of substantial external intrusion into internal affairs that have hitherto been viewed as theirs to control and settle. To begin with, bargaining is almost everywhere conducted in accordance with the terms of statutes: the parties to bargaining must "follow the law" in their dealings with each other. More precisely, there are four points in the bargaining process where external agencies may intervene and either supervise the process of bargaining or make decisions binding on the parties. These are: (1) the labor board's determination of the membership of the bargaining unit; (2) the labor board's supervision of a representation election and certification of a bargaining agent; (3) the arbitrator's ruling in a grievance case, which under certain circumstances is subject to appeal to, and a final ruling in, the courts; and (4) the labor board's ruling that one party or the other has committed an unfair labor practice and must pay a penalty or make some kind of restitution, which ruling is also subject to judicial review.[33] These points of contact between the college or university and external agencies have not been of equal importance up to now. As we have seen, the authority of the labor board to determine the membership of a faculty bar-

33. The extensive body of judicial law that the federal courts, and the U.S. Supreme Court in particular, have made in applying the National Labor Relations Act has largely taken shape in cases reaching the courts from NLRB rulings applying the unfair labor practices provisions of the statute.

gaining unit has had significant consequences for several educational institutions and their employees.

At the other end of things, the unfair labor practice ruling remains an encroachment in theory only. It should be noted here that unfair labor practices are express prohibitions set forth in federal and state collective bargaining statutes. As of June 1972 there was no clear instance where either party to the bargaining process at a four-year institution has finally been found guilty of such a practice, although in at least two instances the matter has come before the NLRB.

An NLRB trial examiner found Lawrence Institute of Technology in Detroit guilty of an unfair labor practice in failing to renew the appointments of three nontenured faculty members who had been active in an unsuccessful effort by the AAUP chapter to organize the faculty and to win designation as bargaining agent. The trial examiner ordered the institute to offer the three faculty members their former jobs or "substantially equivalent positions" and "to make them whole for any loss of earnings." On appeal by the institute, a three-member NLRB panel unanimously reversed the ruling. The Board found that the institute could properly have failed to reappoint the three persons because of its efforts to upgrade its standards of instruction and their failure to meet those standards and, conversely, that the General Counsel of the NLRB had not met the burden of proof test by establishing that the three had been dismissed because of their union activity. The opinions of the trial examiner and the NLRB show sharp contrast in their reactions to the evidence presented. This wide difference suggests that when educational institutions become involved in unfair labor practice cases in any significant number and the issue is whether nontenured teachers have not been promoted because of union activity, this external intrusion into the life of academic communities may have unpredictable and uneven consequences.[34]

In January 1972, an NLRB trial examiner found that Monmouth College in New Jersey also had committed an unfair labor practice in November 1970 in notifying a nontenured faculty member that his contract would not be renewed for 1971–72. The faculty member charged that the negative decision was based on his active role in a faculty labor organization and on his protest of efforts of the college to disci-

34. See Lawrence Institute of Technology and Lawrence Institute of Technology Chapter, American Association of University Professors, 196 NLRB No. 8 (1972).

pline two other faculty members who had been accused of creating a disturbance at a convocation addressed by General Maxwell Taylor. College authorities asserted that the failure to reappoint him was based on his failure to progress satisfactorily toward his Ph.D. and also that it had opportunities "to upgrade the department" by appointing a superior teacher who already held the doctorate. The trial examiner conducted a hearing at which, as is customary, the demeanor of witnesses became a factor influencing his ruling. The examiner did not find the testimony of the department chairman, who had initiated the adverse recommendation, persuasive. He did find the faculty member "to be a truthful witness who gave a forthright version of the circumstances which brought about his discharge." The examiner's judgment of the two adverse witnesses may well have been sound. But institutional and faculty autonomy are subjected to a new and powerful external intrusion when decisions on faculty reappointments and tenure grants can finally be controlled partly by the way a government official views the demeanor, as witnesses before him, of an institution's administrators and faculty members who have participated in actions under review. As of September 1972 a final NLRB order had not been issued in this case.

The frequency with which the parties to bargaining in industry are found to be violating the law through unfair labor practices suggests that this portion of the collective bargaining law will soon become a felt reality in higher education.[35]

At public institutions, collective bargaining may create a "credibility gap" between the employment patterns that management and labor agree to at the campus level and those that public authorities at the state capital are prepared to accept and implement. Thus, faculties may eventually find themselves bargaining, not so much with administrators and trustees within their institutions, as with state administrative officers and agencies, the courts, and the legislature. Indeed, this condition already exists at the State University of New York; it is provided for by law in Hawaii; and it will almost surely take shape in California if faculties at the public institutions there turn to collective bargaining. In Michigan, if faculties and local "management" at the individual state institutions allow their costs to rise sharply because

---

35. The NLRB received 21,038 unfair labor practice complaints in the fiscal year ending June 30, 1971. Of these, 13,601 alleged violations by employers, and 7,330 by unions. See *Thirty-fifth Annual Report of the NLRB*, pp. 1, 10–14.

of collective bargaining, the governor and legislature will likely try to impose additional statutory and administrative controls over institutional costs and productivity. The temptation will also be strong to claim a direct role in the negotiations at the bargaining table, as in the SUNY situation.

These pressures in Michigan may for a while be successfully resisted, for the tradition of autonomy at public institutions is old and respected. When we asked one Michigan university president whether bargaining at the local level might not produce sharp faculty salary differentials among comparable institutions, he replied, "Why not?" and suggested that this trend would be an aspect of the continuing competition to achieve the diversity and excellence among institutions that autonomy is intended to encourage. This kind of answer almost certainly underestimates the likelihood that state legislatures will intervene where the governing boards of some state institutions approve larger salary increases through collective bargaining than do the boards at other institutions, even when the former can find funds to implement generous agreements without asking the legislature for larger appropriations. NEA and AFT, as bargaining agents, boast of the lobbying power they wield at state capitols in winning larger appropriations for education. Their claims may be exaggerated, but neither is likely to remain inactive politically if it sees the other, or their mutual rival, AAUP, making greater gains from institutions than it is able to achieve where it is the bargaining agent. The legislature and the governor will then be tempted not only to eliminate differences in the economic package among institutions, but also to intrude into the trade-off in bargaining by prescribing standards affecting the "hours" and "conditions of employment" sections of contracts. The provision inserted by the Michigan legislature in the 1970 appropriation act setting minimum teaching loads at the several types of public institutions is an example of the kind of legislative interference that may take shape with respect to certain of the educational arrangements that institutions have traditionally viewed as subject to their own control. This particular provision may have been ill-considered, unenforceable administratively, and of doubtful constitutionality. But it is a mistake to assume that, with time and experience, governors and legislatures may not find effective ways of imposing their will on individual institutions.

The argument is heard that government agencies, federal and state, are already establishing dangerous levels of intrusion into the internal affairs of hitherto largely autonomous colleges and universities. The argument continues that unionization and collective bargaining will actually provide faculties and administrations at state institutions (and private institutions as well) with a stronger vantage point in their political confrontations with governors and legislatures, as well as with the federal government. Faculties should, however, be asking themselves whether the mechanism of collective bargaining, limited and colored by forty years of history, is the most effective and productive way for the professionals who staff educational institutions to define and defend their case for public support, both in terms of dollars and of programs and goals. Cannot a university president, as spokesman for an academic community that has worked out a statement of its needs and expectations internally through a well-conceived structure of institutional governance, make a more persuasive and productive presentation of his institution's case at the state capital or in Washington than do or will the dual agents of management and labor defending the requirements of a contract reached through collective bargaining?

In private colleges and universities, if early developments are a forecast, those that turn to collective bargaining will find their autonomy endangered through a succession of confrontations with the National Labor Relations Board and ultimately the federal courts. The rulings that have emerged from NLRB on matters that have traditionally been determined exclusively within an institution (status and role of department chairmen; relations between full-time faculty members and part-time—adjunct—instructors and nonteaching professionals; the operation of the tenure system) suggest that federal officials will not always act out of good understanding of issues or be deterred by even a sense of their own limitations. The Board's rulings may try to reflect the facts of the situation at an institution as the Board sees them, but it is already clear that the rulings will nonetheless seem to many faculty members and administrators to constitute an erosion of their traditional authority to make these policy decisions themselves—in short, to be an erosion of the institution's autonomy.

A Damper on Change and Experimentation?

The continuing search for increased effectiveness and excellence in higher education is said to depend heavily on institutional experimentation and change. Such forward-looking ventures are undoubtedly endangered by collective bargaining although adverse effects have not yet become manifest. The issue is simple: experimentation and change flourish where there is flexibility in the setting and process for a group of people to work together and where individuals are challenged to throw themselves into exciting enterprises without counting personal costs too closely. A collective bargaining contract is by definition a code of work rules. Management and labor are both encouraged, indeed in large measure required, "to go by the book." Will this rigidity not significantly inhibit faculties from undertaking bold and courageous educational experiments, where clock-watching and measurement of worker output could prove fatal? A recent visit by one of the authors of this book to Juniata College, a private liberal arts college engaging in a far-reaching effort to revolutionize its educational program, revealed that faculty members were obviously caught up in the spirit of the venture. They believed in what they were doing and were working hard to perfect and implement a master plan of educational reform. In reporting on the visit to a foundation, attention had to be called to the risk that the faculty was so strongly committed to the venture as to suggest danger it might exhaust itself in the undertaking. Another question suggested itself, though there was no immediate need to answer it. Could such an ambitious educational program be undertaken if the governing board, the administration, and the faculty of the college had agreed to conduct their working relations in accordance with a detailed series of rules covering wages, hours, and working conditions?

That the answer to this question can on occasion be positive is suggested by the experience of CUNY in undertaking its open admissions program, which has necessitated providing instruction to a sharply increased student body, many of whose members require extensive remedial assistance. This ambitious venture has been successfully initiated at a time when the university was bound by the limitations imposed on faculty work patterns by collective bargaining contracts, despite some severe strains in the situation.[36] The next round of contract negotiations at CUNY may place some obstacles in the way of

36. See Leonard Kriegel, "Surviving the Apocalypse: Teaching at City College," *Change*, Summer 1972, p. 54, for a highly personal but significant account of reactions of the City College faculty to the problems created by the open admissions program.

continuing the open admissions experiment, even with both parties to the bargaining claiming to support it.

Will the Parties to Faculty Bargaining Bankrupt their Institutions?

Classical descriptions of collective bargaining attribute to both management and labor a shared concern for the continued well-being of the enterprise itself, but add the qualification that neither the workers nor their bargaining agents should make the continued solvency of the business a part of their major concerns. If management can be persuaded to improve the economic package at each new round of negotiations, labor can assume that management knows where the money is coming from. Presumably the price of the product will be raised or dividends to stockholders will be reduced. The possibility that strikes and high labor costs may have contributed to the demise of some businesses (the newspaper business provides some striking examples) is almost never conceded by the labor movement's economists or examined with care by students of the labor movement.

Can professional people who elect to use collective bargaining to improve their economic status avoid this concern, particularly if they work for nonprofit enterprises? Can they bargain as aggressively as possible for higher wages and better working conditions and simultaneously tell themselves that, in entering into agreements, management will not go beyond the point where survival of the business may be endangered? Or is there reason for apprehension that where the professional employees and the managers of nonprofit educational and cultural enterprises negotiate employment terms through collective bargaining, neither side can be counted on to give adequate attention to the continuing economic stability or viability of the business?

The course of collective bargaining in such cultural enterprises as the Metropolitan Opera Association and the symphony orchestras in Philadelphia, Cleveland, and Washington suggests that such apprehension has some basis in fact. The musicians and other professional groups associated with these organizations have gone on strike for better wage scales when managements were uncertain whether they could find additional income to meet existing deficits, let alone meet additional costs under new contracts. It can be argued that musicians won their strikes against their "employers" in these instances because a social or market judgment was being rendered that, as talented professional people in short supply, they were entitled to more pay and better working conditions.[37] But a troublesome gap may be opening up between such a judgment and the willingness and ability of management to go on "making ends meet." Management undoubtedly tells itself that the enterprises must be kept alive in the expectation that in the long run something will happen to save them. In the short run, every effort will be made to find additional revenues through increased prices at the box office, more intensive search for gift income, and the expenditure of unrestricted endowment or capital funds. The modest salary settlement in 1972 between the Metropolitan Opera Association and the members of its orchestra, already referred to, may indicate that collective bargaining provides a means by which management and labor can, in the face of a bleak financial outlook, reach a sensible agreement that would have been difficult to achieve under any other arrangement. Such a result will be encouraged where both sides (management, in particular) use the opportunity which negotiations at the bargaining table present to share detailed and accurate accounts of their respective financial conditions and needs. The management of a nonprofit enterprise can, if it will, avoid extremes of concealing available income and of minimizing a bleak budgetary outlook. Musicians, as well as academicians, may have to share with management a full accounting of the outside income they earn, gained in some measure from the prestige of their identification with the symphony orchestra or the educational institution. A *quid pro quo* in sharing data at the bargaining table may mean that professional musicians and professors must be willing to report their total incomes.

Faculty members may be more prone to tell themselves "We are the university" than professional musicians are to say "We are the orchestra." At many colleges and universities, faculty members are substantially involved in institutional governance, particularly in the making of policy, whereas in symphony orchestras musicians are still largely excluded from both policy making and administration. For

37. During the Kennedy Center's first season of operation in the nation's capital, stories in the *New York Times* and the *Washington Post* and *Star* reported that some stage hands were earning as much as $1,500 a week under union contracts negotiated with the center's management. The press accounts may have contained inaccuracies or distortions, but one can guess that the musicians of the National Symphony Orchestra, which is the center's resident orchestra, took notice of the stories and gave passing thought to the salary increases they might fairly seek in the next round of negotiations with the orchestra's management. (In actuality, the gains they did win in the next round proved to be quite modest, judging by press reports of the orchestra's new contract.)

another thing, musicians (and such other professionals as doctors and lawyers) can and do find work as self-employed enterpreneurs, although some of their most attractive employment opportunities undoubtedly are on a group-practice basis. To the extent that they choose to work for organizations, they must show concern for the welfare of the enterprises with which they are identified. Professors seldom teach in a noninstitutional setting; it is difficult for them to practice their profession on anything other than a group basis except, of course, where, as economists, chemists, political scientists, and the like, they use their individual competences to earn income through nonteaching activities.

The milieu in which professors work may suggest that they are under greater necessity than are musicians (or than doctors or lawyers would be) to concern themselves with how the latest collective bargaining contract they have won from management is to be funded. It does not appear that many members of the academic profession are yet examining this possibility carefully. The faculty member is still tempted to think that the institution's total income can be increased through larger appropriations from state legislatures, more federal aid, increased tuition charges to students, more generous gifts from the institution's friends and supporters, or an end to administrative extravagances. Or that trustees and administrators can, if they want to or are compelled to do so, make budgetary adjustments or changes in institutional priorities within existing revenue limits, which will enable them to increase faculty salaries.

To put the point differently: members of the academic profession must try to balance their claims for appropriate compensation and working conditions against the limitations that society and the economy may place on costs of higher education, whether measured by the worth of the individual institution or the worth of the system as a whole. So stated, the issue comes back to the fundamental role of the academic profession in institutional governance. Can professors truly share in a system of authority and responsibility for planning and carrying out the work of colleges and universities? Do they wish to share such authority and responsibility to the extent that they too become enterpreneurs not only in helping make bold and enterprising policy decisions but also in sharing the risks to be encountered as the venture moves ahead? Or do they wish to stress the adversary relationship between themselves as employees and the organization's managers, not only using whatever bargaining power they can muster to compel the managers to increase their salaries but also conceding to management the entrepreneurial functions of assuming risks *and* deciding basic policies?

Of course, college teachers may hope to gain the best of two worlds: they may hope through collective bargaining to bring successful pressure on both society and governing boards to improve their salaries and working conditions and, at the same time, retain or even strengthen their roles in shared authority governance systems. More time and experience are needed to reveal the potential inherent in faculty bargaining for any of these results at a given institution. Collective bargaining will be tried at a variety of institutions, public and private. This much is certain. But so, too, should other models of the traditional shared authority approach to operating colleges and universities continue to be tried. Autonomy of the institution and diversity among institutions are still essential to quality in American higher education. As yet, faculty collective bargaining no more deserves to sweep the field that does any other currently popular experiment in higher education, whether it be open admissions, coeducation, abolition of grades and degree requirements, universities without walls, a modular academic calendar, new graduate degrees that qualify academicians for teaching only, or any other new way of ordering and operating the educational process.

The one clear danger posed by the movement toward faculty collective bargaining is that it may quickly come to shape and control the labor-management relationship in higher education as completely as it does in industry. The case for faculty bargaining must be developed and affirmed on an incremental basis over a reasonable period of time. In the end, it will almost certainly develop into an effective model for use at many institutions. But the academic profession can and should develop other effective models, if autonomy and diversity are to remain prized and useful values.

Bibliography

I. Books, Pamphlets, and Reports

AAUP Policy Documents and Reports. 1971 ed. Washington: American Association of University Professors, 1971.

Adell, B. L., and Carter, D. D. *Collective Bargaining for University Faculty in Canada.* Kingston, Ontario: Industrial Relations Center, Queens University, 1972.

Analysis of Faculty Contract Information at Public Community Colleges in Michigan 1969–70. Report prepared for the Michigan Community College Association, April 1970. Lansing: The Association, 1970.

Arian, Edward. *Bach, Beethoven, and Bureaucracy: The Case of the Philadelphia Orchestra.* University: University of Alabama Press, 1971.

Bayer, Alan E. *College and University Faculty: A Statistical Description.* ACE Research Reports, vol. 5, no. 5. Washington: Office of Research, American Council on Education, 1970.

Belcher, A. Lee; Avery, Hugh P.; and Smith, Oscar S. *Labor Relations in Higher Education.* Washington: College and University Personnel Association, 1971.

Bok, Derek C., and Dunlop, John T. *Labor and the American Community.* New York: Simon & Schuster, 1970.

Bufford, Samuel. "University Collective Bargaining Contracts." Dissertation, Eastern Michigan University, 1970.

Carlton, Patrick W., and Goodwin, Harold T. *The Collective Dilemma: Negotiations in Education.* Worthington, Ohio: Charles A. Jones Publishing Co., 1969.

Cole, Stephen. *The Unionization of Teachers: A Case Study of the UFT.* New York: Praeger Publishers, 1969.

Coleman, Daniel R. "The Evolution of Collective Bargaining as It Relates to Higher Education in America." Ph.D. dissertation, Florida State University, n.d.

Collective Bargaining in Higher Education, Bibliography No. 2. Compiled by Joan D. North. University: Manpower and Industrial Relations Institute, University of Alabama, 1972.

Collective Bargaining in Public Employment and the Merit System. Office of Labor-Management Policy Development, U.S. Department of Labor. Washington: Government Printing Office, 1972.

Collective Bargaining in U.S. Higher Education, 1960–1971: A Selective Bibliography. Compiled by Kenneth E. Marks. Ames: Iowa State University Library, 1972.

Collective Bargaining on Campus II: What to Do When the Petition Is Filed. Ann Arbor, Mich.: Institute of Continuing Legal Education, 1972. ("Course Materials.")

"Collective Negotiations and the Academic Senate: A Report to the Faculty Affairs Committee, Academic Senate of the California State Colleges." Multilithed. N.d.

Collective Negotiations in Higher Education: A Symposuim. 1971 *Wisconsin Law Review* (No. 1). [Articles are listed by author in Part II of this Bibliography.]

Davey, Harold W. *Contemporary Collective Bargaining.* Englewood Cliffs, N.J.: Prentice-Hall, Inc., 1972.

Doherty, Robert E., and Oberer, Walter E. *Teachers, School Boards, and Collective Bargaining: A Changing of the Guard.* Ithaca: New York State School of Industrial and Labor Relations, Cornell University, 1967.

Duryea, E. D., and Fisk, Robert S. "Impact of Unionism on Governance." In *The Expanded Campus,* edited by Dyckman W. Vermilye. San Francisco: Jossey-Bass, 1972.

Elam, Stanley, and Moskow, Michael H., eds. *Employment Relations in Higher Education.* Bloomington, Ind.: Phi Delta Kappa, 1969.

Etzioni, Amitai, ed. *The Semi-Professions and Their Organizations: Teachers, Nurses, Social Workers.* New York: Free Press, 1969.

Faculty Collective Bargaining in Postsecondary Institutions: The Impact on the Campus and on the State. Prepared by the Higher Education Services Division for the 1972 Annual Meeting of the Education Commission of the States. Denver, Colo.: The Commission, 1972.

Faculty Participation in Academic Governance. Report of AAHE Task Force. Washington: American Association for Higher Education, 1967.

Fleming, Robben W. *The Labor Arbitration Process.* Urbana: University of Illinois Press, 1966.

"An Impartial Review of Collective Bargaining by University Faculties." Prepared by the Michigan State University Faculty Affairs Committee, March 1971. Multilithed.

"Interim Report." Committee to Study Faculty Collective Bargaining. Faculty Senate, Western Michigan University. Mimeographed. April 1972.

"Issues and Answers on Collective Bargaining." The Ad Hoc Committee on Collective Bargaining of the Academic Senate, California State Colleges. Multilithed. N.d.

Lieberman, Myron, and Moskow, Michael. *Collective Negotiations for Teachers.* Chicago: Rand-McNally & Co., 1966.

Mason, Henry L. *College and University Government: A Handbook of Principle and Practice.* New Orleans: Tulane University, 1972.

Michigan, University of, Senate Assembly. *Report of the Committee on Faculty Rights and Responsibilities.* Ann Arbor: The Senate Assembly, 1971.

Morris, Charles J., ed. *The Developing Labor Law*. Washington: Bureau of National Affairs, 1971.

Moskow, Michael H.; Loewenberg, J. Joseph; and Koziara, Edward C. *Collective Bargaining in Public Employment*. New York: Random House, 1970.

Nolte, M. Chester. *Status and Scope of Collective Bargaining in Public Education*. Eugene: Eric Clearinghouse on Educational Administration, University of Oregon, 1970.

Primer of Labor Relations: A Guide to Employer-Employee Conduct. 18th ed. Washington: Bureau of National Affairs, 1971.

Scope of Bargaining in the Public Sector: Concepts and Problems. Report by Paul Prasow and others, submitted to Office of Labor-Management Relations Services, U.S. Department of Labor. Washington: Government Printing Office, 1972.

Selznick, Philip. *Law, Society, and Industrial Justice*. New York: Russell Sage Foundation, 1969.

Shulman, Carol H. *Collective Bargaining on the Campus*. Prepared by Eric Clearinghouse on Higher Education. Washington: American Association for Higher Education, 1972.

Smith, G. Kerry, ed. *Agony and Promise*. San Francisco: Jossey-Bass, 1969.

Smith, Robert; Axen, Richard; and Pentony, Devere. *By Any Means Necessary*. San Francisco: Jossey-Bass, 1970.

Stanley, David T. *Managing Local Government Under Union Pressure*. Washington: Brookings Institution, 1972.

Thirty-fifth Annual Report of the National Labor Relations Board. Washington: Government Printing Office, 1971.

Tice, Terrence N., ed. *Faculty Power: Collective Bargaining on Campus*. Ann Arbor, Mich.: Institute for Continuing Legal Education, 1972.

Wellington, Harry H. *Labor and the Legal Process*. New Haven: Yale University Press, 1968.

Wellington, Harry H., and Winter, Ralph K., Jr. *The Unions and the Cities*. Washington: Brookings Institution, 1971.

Wollett, Donald H., and Chanin, Robert H. *The Law and Practice of Teacher Negotiations*. Washington: Bureau of National Affairs, 1970.

Zagoria, Sam, ed. *Public Workers and Public Unions*. Englewood Cliffs, N.J.: Prentice-Hall, Inc., 1972.

II. Articles and Papers

Andes, John, and Goodwin, Harold. "Emerging Trends in Faculty Collective Bargaining Agreements." 1 *Studies in Management* (June 1972).

"At the Brink: Report on the Economic Status of the Profession, 1970–1971." 57 *AAUP Bulletin* (June 1971).

Bain, Trevor. "Precarious Professors: New Patterns of Representation: A Comment"; *and* Garbarino, Joseph W. "Reply to Professor Bain." 10 *Industrial Relations* (May 1971).

Barrett, Jerome T. "Governmental Response to Public Unionism and Recognition of Employee Rights: Trends and Alternatives for Resolving Issues." 51 *Oregon Law Review* (Fall 1971).

Begin, James P. "Collective Bargaining Agreements in Colleges and Universities: Union Security Provisions." 22 *Journal of the College and University Personnel Association* (March 1971).

Bernstein, Merton C. "Alternatives to the Strike." 85 *Harvard Law Review* (December 1971). Reprinted in 58 *AAUP Bulletin* (December 1972).

Boyd, William B. "Collective Bargaining in Academe: Causes and Consequences." 57 *Liberal Education* (October 1971).

Brown, Martha A. "Collective Bargaining on the Campus: Professors, Associations and Unions." 21 *Labor Law Journal* (March 1970).

Brown, Ralph S., Jr. "Collective Bargaining for the Faculty, I." 56 *Liberal Education* (March 1970).

———. "Collective Bargaining in Higher Education." 67 *Michigan Law Review* (March 1969).

———. "Representation of Economic Interests: Report of a Conference." 51 *AAUP Bulletin* (September 1965).

Brown, Ronald C. "Professors and Unions: The Faculty Senate, An Effective Alternative to Collective Bargaining in Higher Education?" 12 *William and Mary Law Review* (Winter 1970).

Bucklew, Neil S. "Administering a Faculty Agreement." 22 *Journal of the College and University Personnel Association* (May 1971).

———. "Collective Bargaining in Higher Education: Its Fiscal Implications." 57 *Liberal Education* (May 1971).

———. "Fiscal Judgment in Bargaining Can Uncover Hidden Costs." 50 *College and University Business* (March 1971).

Bunzel, John H. "The Faculty Strike at San Francisco State College." 57 *AAUP Bulletin* (September 1971).

Buys, L. M. "Collective Bargaining in Michigan Community Colleges." 21 *Journal of the College and University Personnel Association* (May 1970).

Cartter, Allan M. "Scientific Manpower for 1970–1985." 172 *Science* (April 9, 1971).

Christenson, Arlen. "Collective Bargaining in a University: The University of Wisconsin and the Teaching Assistants Association." 1971 *Wisconsin Law Review* (No. 1).

Collective Bargaining: New Faces at the Bargaining Table. 6 *Compact* (June 1972). [Thirteen articles on bargaining in higher and public school education.]

"Coping with Adversity: Report on the Economic Status of the Profession, 1971–72." 58 *AAUP Bulletin* (June 1972).

Davis, Bertram H. "Unions and Higher Education: Another View." 54 *AAUP Bulletin* (September 1968).

Drotning, John; Lipsky, David; and Foster, Howard. "The Analysis of

Impasse Procedures in Public Sector Negotiations." *Management of Personnel Quarterly,* Summer 1971.

"Faculty Participation in Strikes." 54 *AAUP Bulletin* (June 1968).

Feinsinger, Nathan P., and Roe, Eleanor J. "The University of Wisconsin Madison Campus—TAA Dispute of 1969–70: A Case Study." 1971 *Wisconsin Law Review* (No. 1).

Ferguson, Tracy H. "Collective Bargaining in Universities and Colleges." 19 *Labor Law Review* (December 1968).

Finkin, Matthew W. "Collective Bargaining and University Government." 1971 *Wisconsin Law Review* (No. 1). Reprinted in revised form in 57 *AAUP Bulletin* (June 1971).

Fuller, Lon L. "Collective Bargaining and the Arbitrator." 1963 *Wisconsin Law Review* (No. 1).

―――. "Mediation—Its Forms and Functions." 44 *Southern California Law Review* (1971, No. 2).

Garbarino, Joseph W. "Creeping Unionism and the Faculty Labor Market." Mimeographed. 1971. Prepared for *Higher Education and the Labor Market,* forthcoming publication of the Carnegie Commission on Higher Education.

―――. "Faculty Unionism from Theory to Practice." 11 *Industrial Relations* (February 1972). Reprinted by Carnegie Commission on Higher Education, 1972.

―――. "Precarious Professors: New Patterns of Representation." 10 *Industrial Relations* (February 1971). Reprinted by Carnegie Commission on Higher Education, 1971.

―――. "Reply to Professor Bain." 10 *Industrial Relations* (May 1971).

Getman, Julius G.; Goldberg, Stephen B.; and Herman, Jeanne B. "The National Labor Relations Board Voting Study: A Preliminary Report." 1 *Journal of Legal Studies* (June 1972).

Gianopulos, John. "Collective Bargaining: What Part Should College Presidents Play?" 49 *College and University Business* (September 1970).

Gillis, John W. "Academic Collective Bargaining: Comment and an Annotated Bibliography." 56 *Liberal Education* (December 1970).

―――. "Continuing Development of Academic Collective Bargaining." 57 *Liberal Education* (December 1971).

Grobman, Arnold B. "Collective Bargaining on Campus." 175 *Science* (March 31, 1972).

Grodin, J. G., and Hardin, M. A. "Public Employee Bargaining in Oregon." 51 *Oregon Law Review* (Fall 1971).

Hanley, Dexter L. "Issues and Models for Collective Bargaining in Higher Education." 57 *Liberal Education* (March 1971).

Helper, John C. "Time Table for a Take-Over." 42 *Journal of Higher Education* (February 1971).

Hixon, Richard A. "Problems in Negotiating for Professors." *Colleges and Universities Department, American Federation of Teachers,* November 1970.

Howe, Ray A. "The Bloody Business of Bargaining." 48 *College and University Business* (March 1970).

———. "Faculty-Administrative Relations in Extremis." 37 *Junior College Journal* (November 1966).

Kadish, Sanford. "The Strike and the Professoriate." 54 *AAUP Bulletin* (Summer 1968).

———. "The Theory of the Profession and Its Predicament." 58 *AAUP Bulletin* (June 1972).

Keck, Donald J. "Faculty Governance and the 'New Managerial Class.'" 5 *NEA Reports* (November 1971).

Kennelly, J. R. "Collective Bargaining in the Community College." 52 *Educational Record* (Winter 1971).

Kerr, J. David. "Faculty Organizing and Bargaining in Higher Education." 6 *College Counsel* (1971).

Kleinsorge, Paul L., and Harter, Lafayette G., Jr. "Criteria for Impasse Resolution in Public Employee Labor Disputes: An Economic Analysis." 51 *Oregon Law Review* (Fall 1971).

Kriegel, Leonard. "Surviving the Apocalypse: Teaching at City College." *Change*, Summer 1972.

Kugler, Israel. "Collective Bargaining for the Faculty, II." 56 *Liberal Education* (March 1970).

———. "The Union Speaks for Itself." 49 *Educational Record* (Fall 1968).

Lemmer, William P. "Collective Bargaining Report—Non-Academic." 5 *College Counsel* (June 1970).

Leslie, David W. "NLRB Rulings on the Department Chairmanship." 53 *Educational Record* (Fall 1972).

Lesnick, Howard. "Establishment of Bargaining Rights Without an NLRB Election." 65 *Michigan Law Review* (March 1967).

Lieberman, Myron. "Faculty Senates: Institutionalized Irresponsibility." 51 *Phi Delta Kappa* (September 1969).

———. "Professors, Unite!" *Harper's Magazine*, October 1971.

Livingston, Frederick R., and Christensen, Andrea S. "State and Federal Regulation of Collective Negotiations in Higher Education." 1971 *Wisconsin Law Review* (No. 1).

Livingston, John C. "Collective Bargaining and Professionalism in Higher Education." 48 *Educational Record* (Winter 1967).

Macy, John W., Jr. "The Role of Bargaining in Public Service." In *Public Workers and Public Unions*, edited by Sam Zagoria. Englewood Cliffs, N.J.: Prentice-Hall, Inc., 1972.

Malamud, Phyllis. "Faculty: Labor or Management?" *Change*, September 1971.

Marmion, Harry A. "Unions and Higher Education." 49 *Educational Record* (Winter 1968).

McHugh, William F. "Collective Bargaining and the College Student." 42 *Journal of Higher Education* (March 1971).

———. "Collective Bargaining with Professionals in Higher Education:

Problems in Unit Determinations." 1971 *Wisconsin Law Review* (No. 1).

———. "Collective Negotiations in Public Higher Education." 47 *College and University Business* (December 1969).

———. "Faculty Unionism." In *The Tenure Debate*, edited by Bardwell L. Smith. San Francisco: Jossey-Bass, 1973.

———. "Recent Developments in Collective Bargaining in Higher Education." 5 *College Counsel* (October 1970).

Millett, John D. "Tenure and Collective Bargaining." In *Personnel Management in Higher Education*. Washington: Management Division, Academy for Educational Development, 1972.

Mintz, Bernard, "The CUNY Experience." 1971 *Wisconsin Law Review* (No. 1).

Moore, John W. "Attitudes Toward Collective Negotiations." In *Pennsylvania Community College Faculty*. University Park: Center for the Study of Higher Education, Pennsylvania State University, 1971.

Moskow, Michael H. "The Scope of Collective Bargaining in Higher Education." 1971 *Wisconsin Law Review* (No. 1).

"National Education Association Memorandum on Teacher Strikes, Work Stoppages, and Interruptions of Service, 1970–71." 71 *Government Employment Relations Reporter* 1051. Washington: Bureau of National Affairs, 1972.

Pitts, Jesse R. "Strike at Oakland University." *Change*, February 1972.

Polishook, Sheila S. "Collective Bargaining and the City University of New York." 41 *Journal of Higher Education* (May 1970).

Proulx, Pierre-Paul. "Collective Negotiations in Higher Education— Canada." 1971 *Wisconsin Law Review* (No. 1).

Rehmus, Charles M. "Collective Bargaining and the Market for Academic Personnel." *Quarterly Review of Economics and Business*, Autumn 1968.

"Representation of Economic Interests." 52 *AAUP Bulletin* (June 1966).

"Rising Costs and the Public Institutions: The Annual Report on the Economic Status of the Profession." 56 *AAUP Bulletin* (June 1970).

Sabol, Geraldine G. "NLRB's Assertion of Jurisdiction Over Universities." 32 *University of Pittsburgh Law Review* (Spring 1971).

Sands, C. Dallas. "The Role of Collective Bargaining in Higher Education." 1971 *Wisconsin Law Review* (No. 1).

Scully, Malcolm G., and Sievert, William A. "Collective Bargaining Gains Converts Among Teachers." *Chronicle of Higher Education*, May 10, 1971.

Shaw, Lee C. "The Development of State and Federal Laws." In *Public Workers and Public Unions*, edited by Sam Zagoria. Englewood Cliffs, N.J.: Prentice-Hall, Inc., 1972.

Shaw, Lee C., and Clark, R. Theodore, Jr. "Determination of Appropriate Bargaining Units in the Public Sector: Legal and Practical Problems." 51 *Oregon Law Review* (Fall 1971).

Sherman, Frederick E., and Loeffler, David. "Universities, Unions, and the Rule of Law: The Teaching Assistants at Wisconsin." 1971 *Wisconsin Law Review* (No. 1).

Simpkin, William E. "Fact-Finding—Its Values and Limitations." 61 *Government Employment Relations Reporter* 511. Washington: Bureau of National Affairs, 1970.

Spigler, Manual A. "NLRB Jurisdiction Over Private Colleges and Universities—Toward Elimination of the Good Works Exclusion." 44 *Temple Law Quarterly* (Spring 1971).

"Statement on Collective Bargaining." 58 *AAUP Bulletin* (December 1972). [Approved for publication by the AAUP Council in October 1972.]

"Statement on Government of Colleges and Universities." 52 *AAUP Bulletin* (December 1966).

Stevens, Carl M. "The Management of Labor Disputes in the Public Sector." 51 *Oregon Law Review* (Fall 1971). Reprinted in 58 *AAUP Bulletin* (December 1972).

"The State of Higher Education in Michigan." Report of Special Committee of AAUP Michigan Conference. 54 *AAUP Bulletin* (December 1968).

"The Threat of Inflationary Erosion: The Annual Report on the Economic Status of the Profession, 1968–69." 55 *AAUP Bulletin* (June 1969).

Tyler, Gus. "The Faculty Joins the Proletariat." *Change*, Winter 1971–72.

"Unions Woo the College Faculties." *Business Week*, May 1, 1971.

Wellington, Harry H., and Winter, Ralph K., Jr. "The Limits of Collective Bargaining in Public Employment." 78 *Yale Law Journal* (June 1969). Also: Brookings Institution Reprint No. 167.

———. "More Strikes by Public Employees." 79 *Yale Law Journal* (June 1970).

———. "Structuring Collective Bargaining in Public Employment." 79 *Yale Law Journal* (April 1970). Also: Brookings Institution Reprint No. 185.

Wildman, Thomas R. "The Legislation Necessary to Effectively Govern Collective Bargaining in Public Education." 1971 *Wisconsin Law Review* (No. 1).

Wollett, Donald H. "The Bargaining Process in the Public Sector: What Is Bargainable?" 51 *Oregon Law Review* (Fall 1971).

———. "The Status and Trends of Collective Negotiations for Faculty in Higher Education." 1971 *Wisconsin Law Review* (No. 1).

Wright, John C., Jr. "The Pennsylvania Public Employee Relations Act." 51 *Oregon Law Review* (Fall 1971).

Young, Edwin. "Management and Collective Bargaining on the Campus." 13 *Association of Governing Boards Reports* (November 1970).

Zack, Arnold M. "Impasses, Strikes and Resolutions." In *Public Workers and Public Unions*, edited by Sam Zagoria. Englewood Cliffs, N.J.: Prentice-Hall, Inc., 1972.

Index

AMERICAN COUNCIL ON EDUCATION

ROGER W. HEYNS, *President*

The American Council on Education, founded in 1918, is a
council of educational organizations and institutions. Its purpose is to advance education and educational methods through
comprehensive voluntary and cooperative action on the part of
educational associations, organizations, and institutions.